j

Perspectives in Child Care Policy

Lorraine Fox Harding

2nd Edition

An imprint of **Pearson Education**

Harlow, England · London · New York · Reading, Massachusetts · San Francisco · Toronto · Don Mills, Ontario · Sydney
Tokyo · Singapore · Hong Kong · Seoul · Taipei · Cape Town · Madrid · Mexico City · Amsterdam · Munich · Paris · Milan

Pearson Education Limited,
Edinburgh Gate, Harlow
Essex CM20 2JE, England
and Associated Companies throughout the world.

Visit us on the World Wide Web at:
http://www.pearsoneduc.com

First published 1991
Second Edition 1997

ISBN 0 582 276845   PPR

British Library Cataloguing-in-Publication Data

A catalogue record for this book is available from the British Library

Library of Congress Cataloging-in-Publication Data

A catalogue record for this book is available from the Library of Congress

Set by 8 in 10/11 Times

10   9   8   7   6   5   4   3   2
04   03   02   01   00

Printed in Malaysia, GPS

To two friends called Mary

CONTENTS

PREFACE

In the first edition of this book, I suggested that it would be very helpful to those who, over the years, have struggled with the underlying ethical issues which constantly arise in the practice of child welfare. I have no reason to change my mind on reading the second edition. The author has updated and expanded her analysis in a fast developing field of knowledge and argument. The result is a refreshing (and very thorough) attempt to analyse objectively four powerful themes which recur in the analysis of policy – *laissez-faire* and patriarchy; state paternalism and child protection; the birth family and parents' rights, and children's rights. It will be a godsend to students and teachers who should not be deterred by the unhelpful Harris and Timms critique to which the author responds. But it will also be valued by those many practitioners and managers who want to work on their underlying philosophy of child care, to inform their discussion making and counteract the arbitrary shifts of emphasis to which we have been so prone since the war. The next stage in this unending process will be an examination of the implications of the raft of research, sponsored by the Department of Health which appeared in 1995.

The author presumably believes in the power of reason. Indeed, academics have to or we would be out of business! Yet it is observable that arguments concerning children in families rouse deep emotions. We can all point to examples of literature in which feelings masquerade as reason and in which one senses a powerful need to persuade readers that one side of the story of families is paramount. Adopters, foster parents, birth parents, children – each take their turn in being placed at the top of the moral tree, to be accorded special priority in law, policy and practice. Even when child protection is afforded unequivocal priority, hidden identification with parental rights and needs can affect practice or there can be genuine doubt as to the extent to which specific children's needs are best met within their birth family. The shifts in emphasis in the law, as the pendulum sways, illustrates this vividly; they both mirror and influence public opinion. The latest Children Act will affect the debate significantly.

We have to learn to live with the tension and ambivalence in this sphere of social welfare policy, possibly more affected by underlying emotion than any other. Those who, as part of the management of ambivalence, have the will to understand intellectually will benefit greatly from an appraisal of the different perspectives which this book offers. Objectivity in the social sciences is a phantasy but at least we can examine our underlying biases more rigorously with the help of such a text.

Olive Stevenson
Professor Emeritus of Social Work Studies
University of Nottingham
July 1996

FOREWORD

The idea for this book originated in an article published by the author under the name of Lorraine Fox in 1982 in the *British Journal of Social Work* (reprinted in the Open University Reader edited by Morgan and Righton, *Child Care: Concerns and Conflicts*, 1989). The article set out two schools of thought or 'value positions' in relation to child care policy, and has been quite widely referred to. The 1991 edition of this book developed the ideas further, and explored a four-fold division of positions or 'value perspectives', building on and elaborating the original two-fold classification. This edition of the book updates the 1991 edition, with an expanded section on 'children's rights' in practice, as this has been an area of rapid development and is possibly the direction for the future.

A note on the national focus of the book

The book is written mostly with child care law and policy in England and Wales in mind as a context (referred to usually as England/English policy for shortness). References to British policy are on the whole not made, as it is recognised that Scotland, while it shares some of the English child care legislation, also has some Acts of its own (including one in 1995), and in particular has a very different system, based on informal children's hearings, for children in need of compulsory care. Scotland, it is felt, is worthy of a study in its own right, as indeed is Northern Ireland.

A note on terminology

Since the implementation of the Children Act 1989 in October 1991 it has been necessary to distinguish between children 'in care', that is away from home under a court order, and those 'in accommodation', where the local authority looks after children away from home but there is no order. Both groups, however, may be referred to as children who are 'looked after'.

Therefore 'in care' before 1991 means being in the care of the local authority, whatever the legal situation. 'In care' after 1991 means being looked after under an order, 'in accommodation' means being looked after with no order.

CHAPTER 1

The importance of child care law and policy

In modern societies it may be thought self-evident that the state should use its power to intervene between parents and their children in order to defend the children from various kinds of ill-treatment, inadequate care or poor upbringing. It is widely known and accepted that not all parents care for and socialise their children well. There is much evidence of various kinds of abuse. From time to time extreme cases of child cruelty leading to death hit the headlines and provoke much media condemnation of the agents of the state. The most famous examples in a British context would be Maria Colwell in the 1970s and Jasmine Beckford, Tyra Henry and Kimberley Carlile in the 1980s (Secretary of State for Social Services 1974, London Borough of Brent 1985, London Borough of Lambeth 1987, London Borough of Greenwich 1987). In the United States there was the case of Melisha Gibson in the 1970s (Goldstein, Freud and Solnit 1980) and in Canada Kim Popen in the 1980s (Levitt and Wharf 1985). In the 1980s sexual abuse of children by parents was discovered to be more common than was thought (see, for example, Creighton 1989). In the 1990s 'satanic' or ritual abuse began to emerge as a possible problem (see, for example, La Fontaine 1994). Becoming a parent in the biological sense hardly ensures that an adult will consistently maintain the standards of upbringing which are widely regarded in society as necessary or desirable.

It seems legitimate for society – through the force of law if necessary – to act, when such standards are not achieved. As suggested, in particularly severe cases of abuse leading to death there is often an outcry to the effect that the state and its legal machinery should have done more. This can be so marked that attention is deflected from the actual killer of the child. There is a strong popular sense of society's duty to protect children, and social workers already involved with families where a child is killed may be bitterly accused of negligence and incompetence for not having anticipated the severe injury and death and for not having safeguarded the child by removing her or him. That is, they are criticised for not having used more fully and willingly the powers of the state. Sometimes the actual limits of these powers are misunderstood, but it appears – at first glance – that there must be a consensus here that the state should indeed have, and use, extensive legal powers to act against and overrule the apparently 'natural' powers of parents where there is a need to protect the child. Surely there can be no dispute about this?

Such a position, however, becomes increasingly problematic the closer we look at it, and some awkward questions arise. For example, just when is the state to intervene? Outright cruelty to, and neglect of, children shade into merely careless or casual care; unacceptable violence shades into methods of discipline accepted by some people; one person's or culture's notion of a 'good upbringing' is not another's; and one person's 'good' decision about a child's life and future might be a fearful mistake from another perspective. Should the state act to protect only when harm to a child has occurred – or when it is likely to occur – and how is such harm to be decided and by whom? How can there be clear guidelines – so that everyone knows where they are – indicating when the state should use its coercive powers, when it should merely offer supportive help, and when it should stay out of the family altogether?

Secondly, how is the state to know when poor quality child care is going on and how are the mechanisms for identifying it to be applied throughout the population? Presumably the powers of the state should be applied consistently to all children, all parents, yet it can be argued that the system is haphazard: while some groups are under greater state surveillance and are more likely to suffer the loss of their family autonomy and integrity to the state's control, others, protected by relative wealth and high social status, may get away, almost literally, with murder. Yet to identify and respond exhaustively to all child maltreatment would be likely to involve state surveillance on a scale which most people would regard as unacceptable in terms of civil liberties, the costs of which (both in financial and other terms) would be incalculable.

Thirdly, some poor child care is certainly due to circumstances over which parents have no control. They may be struggling with low incomes and/or jobs which militate against proper child care, living in appalling housing and deprived neighbourhoods, or be in poor mental or physical health. They may have been victims of poor child care and depriving environments themselves. Are these parents to be 'punished' by having their children taken away, perhaps permanently? What is the justification when parents are victims themselves?

Fourthly, is the action that the state takes in cases of improper care always helpful, and the alternative care that the state itself may provide necessarily superior to the birth parents' care? It may be additionally damaging to children to split up the family and/or remove them to a 'substitute home', perhaps depriving them of all contact with their original parents. It is salutary to remember that one of the most notorious child abuse cases in Britain this century – and one that had some influence on the reform of law and practice – the case of Dennis O'Neill, who died in 1945, was of a child *already* in the care of the state because of parental mistreatment, placed with foster parents supposedly 'chosen' and 'supervised' by a local authority (although in fact seized on in desperation and supervised barely at all) (Monckton 1945).

These 'awkward questions', and many others, give rise to a situation where there can be no certainty as to what the state should do, when it should do it, or how. Consensus is illusory once the complexities are probed, and differing perspectives on the many problematic aspects of the state's child care role can be identified, while the debate between the proponents of the various views is often heated and emotional. It is difficult to be detached: after all, everyone has been a child and most people have parented one. Disagreements are not merely intellectual therefore, but are bound up with personal feelings and experiences. The debates are significant, because of the serious dilemmas that arise in policy, and because different perspectives point to different policy consequences.

The study of child care policy

The study of child care policy and the debates surrounding it can be useful and important for a number of groups: first, for social scientists, secondly, for various professionals and policy-makers, and thirdly, for a wider audience. As far as social science is concerned, one aspect of the study of society is the study of childhood and its construction by society, of the place and condition of children in society, and by extension the study of age itself: questions of development and maturation over time, of how experience at different ages is defined, and of how society responds to differences in age. The meaning of age and the treatment of different ages are found to vary between societies, between social groups, and over time. Such meanings and practices may be argued to have only a limited connection with biological factors and much to do with the nature of society and the role of different age groups within it.

The study of child care law and policy may have much to contribute to the more general study of childhood. While it is true that the formal child care machinery of the state only involves a minority of children (in England, for example, well under 1 per cent of the under-18 population are actually in the care of the state at any one time – Department of Health 1991d – although others would be under supervision and helped in other ways), the role of the state – in providing care for children as an alternative to parental care, in intervening between parent and child in various ways, and in prescribing certain rules surrounding childhood – can tell us much about childhood in society and how children are perceived and treated. For example, in modern Western societies children are not seen as being as fully responsible for themselves as adults are. They are seen as dependent, vulnerable and in need of some protection. Their rights are recognised to a degree, yet are also highly circumscribed. They are seen as needing to be controlled. They cannot be passed from adult to adult in an unrestricted way. Childhood's special status is reflected in the laws and policies which have been formulated over time, the changes which have been made in these, and the debates surrounding such changes and attempted changes. Where disagreements arise, they may reflect conflicting notions of childhood, as discussion of the four perspectives outlined in this book will attempt to show. Nevertheless, despite disputes, there seems to be a broad consensus about the importance of children and of safeguarding their welfare. This reflects something of the general position of children in society.

A second reason for an interest in child care policy in the social sciences concerns such policy's relation to the family. The family may be seen as a central social institution, carrying *inter alia* the function of reproducing the next generation and hence the society of the future. The family has excited a great deal of recent interest and study. Two features of this interest have been, first, a focus on family change, in response to the many changes which are perceived to be occurring, and to be of significance, in Western societies, such as a markedly increased incidence of divorce and its consequences (for family change, see Fox Harding 1996); and secondly, a focus on diversity, not only of actual family forms, but of norms and beliefs concerning the family. Debates on family change and diversity have been particularly intense during the 1990s, generating many publications of a polemical kind (see, for example, publications from the Institute of Economic Affairs such as Dennis and Erdos 1992, Davies 1993, Dennis 1993, Morgan 1994). The interest for social science is perhaps essentially that there seems to be no universal consensus either on what 'the family' is, or on what it ought to be.

Children are central to most notions of the family unit. Here again there is both change and diversity of family patterns and approaches. For example, the increased fragmentation and realignment of parent couples may affect children's experience and upbringing profoundly (for some recent findings on children and family disruption, see, for example, Burghes 1994, Cockett and Tripp 1994). Also children's lives are probably also more heterogeneous than they were, and conflicting beliefs about what is good for the family, and for individuals in families, overlap with the question of what is good for children as a special group. The study of child care law and policy, then, can add another dimension to the understanding of shifting family forms and ideas about the family. Law and policy usually attempt, to some degree, to respond to changes in the family and to the rich variety of family forms and circumstances. They will also be informed by different concepts of, and beliefs about, the family; and the different child care perspectives discussed in this book will also reflect different family concepts and beliefs. For example, different views may be taken of whether the family is primarily a biological or a psychological unit, of the importance of early bonds and of stability over time, and of the relative importance of family autonomy as opposed to support and intervention from outside.

A third point concerns the role of the state and the inter-relationship between the state and citizens. As indicated, there is a widespread acceptance that the modern state should have *some* legal powers to intervene coercively between parents and children where there has been clear maltreatment. In England, for example, there have been such powers on the statute book for about a century. Intervention may take the form of both prosecution of the offender and removal (or supervision) of the child. Yet the popular concern about child welfare is balanced by a perhaps equally strong concern, which manifests itself in some circumstances, about the dangers of the state having excessive powers and making unwarranted intrusions into the privacy of domestic life. The family may be seen as some kind of 'bastion' against the power of the state. This is neatly illustrated in some cases where it appears that the state, acting through courts, social workers, medical staff and so on, has forcibly removed children from parents without sufficient justification. Here the public and media response is the mirror image of that in cases of child deaths – the agents of the state are execrated for doing too much. An example would be the Cleveland child sex abuse cases in England in 1987 (Secretary of State for Social Services 1988) and similar cases in Orkney in 1991 (Clyde 1992).

The inconsistency over state intervention arises in societies where there has traditionally been a marked distrust of too large-scale or authoritarian a role for state bodies. This distrust may be in tension with the desire to protect the most vulnerable. A further tension arises between this desire to protect the vulnerable and the reluctance to commit sufficient societal resources, via state or other bodies, to make such protection effective. The point to bear in mind here is that consideration of the workings of the child care laws and machinery of the state, and the ideas underlying them, may contribute to an understanding of the role of the state in general.

The importance of child care law and policy for those who are involved in the child care field as professionals, practitioners, decision-makers, policy-makers and law-makers – those who create, analyse, discuss, influence and implement law and policy at every level – should be self-evidently clear. Within the category of professionals and practitioners might be included, most obviously, the social workers employed by local authorities and their managers, also social workers with voluntary bodies, doctors and other health professionals, education and other professionals working with children, and magistrates and judges called on to make decisions in a variety of child care cases. In so far as elected representatives in public authorities are involved in decisions in child care practice, they may also be included in this category. Those who train professionals and practitioners are another important group. That there is an overlap with the 'policy-maker' category should be clear. 'Policy' here is taken to mean the ongoing actions of the state of a significant kind and the thinking underlying them. The middle and higher levels of the state organisations responsible for child care may be involved in policy-making. Child care legislation in many respects leaves a wide area of discretion to the implementing authorities. For example, decisions and judgements have to be made as to when to bring into operation particular sections of the law, or as to how particular principles enshrined in the law (such as the 'welfare of the child') should be interpreted. Policy is created within agencies as well as at a more centralised level of the state. Similarly, courts which regularly deal with child care cases may evolve particular 'policies' or approaches. Elected representatives at a local and central level are policy-makers in a broader sense, particularly those at the level where laws are passed, along with the state employees who advise them. Various pressure groups and professional bodies may also have a role in policy-making. Members of investigating committees and enquiries, and other experts, specialists, advisers and commentators, also have a policy-making role.

Three specific aspects of a study of child care law and policy suggest themselves as helpful to these groups. First, there is the acquisition of factual knowledge based on, for example, research into child care, historical accounts of law and policy, and accounts of individual cases. Secondly, there is the analysis of the principles, values, beliefs, assumptions and preferences underlying policy and law, which might lead to greater clarity and more meaningful choices. It is in this second field that the analysis of the four competing value perspectives in this book will, it is hoped, make the greatest contribution. Thirdly, there is the more detailed analysis of particular pieces of legislation and decisions in individual cases which can help also to clarify values, assumptions and policy outcomes, while indicating both current trends and problems and possible likely developments in the future. And where wide publicity is given to individual 'scandal' cases, it is important for professionals and policy-makers to be able to disentangle in an informed and thoughtful way the arguments, ideas and criticisms embodied in the response. There is the same need where official enquiries investigate and report and when specific legislative changes are proposed. In particular, emotive and ill-informed social responses to single issues and cases require careful and knowledgeable dissection and evaluation.

However, it can be argued that an interest in child care law and policy cannot realistically be seen as solely the province of specialists. The actions of child care professionals, courts, legislators and so on, are clearly of interest to a broad section of the general public, or individual cases of children either killed/abused or taken away from home 'unnecessarily' would not attract the degree of media attention that they do. As indicated, the perception of child care issues is sharpened emotionally by the fact that everyone has been a child and most people have had one (or would like to have one). In the contemplation of particular problems and disputes, it appears that onlookers may emotionally identify with the interests of just one party in the dispute. This may, for example, be the child. It is suggested that the majority of media reports of severe child abuse cases in Britain both reflect and encourage an identification with the child, who is portrayed entirely as victim, while little or no identification is made with the abusing parent. Alternatively in some –

though probably fewer – cases, the story is implicitly or explicitly presented entirely from the (supposedly innocent) parents' point of view, encouraging identification with them. An example of an emotional identification by a stranger with the parents, to the exclusion of the child, was the Rayner case in Tameside in England in 1987. A local authority planned to take away a baby at birth from a family where there had been three unexplained child deaths already. A businessman who did not know the family was moved to offer financial aid to help meet their legal bills (*Guardian*, 18 November 1987). More rarely, perhaps, an onlooker in a child care case might identify emotionally with a foster or adoptive parent, with a non-resident or step-parent, or with the social worker responsible for the case. It might be hypothesised that factors in individuals' own psychological histories would have a bearing on which party they feel closest to. Child care is an area of state policy where it is extremely difficult to remain neutral and detached, because of the emotional processes which appear to be involved.

This state of affairs appears to have two consequences. First, there is a high level of general interest in child care matters, as indicated, and from the amount of media focus this would appear to have increased in extent in the 1970s, 1980s and early 1990s. Secondly, while there is a high level of interest, much of the debate and discussion is pitched at a low level in terms of knowledge, understanding, fairness to all parties involved, balance in considering arguments, awareness of how much is not known, and an ability to consider a number of different interpretations of the given facts. Emotion lowers the quality of debate, possibly to the detriment of the quality of decision-making and policy-making. And the area is seemingly not widely recognised as one in which specialist knowledge and experience is needed in order to reach a conclusion. It is suggested that there is a public education need here, so that public and media responses to well-publicised cases at least become more sophisticated and balanced.

The importance to society of developing appropriate laws and policies in the child care field should be readily apparent. Children constitute future generations of adults, and the continuities between childhood experience and adult behaviour are widely recognised. For example, those who abuse children have been thought to be disproportionately those who were abused or neglected as children themselves (for example, Wasserman 1967 cited in Parton 1985a, Strauss, Gelles and Steinmetz 1980 cited in Elliot 1996). There is a strong social investment in ensuring the adequate care and socialisation of the young in order to safeguard the future social order, and the high level of interest and concern about child care matters surely reflects this wider awareness of the needs of society. Unfortunately, however, there can be no clearcut consensus as to what kind of adult – or what kind of social order – it is desirable to produce, or precisely what sort of child upbringing will bring the desired ends about. In considering the importance of child care law and policy we are inevitably drawn back to the question of values – what kind of people and what kind of society? Child care may be important, but recognising this does not tell us what kind of child care we should provide. For example, it might be thought obvious that abuse is a 'bad thing' and that if abused children tend to become abusing adults, abuse is doubly a 'bad thing'. Yet this position presupposes a value judgement about physical violence and social control. In some times, places and cultures, severe physical chastisement might be seen as a legitimate tool of socialisation. If the chastised then go on to chastise others, this would not be construed negatively. The point is that fundamental norms are bound up with notions of effectiveness in child upbringing.

Child care and the role of society acting through the state are rightly seen as of crucial importance to society, but the issues are complex and tied to deep-seated values and feelings. An attempt at systematic analysis of different perspectives in this area may be helpful.

Introduction to the four value perspectives in Chapters 2–5

To recapitulate, there is no certainty and no consensus as to the state's role in child care, and different perspectives can be identified. In an attempt to make sense of the differences, a four-fold classification is put forward in this book. This framework is based on an article published by the author under the name of Fox in 1982, 'Two value positions in recent child care law and practice'. The article outlined only two schools of thought in the child care field: the first, referred to as the 'kinship defenders', stressed the value of biological families for children and the need for state intervention to support and preserve the family unit, rather than putting children into state or substitute care; while the second, called the 'society-as-parent protagonists', stressed a protective role for the state where parental care of children is poor, favouring good, secure foster and adoptive homes, with the exclusion of the birth parents if the child is not to return to them, and a general diminution of parental rights. However, this two-fold framework was subsequently found to be an unsatisfactory over-simplification: it did not adequately incorporate the range of diverse views found in child care law and policy, and in particular did not fully accommodate those authors, commentators and pressure groups inclined to a *laissez-faire* or to a 'children's rights' perspective. A four-fold classification was therefore developed. The four-fold typology is no doubt not the only possible classification; there may be some blurring of the boundaries between categories; and other categories of view might also be argued to exist. But the four polarities seem currently to be the most significant in understanding child care law and policy. The four positions have been influential to different degrees, and particular positions have been in the ascendant at different historical periods.

Because concepts of the state's role in relation to children hinge partly on underlying values – values to do with children, with adults as parents, with the family as a unit, with welfare and suffering, and with the state itself – the four positions are referred to as value positions or perspectives. The term perspective is favoured because each category incorporates a range of views in itself, and 'position' perhaps implies something more definite, fixed and monolithic than is actually found from an examination of the literature and policy. The perspectives are labelled here as follows:

1 Laissez-faire *and patriarchy*

This perspective is broadly identified with the nineteenth century but has enjoyed some renaissance in the late twentieth century. It is essentially the view that power in the family should not be disturbed except in very extreme circumstances, and the role of the state should be a minimal one.

2 *State paternalism and child protection*

This perspective may be associated with the growth of state intervention in welfare in the late nineteenth and twentieth centuries. Here extensive state intervention to protect and care for children is legitimated, but state intervention itself may be authoritarian and biological family bonds undervalued. Good quality substitute care is favoured when the care of the biological parents is found to be inadequate.

3 *The modern defence of the birth family and parents' rights*

This perspective may be associated more with the expansion of Welfare States in the post-Second World War period. It is to be distinguished from *laissez-faire* in that state intervention is legitimated, but this intervention is seen as ideally of a supportive kind, helping to defend and preserve birth families. Poorer and socially deprived parents are seen as often victims of heavy-handed state action, rather than – as they should be – objects of help and support.

4 *Children's rights and child liberation*

This perspective, certainly in its extreme form, is more marginal to law and policy, but has been influential in some times and places and is apparently becoming increasingly so in the last decade of the twentieth century. The perspective advocates the child as a subject, as an independent person with rights which, at the extreme, are similar to the rights of the adult. Children are to be freed from adult oppression by being granted a more adult status.

Each perspective will be related to examples of law, policy and practice.

CHAPTER 2

Laissez-faire and patriarchy

Introduction

The terms *laissez-faire* and *minimalism* are used here to describe the view that the role of the state in child care should be a minimal one, while the privacy and sanctity of the parent–child relationship should be respected. Some who take this view would also argue that in extreme cases of poor parental care, state intervention is not only acceptable but preferably of a strong and authoritative kind, transferring the child to a secure placement with a new set of parent figures.

Patriarchy here refers to the power of adult males over women and children, particularly of the 'private' sort, that is in the family. (For private and public patriarchy see, for example, Walby 1990.)

The main elements of the perspective

Underlying this first value perspective lies a mistrust of the state and an acute awareness of the dangerousness of its powers. It reflects a liberal democratic culture such as is broadly found in Western industrial societies, where there is a strong undercurrent of feeling that the state should in general keep out of certain 'private' areas of citizens' lives, with restricted exceptions. In this perspective, citizens have – or should have – strong rights held against the state. In particular, domestic and family life, the home and hearth, are seen as a relatively private arena which should not be invaded by the agents of the state except with due cause, such cause usually being associated with criminality. There is a pervading sense that personal relationships are in general no business of the state's. There is an ideology implied here of a dichotomy between a private domain, encompassing the family and seen perhaps as some kind of retreat, a domain particularly associated with a special role for women, and a contrasting public arena, in which individuals interact with the wider society and the state, an arena seen as the particular province of men. These two spheres of the private and the public may be seen as somewhat in tension and in opposition to each other. Mount (1982) is one writer on the family (not one focusing on the child care field specifically) who sees the family over the centuries as a desired private unit which individuals have valued and fiercely protected against the incursions of larger institutions, both the state and the Church. He comments: 'Only the family has continued throughout history and still continues to undermine the state. The family is the enduring permanent enemy of all hierarchies, churches and ideologies' (p. 1).

A general emphasis on the desirable separateness of the family from the power of the state appears to mean, in effect, that power within the family should lie where it is allowed to fall. In the societies considered here, adults are powerful in relation to children and men in relation to women. This power is partly based on generally superior physical size and strength, but is also, clearly, socially and legally structured and determined. One aspect of such male and adult power would be the relative economic dependence of women and children; another would be legal provisions which allot children, in particular, a less independent status; and other aspects would include institutions such as labour and housing markets, political institutions, education and social security systems, as well as social norms and attitudes, and informal sanctions. The relative power positions of men and women in the family have been extensively analysed by feminist writers (see, for example, Barrett and McIntosh 1991, Gittins 1993, Walby 1990, Delphy and Leonard 1992). The weaker power position of children has been taken up most obviously, perhaps, by those authors who will be categorised in this book as belonging to the 'children's rights' perspective (the fourth perspective, to be discussed in Chapter 5), and, perhaps to a lesser degree, those belonging to the 'state paternalism and child protection' school (the second perspective, to be discussed in Chapter 3). The two streams of writing – on women and on children – come together in feminist analyses of child sexual abuse, which take the institution of patriarchy as a major factor in the abuse of (largely female) children by (largely male) adults (see, for example, Finkelhor 1984, Metcalfe and Humphries 1985, Gordon 1989).

The point to be made here, however, is that a strong emphasis on the value of not intervening directly in the family via the state will mean in practice that family power will lie where it falls according to various other institutions and practices, and where it falls, on the whole, is on adults, and, particularly, on men in their role as husbands/partners and fathers/stepfathers.

It may be argued that in modern Western cultures such beliefs about the protection of the autonomy of the family from the encroachments of the state remain deeply embedded, notwithstanding the proliferation of modern statutes which do give the state a certain amount of power over the workings of the family. For example, in the English context, Dingwall, Eekelaar and Murray (1983a) in their study of social work practice in child care cases, found that the social workers (who, it must be noted, were agents of the state who had as one of their special tasks the intervention, on a compulsory basis if need be, between parent and child) were in practice reluctant to use their coercive powers. They readily and optimistically accepted parental explanations and excuses regarding the children, and interpreted events in the way most favourable to the parents. Dingwall *et al.* outline the dilemma facing the 'liberal society' which places a high value on family autonomy and privacy (as a check on state power), yet must be concerned with the socialisation of future generations of citizens. In such a society there are considerable structural and cultural limitations to the degree of state surveillance possible.

The main elements of the position of those who, having looked at child care questions, explicitly support a *laissez-faire* role for the state in child care, appear to be:

1. A belief in the benefits for society of a minimum state, a state which engages in only minimal intervention in families. A weaker state entails stronger families, freer individuals, and is generally advantageous, in this view.
2. A complementary belief in the value to all, including children, of undisturbed family life where adults can get on with bringing up their children in their chosen way. It is argued that adults have a right to do this, and in any case it is better for the children too. The bearing and rearing of a child produces a special bond between parents and child, and it is damaging to disrupt it, though it is accepted that it may be necessary to do so in extreme cases to avert a greater evil. Where extreme cases do occur, for some of these authors the function of the state, ideally, is to find a new, permanent, secure home for the child, with severance of contact with the family of origin. The state, having intervened authoritatively in this way, then withdraws, according the new home the same autonomy as the original one.

The *laissez-faire* approach to child care does not necessarily entail patriarchy, that is, institutionalised power of males over females and children, and in modern child care literature the argument about undisturbed family functioning tends to be put more about parents generically than fathers in particular. In this value position in its modern form, it is relatively unfettered parental control which is seen as desirable; the state cannot do the parents' job for them in any effective way. Parents' and children's interests are, largely, identified, and by implication the interests of the two separate parents are also identified; the family as a whole has a life as a unit whose boundaries the rest of the community should respect. Yet, as indicated, *laissez-faire* tends to be linked with patriarchy in societies where men already have greater power than women. This was very obviously the case, for example, in mid-nineteenth century Britain when the family – though with some class variations – was more overtly and formally patriarchal than it is now (see Walby 1990). The vastly superior power of men in society was both reinforced by, and explicitly reflected in, the family, and the husband/father's rights and powers were almost absolute under the common law. There was also a belief that such male authority was divinely ordered and 'natural'. In this situation, a weak child care role for the state in effect reinforced private patriarchy by only very limited intervention in the patriarchal family, while belief in the value of patriarchy could be used to reinforce the notion of a weak, non-interventionist state in child care matters. So justificatory arguments about the divinely inspired nature of patriarchy could be deployed when the state was asked to exercise power in relation to children. Paternal power should not be interfered with because of its 'natural' and God-given quality.

In modern society patriarchy in the family is less overt and support for it less blatant. It is not reinforced by the law in the way it was in the nineteenth century. Yet it may be argued that the difference is only one of degree, and that patriarchy and notions of minimalism or *laissez-faire* continue to support and reinforce one another. Also patriarchal authority today is not without its defenders, as will be shown later. There are elements of support on the political right and elsewhere for a return to a 'traditional' patriarchal family which is freer from state intervention, while academic authors not necessarily on the right have also appeared to regret the passing of the more obviously patriarchal family and the extension of intervention in the family by the state.

Some authors associated with the perspective

The most notable child care authors associated with the minimalist and *laissez-faire* position on child care are Goldstein, Freud and Solnit, who set out their views in two works, *Beyond the Best Interests of the Child* (1979) and *Before the Best Interests of the Child* (1980). While these works may now seem somewhat dated, they state a coherent case which is still worthy of detailed consideration. No more recent authors advocating this perspective and of similar stature have been identified. In their earlier work Goldstein *et al.* note first that the law distinguishes between adults and children, with the law for adults being by and large designed to safeguard their right to order their personal affairs free of government intrusion, while for children, who are presumed to be not fully competent to safeguard their interests but dependent on adults, the state 'seeks to assure each child membership in a family with at least one such adult whom the law designates "parent"' (p. 3). The degree of state intervention in parent–child relationships varies, but the traditional goals of such intervention have been to serve 'the best interests of the child'. However, Goldstein *et al.* feel that, while decision-makers have recognised the need to protect the child's physical well-being, they have not understood, or have undervalued, the need to safeguard psychological well-being. The authors use psychoanalytic theory to develop child placement guidelines which would safeguard the child's psychological needs. Such theory, they believe, shows the child's need for continuity of relationships. Of importance here are two 'value preferences' which the authors state. The first is that the law must make the child's needs paramount (this being in society's best interests), and the second is a value preference for privacy and minimum state intervention. This stems from the need to safeguard the child's need for continuity, and therefore to safeguard the right of parents to raise their children as they see fit, free of government intrusion except in cases of neglect and abandonment. The value preference is reinforced by the view that the law is a crude instrument, incapable of effectively managing complex parent–child relationships.

Goldstein *et al.* delineate five guidelines for decision-makers concerned with placements, based on the beliefs that children whose placement becomes the subject of controversy should be placed with adults who are, or are likely to become, their psychological parents, and that the least detrimental available alternative should be found for the child. The guidelines they put forward are as follows:

1. Placement decisions should safeguard the child's need for continuity.
2. Placement decisions should reflect the child's, not the adult's, sense of time. The younger the child, the shorter the interval before absence is experienced as a permanent loss. Speedy decision-taking is thus more important the younger the child.
3. Placement decisions must take into account the law's incapacity to supervise inter-personal relationships and the limits of knowledge to make long-term predictions.

These are three component guidelines for a fourth, more general one:

4. Placements should provide the least detrimental alternative for safeguarding the child's growth and development, this being the placement which maximises the child's opportunity for being wanted and maintaining a continuous relationship with a psychological parent. The traditional standard, 'in the best interests of the child', fails to convey that in these cases the child is already a victim of adverse circumstances. It is damage limitation which is required, it seems.
5. The child in any contested placement should have full party status and the right to be represented by counsel. This guideline has much in common with the children's rights perspective which will be discussed in Chapter 5. Goldstein *et al.* note that the law presumed that parents were generally best suited to represent and safeguard the child's interests, but that such a presumption should not prevail in disputes over placement. Nor should it be presumed that the state or child care agency necessarily represents the child's interests. The child's interests should therefore be represented independently. However, in their later book they appear to retreat somewhat from this position.

Goldstein *et al.* then devote a chapter to rewriting a judge's decision in an actual case in accordance with their fourth guideline, the overall guideline of the least detrimental alternative. A final chapter asks 'Why Should the Child's Interests be Paramount?' (p. 105). The answer put forward is, firstly, that these interests should be paramount once the child's placement becomes the subject of official controversy, but not before. *Before* this, the law must safeguard the rights of parents to raise their children as they see fit, free of state intervention and of harassment by other adults, in order to accord with the continuity guideline.

In their later work, *Before the Best Interests of the Child*, Goldstein *et al.* develop further their theme of parental control undisturbed by state intervention except in extreme cases. They reiterate their view that *before* state intervention occurs, family autonomy and minimum state intervention should be supported, commenting: 'So long as a child is a member of a functioning family, his paramount interest lies in the preservation of his family' (p. 5). The question posed in their book is essentially *when* the state is justified in overriding the autonomy of families, but first the authors defend further the principle of minimum intervention. They argue that the dependence of childhood requires day-to-day care which provides the basis of attachment. This attachment is an essential element in socialisation. The 'complex and vital developments' of childhood and adolescence 'require the privacy of family life under guardianship by parents who are autonomous' (p. 9) Thus:

> When family integrity is broken or weakened by state intrusion, his [the child's] needs are thwarted and his belief that his parents are omniscient and all-powerful is shaken prematurely. The effect on the child's developmental progress is invariably detrimental. The child's need for safety within the confines of the family must be met by law through its recognition of family privacy as the barrier to state intrusion upon parental autonomy in child rearing.
>
> (Goldstein *et al.* 1980:9)

Two underlying purposes here are to provide parents with an uninterrupted opportunity to meet their child's needs, and to safeguard the continuing maintenance of family ties. Psychological bonds which are not based on biological ties also merit protection, for the same reasons. So 'rights which are normally secured over time by biological or adoptive parents may be lost by their failure to provide continuous care for their child and earned by those who do' (p. 10). Thus long-term substitute caretakers should be granted the same respect for their autonomy as biological parents.

The authors' position is thus that: 'A policy of minimum coercive intervention by the state thus accords not only with our firm belief as citizens in individual freedom and human dignity, but also with our professional understanding of the intricate developmental processes of childhood' (p. 12). The authors recognise, however, that parents may fail, and that 'Family privacy may become a cover for exploiting the inherent inequality between adult and child' (pp. 12–13). Where family privacy becomes a threat to the child's well-being, state intervention is justified. Yet even then state intrusion may make things worse – what is offered by the state or other agencies as alternative care is not necessarily better, or able to compensate children for what they lose in their own homes. In every case the law should ask 'whether removal from an unsatisfactory home is the beneficial measure it purports to be' (p. 13). In their quest for minimum intervention, the authors ask and seek to answer the question: what ought to be established before the 'best interests of the child test' is invoked over rights to parental autonomy and family privacy?

In subsequent chapters Goldstein *et al.* 1980 set out a framework for the law's response to the question of justifying coercive state intervention, including here fair warning to parents, restriction of the power of state officials, and greater precision; they then outline appropriate grounds for such intervention. There are seven very restricted grounds where compulsory intervention between parent and child would in their view be acceptable:

1. Where a parent has asked the state to terminate their rights (without further justification required) or to determine custody. But custody agreements between parents would be respected.
2. Where psychological bonds existed between a long-term parental caretaker and a child, and the caretaker sought to retain the child or to become the legal parent. Goldstein *et al.* specify time periods for children of different ages after which legal recognition could be granted to the new parent–child relationship, and the old one terminated with the original parents losing their rights. In this event, adoption is seen as the most favourable outcome, or failing that, 'care with tenure' which appears to be close to the notion present in English law in the late 1980s of custodianship, a form of legal custody less comprehensive and irreversible than adoption. Placements without tenure are seen as producing insecurity in the child, although some placements are recognised as genuinely temporary.
3. The death, disappearance, hospitalisation or imprisonment of parents, together with their failure to make provision for the child's care.
4. The parent's conviction of a sexual offence against the child, also seen as a gross failure of care, producing emotional harm. It should be noted that conviction or acquittal because of 'insanity' is required.
5. Serious bodily injury, interpreted narrowly. Where such harm has been inflicted by the parent, parental rights should always be terminated, and the child should be permanently placed elsewhere. Corporal punishment is condemned by the authors, but is not included in the ground; emotional damage alone is also not included.
6. Failure to authorise medical care, but only where denial of such care would result in death *and* where supplying such care would give the child a chance of a normal life or a life worth living. The narrowness of the ground is said to acknowledge the law's limited capacity for making more than gross distinctions in this field, and to respect diverse parental beliefs and values.
7. Where the child needs legal assistance, and the parents request it or there is an establishment of any of the other grounds for modifying or terminating parental relationships.

The seven grounds are on the whole narrow and relatively clearcut. And in cases stopping short of the grounds, usually *no* intervention is seen as justified. Where they do apply, the original parent–child relationship would often be severed and a new one created.

Running throughout *Before the Best Interests* is the theme of the adverse effects of state action on the parent–child relationship, and the need to keep such action to a minimum. Children react to the infringement of parental autonomy 'with anxiety, diminishing trust, loosening of emotional ties, or an increasing tendency to be out of control' (p. 25). The final chapter is entitled 'Too Early, Too Late, Too Much or Too Little' (p. 133). Noting that there is no consensus about what is best for children, the authors discuss the tension between fear of encouraging the state to violate family integrity before intervention is justified, and fear of inhibiting the state until it is too late to protect the child. Under the existing grounds for intervention at the time (the authors were writing in an American context) agencies could be held to do too little, too late, for example, in returning battered infants to parents, *or* to do too much or to do it too early on insufficient evidence, for example, in the duty to report cases of suspected child battering. Goldstein *et al.*'s own emphasis is clear. They seek 'to hold in check our rescue fantasies and to ensure that the state be authorised to intervene if and only if it provides the child in jeopardy with a less detrimental alternative' (p. 136). Coercive intervention – intervention by force of law – should be restricted to 'objectively' definable grounds. This means leaving out some children we would wish to protect; but over-inclusion on the other hand means that state agents have too much discretion. Harm is inherent in every violation of family integrity; so the preferred error is on the side of non-intrusiveness.

Goldstein *et al.* will be discussed further below. Brief mention can be made here of two groups of British child care authors writing around the same time who may also arguably be put in the *laissez-faire* camp, although they also have points in common with other value perspectives.

First, Morris *et al.* (1980) in *Justice for Children* evince concern for parents' civil liberties and call for less compulsory state intervention. These authors are associated with a pressure group of the same title as their book, which will be referred to in discussing the children's rights perspective. Their argument is put on the grounds that the state does not necessarily act in the best interests of children. Not only does state intervention and 'treatment' not work, but the costs to the child may outweigh those of leaving well alone. Morris *et al.* say: 'Parental autonomy in child-rearing must be respected ... there is no "proper" way to raise children' (p. 127). They propose six interrelated principles as a basis for intervention with non-offending children, to replace the subjective 'best interests' test. These are:

1 The principle of respect for family autonomy. Here diversity in child-rearing, and the importance of respecting it, is stressed. The presumption in favour of parental autonomy should only be rebutted

where there is specific harm or the disruption/absence of parental ties; even then, there should be a presumption against removing the child.

2 The principle of voluntary services. That is, help should be given on a non-compulsory basis to assist parents to keep their children.

3 The principle of limited intervention in the lives of children and families. Criticising certain grounds for compulsory intervention in the English system at the time, the authors advocate more restricted intervention on narrower, strictly defined criteria – where there has been physical harm or neglect or sexual abuse or abandonment. There may also be a need for some intervention with the siblings of abused children. The alleged criteria would have to be proved in court.

4 The principle of least restrictive alternative. Where there is a case for compulsory intervention, such intervention should minimise disruption and promote the child–family relationship. Various forms of substitute care are seen as damaging to the child. Thus the proving of a criterion for intervention would not automatically lead to intervention, let alone removal from home.

5 The principle of the parties' right to legal representation. The child should be a full independent party to the proceedings, as should the parents.

6 The principle of visibility and accountability of decision-making. Discretion should be limited and there should be firm guidelines for decisions and scope for appeal.

These six principles are broadly in line with the minimum intervention position of Goldstein *et al.* However, there is also in Morris *et al.*'s approach an element of the fourth value perspective to be described in Chapter 5, the children's rights perspective. This is seen in their emphasis on the child as subject rather than object, for example, in their fifth principle that the child should have separate legal representation. Morris *et al.* also say: 'Our proposals are not a legitimation of a *laissez-faire* approach *towards social inequalities* [my italics] ... limiting compulsory intervention means the corresponding expansion of voluntary services' (p. 8). Their second principle of intervention stresses the importance of assistance to parents on a non-compulsory basis to keep families together. There are echoes here of the third value perspective, to be discussed in Chapter 4, the modern defence of the birth parents, which advocates supportive intervention to help parents fulfil their role.

Secondly, Taylor, Lacey and Bracken (1979) in *In Whose Best Interests* argue in a broadly similar vein to Morris *et al.*, although concerned mainly with young offenders. They defend 'natural justice' and parents' and children's rights and liberties held against the state, and propose restricted grounds for compulsory state intervention based on a limited list of specific harms to the child. Again, the 'best interests' principle is criticised. Taylor *et al.*, using the terminology of the time, state the principle: 'No child should be received into care or committed to the care of a local authority unless it has been previously determined that such a course of action constitutes the least restrictive, or least detrimental available alternative' (p. 31). They put forward proposals, based on a formulation by the American author Wald (1976), for grounds for intervention with non-offending children. First the statement is made that 'Coercive societal intervention should be premised upon specific harms to a child, not on the basis of parental conduct' (p. 87). Intervention would only be permitted where it would not cause a greater harm; and would only be permitted for the following specific harms:

1. Injury causing disfigurement, impairment of bodily functioning or severe bodily harm, or the substantial likelihood of this;
2. Serious emotional damage where the parents are unwilling or unable to provide or permit the necessary treatment;
3. Sexual abuse by a member of the household;
4. Need for medical treatment to prevent serious physical harm where the parents are unwilling or unable to provide or permit this.

The slightly broader grounds for intervention accepted by these authors may be noted. Emotional damage is acknowledged as a justification for compulsory intervention, as is refusal of medical treatment in other than life-or-death situations. The (substantial) likelihood of injury is also accepted as a ground. On the other hand the parents' disappearance from the child's life and/or the formation of strong bonds with a substitute caretaker are not referred to. There is an attempt to narrow the grounds for coercive state intervention, which is in keeping with a general *laissez-faire* approach.

The child's right to separate legal representation is supported and Taylor *et al.* include in their book charters of rights for children in care and in institutions. There is an affinity with the children's rights school again. Taylor *et al.*, like Morris *et al.* (1980), favour state intervention stopping short of compulsory measures; families should be helped before the point of legal action. This emphasis is in keeping with the third, pro-parent value perspective. Nevertheless, the views of Taylor *et al.*, like those of Morris *et al.*, seem to have more in common with *laissez-faire* than with the other schools of thought.

The absence of more recent prominent authors who correspond specifically to the *laissez-faire* approach may be noted. It may be that writing on this perspective is associated particularly with the 1970s, while finding expression also in the 1980s. This may also be seen as a characteristically American approach.

Rationale and underlying values

A number of elements of Goldstein *et al.*'s rationale may be outlined. An article by Freeman (1983b) is helpful here and will be drawn on in identifying the different elements. The first element is the psychological aspect of the rationale. This concerns the notion of psychological parenthood, which has been touched on. Goldstein *et al.* argue for the sanctity, not of the biological parent–child link *per se*, but of the psychological bond between children and whoever parents them, based on day-to-day caring, interaction and attachment. The psychological parent role may indeed be carried by the biological parent, and in practice often is, but it can equally well be played by unrelated adults who want the child and are the child's principal carers. It is thus the psychological aspects of the relationship, rather than its biological or legal basis, which are important. In *Beyond the Best Interests* (1979) Goldstein *et al.* argue that children have no psychological conception of relationships by blood tie till quite late in their development; it is day-to-day interchanges with people who care for them which are more important. They comment that while having produced a child normally has far-reaching psychological meaning for the parents, for children the physical realities of their conception and birth are not the direct cause of their emotional attachments. Attachment results from day-to-day attention to their physical and emotional needs. Only a parent who provides for these needs will build a psychological relationship to the child, will become the psychological parent. The absent biological parent is a stranger. In discussing the 'wanted child' the authors say that only children who have a person they can love, and who feel love, can develop healthy self-esteem. If such a positive emotional environment is missing from the start, individuals' love and regard for themselves – and therefore their capacity to love and care for others – are damaged.

In *Before the Best Interests* (1980) the concept of psychological parenthood is emphasised again. The authors comment that 'constantly ongoing interactions between parents and children become for each child the starting point for an all-important line of development that leads towards adult functioning. What begins as the experience of physical contentment or pleasure that accompanies bodily care develops into a primary attachment to the person who provides it' (p. 8). The assignment of parental rights does not guarantee that either biological or adoptive parents will establish significant psychological ties to their child. And in cases of separation of parent and child, legal entitlement cannot prevent the establishment of psychological bonds between children and others – their longtime substitute caretakers.

In a sense this view departs from the traditional or conventional one of the family, in that the importance of the family is construed in social and psychological rather than genetic terms. As Hodges (1981) comments in a review of Goldstein *et al.*'s works: 'importantly, they reorganise the notion of the family around psychological ties rather than birth or the "blood tie" ' (p. 53). This means that Goldstein *et al.*'s approach differs significantly from earlier forms of *laissez-faire*, which saw the sanctity of the blood tie itself as requiring protection. Such thinking about the importance of the blood tie as a separate factor does still emerge in some modern judicial decisions however, and it is also present in some recent policy trends such as the increased importance placed on the role of the unmarried father in the Children Act 1989 and elsewhere. It can also be noted that Goldstein *et al.* do clearly recognise that in practice in most cases the psychological/biological distinction does not need to be made: the biological parent is also the psychological parent. In these cases the biological parent, except in extreme situations, should be left undisturbed.

But it is the notion of psychological parenthood which is deployed by Goldstein *et al.* to defend the policy of minimum state intervention. True psychological parenthood – necessary to the child – cannot be achieved unless the family's sanctity is respected. Psychological parents must be autonomous, within certain broad limits. *Beyond the Best Interests* makes the point that interference with the tie with the psychological parent is extremely emotionally painful for the child, and this may be so even where the tie is to a psychological parent who seems 'unfit'. The authors comment: 'Whatever beneficial qualities a psychological parent may be lacking, he offers the child the chance to become a wanted and needed member within a family structure' (p. 21). This, according to the authors, is usually not provided in an institution, where there are no psychological parents. The fostering situation also has little chance of 'promoting the psychological parent – wanted child relationship' (p. 25). Foster parents are deprived of the usual base of parental devotion, that is being the 'undisputed sole possessor' (p. 25) of the child, while children feel the insecurity of the arrangement, which clashes with their need for emotional constancy. It is also difficult for a child to react to two sets of parents for more than a short time. The second ground for compulsory intervention, that there are bonds between the child and a longtime caretaker, as set out in *Before the Best Interests*, also derives its justification from the concept of psychological parenthood. Children should not be kept 'in limbo' or separated from psychologically real parents who wish to continue to care for them. These bonds also deserve protection from state interference.

The notion of psychological parenthood is the main plank in Goldstein *et al.*'s justification for their policy position; others will be briefly discussed. There is a philosophical rationale to their viewpoint: minimum state intervention, as mentioned, accords with a belief 'in individual freedom and human dignity' (p. 12). Freeman (1983b) sets the emergence of Goldstein *et al.*'s ideas in the context of the early 1980s popularity of libertarianism and the minimal state. While Goldstein *et al.* do not make an explicit connection between their arguments on child care and those political authors who advocate a more limited role for the state in general, there is, argues Freeman, a strong compatability between their views and a 'philosophy of extreme liberalism, of an individualism which treats all rights as though they were private property' (p. 70). The state is seen here as having (ideally) very limited functions, for example, enforcing contracts and protecting individuals against crime. The family is seen as 'a private area outside the law' (Freeman 1983b:71). There may be an unstated economic rationale here also – highly limited state intervention is consonant with lower levels of public expenditure.

Then there are the more pragmatic arguments. The law is too blunt and too slow an instrument to supervise complex parent–child relationships; and the legal system itself cannot act like a decision-making parent. Furthermore, state intervention is often not effective in averting the ill-treatment of children. A further line of argument stresses the injustice of using vague standards in assessing the adequacy of parental care: parents may not know what is expected of them. Also, the child-rearing standards of one class or ethnic group may be unfairly imposed on another. When the various legal powers are used against parents, the assessments made of the parents may have much to do with subjective perceptions, personalities, and the relationship between the parents and those doing the assessing. The civil liberties of parents are thus under threat from the discretion of those who define the situation – the agents of the state – and from the absence of consistent, objective yardsticks for the care of children. And once particular parents have been labelled as inadequate, or their children as at risk of abuse and neglect, subsequent events may be interpreted to fit the label. A related problem is the difficulty of predicting the long-term damage to children of leaving them in an inadequate home or removing them to an alternative. This is particularly so when emotional as opposed to physical abuse or deprivation is the issue.

It would be tempting to identify the underlying political values of the *laissez-faire* or minimalist position in child care with the values of the radical right concerning the state, individuals and the family more generally (on the latter, see, for example, Abbott and Wallace 1992). In both cases the freedom of individuals from state control is stressed; the state is seen as threatening, as a force to be kept within bounds; and counterweights to state power are highly valued. The family may be seen as a locus of alternative power. It is also seen as a locus of serious responsibility. However, not all of those who support a more restricted state role in intervening compulsorily between parent and child belong, politically, on the right. Morris *et al.* (1980) and Taylor *et al.* (1979) put their critique of state intrusion more from a radical left point of view. For example, Morris *et al.* seem to see the development of compulsory intervention in children's lives as part of a more general class-linked structure of social control, stating: 'The recognition of childhood was one device by which control of the property-less class was achieved' (p. 5). They are also conscious of class dominance in models of what 'good' child-rearing practices are. Taylor *et al.* emphasise that they do not 'subscribe to some crude "self-help" theory of society' (p. 9), but that any concern with natural justice and rights in child care involves confronting present social work ideology and practice (the implication being that such state intervention could be improved). It is perfectly possible from a left-wing perspective to see the exercise of state power in a capitalist society as potentially oppressive to most people, as consideration of the third position, to be discussed in Chapter 4, will hopefully make clear. Thus it is not necessarily a conservative world view which underlies the minimalist approach and its distrust of the state.

A final point about underlying values is that at least in the Goldstein *et al.* version of *laissez-faire* – and particularly their latter work – the child as a discrete individual with a viewpoint of his or her own does not make much of an appearance. Decisions and judgements are made on behalf of children by parents and other adults. The child's different sense of time is emphasised, as are other aspects of the child's perceptions, but generally children's interests are imputed to them by others, and conflict is seen as lying between parents and the state. True, in *Beyond the Best Interests* (1979) the authors put forward the guideline that the child in a contested placement should have party status and the right to be represented. It is said here that the presumption that parents or the state represent the child's interests should not prevail in disputes; children need their own counsel whose goal is to determine the least detrimental alternative for the client. However, in *Before the Best Interests* (1980), a somewhat different position is put. Legal assistance is only seen as appropriate for children whose parents believe they need a lawyer and cannot get one for them, *or* whose parents have been disqualified as the exclusive representatives of their interests. It is argued that the appointment of a lawyer for a child without regard to the wishes of the parents should not take place, unless and until the presumption of parental autonomy is overcome with the establishment of one of the grounds for intervention. Short of this situation (for example, where there is only a *charge* of one of the grounds) the same lawyer can usually represent both parents and child. Thus parents' and children's interests are to a great extent identified. This is very different from the approach of the children's rights perspective. This identification of parent and child is less marked with Morris *et al.* (1980) and, especially, Taylor *et al.* (1979), both of whom support separate representation for the child, for example.

Criticisms of *laissez-faire*

Empirical support

Beyond the Best Interests of the Child (1979) has been criticised by Katkin, Bullington and Levine (1974) for lack of empirical support for its propositions. They point out that the book 'does not contain a single reference to any empirical study in the extensive literature on adoption and foster placement. In fact, its references to material from the social sciences include only a single citation to non-psychiatric or non-psychoanalytic literature' (p. 672). Goldstein *et al.* do, however, quote some child studies, such as those by Bowlby and others on the effects of maternal deprivation, and some on child abuse; but in the view of Katkin *et al.* they are not sufficiently aware of the criticisms of these studies. They also, it is argued, overlook the limitations on what can be inferred from the evidence they introduce; for example, they base assertions on a single case study and confuse causality and correlation. The issue here, Katkin *et al.* say, is whether Goldstein *et al.* 'fulfilled the responsibility, implicit in all scholarly efforts to influence social policy, to demonstrate not only the justifications for action, but also the bases for uncertainty' (p. 674). Katkin *et al.* also find that some of the Goldstein unsubstantiated claims contradict everyday experience, for example, the assertion that separation from the parent for more than just a few days may result in permanent emotional scarring in a pre-oedipal child, regardless of the adequacy of the interim care. Nor do Goldstein *et al.* always acknowledge where, among the views they take, there is controversy about what actually is the case. For example, they fail to do this with the question of the harmful effects of separation from the parent *per se*, regardless of subsequent deprivation. In fact, Katkin *et al.* say, many of the studies cited in support of this position deal with deprivation, not separation. An additional criticism is that the authors do not deal with the totality of psychoanalytic theory and literature relevant to their study. Nor do they examine competing explanations and positions but merely advocate their own. Perceptively, Katkin *et al.* comment that in law advocates are expected to amass only the evidence that supports their own position, but in *Beyond the Best Interests* 'neither Professor Goldstein nor the others is practising law; and in any event the usual condition of advocacy – that another side be present – has not been fulfilled' (p. 676). In their conclusion, Katkin *et al.* ask: 'Why was such a limited range of literature consulted, and why did the authors ignore evidence of the weakness of basic studies used to support their propositions?' (p. 681). Relating the problem to the sociology of knowledge, they see the answer as lying partly in the fact that the three authors are particularly prestigious psychoanalysts who may have become insulated and protected from outside criticism.

So Goldstein *et al.* in their earlier book are open to some degree of criticism for their disregard of evidence and its limitations; indeed, the charge is a serious one given the importance and the firmness of their recommendations. *Before the Best Interests of the Child* (1980) refers to more studies of children and their development – for example, the notes list studies on maternal deprivation and early childhood development, on later childhood, on adoption, institutional care, sexual and other forms of abuse, as well as legal material, psychoanalytic writings, and their own earlier works. Nevertheless, it seems that the evidence of some child studies is dismissed in this book (see Freeman 1983b), and that Goldstein *et al.*'s position derives largely from psychoanalytic theory, from findings in individual cases in clinical practice, and from analysis of court cases and other individual cases.

To consider the other authors briefly, Morris *et al.* (1980) make use of government figures relating to children and the interventions of the legal system, and of research studies, including their own. Examples would be the finding by Cawson *et al.* (1978) that over 30 per cent of young offenders subject to care orders in 1975 had no previous court appearances, Millham's (1978) study of secure units, and Holman's (1980) evidence of the under-use of the powers to do preventive work. The authors also quote individual cases. They aim to show, broadly, that the state system for dealing with both offending and non-offending children and young persons is unsatisfactory and more coercive than it needs to be. A problem arises with the interpretation of the data, however. If, for example, Cawson's figure of 31 per cent is higher than might be expected or hoped, what is the yardstick that is being used to reach this conclusion?

Taylor *et al.*'s (1979) initial concern arose from experience of about a hundred child care cases handled by the British mental health pressure group MIND, which provided a social work advocacy service for parents and children involved in care and other proceedings in the juvenile court. The authors also quote extensively from research and government statistics to support various aspects of their case. Examples would be the finding by Thorpe, Paley and Green (1979) that a third of young offenders apparently not requiring residential care received a care order on their first court appearance, Cawson *et al.*'s (1978) finding again, figures showing the increased number of young offenders sent to penal institutions over the 1970s, and evidence of life inside institutions. The type of data used, and the intention in using it, are similar to Morris *et al.*'s approach. It is aimed to show that state intervention is too coercive and could and should be less so. Similar problems arise as with Morris *et al.*'s work: what do the statistics actually tell us? Differences of view arise about the appropriate disposition for children appearing before the courts (whether for offences or because of their own need for protection). Differences of view mean that from one angle a given set of statistics makes the system look too coercive, and from another angle not coercive enough. A similar reservation must be entered about the use of individual cases. Judicial decisions, for example, *may* reflect a current trend or presage a new one, but do not necessarily do so; and different judges arrive at different judgements when faced with similar cases in the same historical period (indeed, the existence of an appeals system reflects and assumes such differences). Consideration of one case may suggest that the system is too coercive, and consideration of another that it is not coercive enough. Overall conclusions are difficult to arrive at from isolated instances, although such instances may be useful to illustrate particular ways of thinking and are usually of intrinsic interest in themselves.

Problems with the implications for policy

The implications for policy arising from Goldstein *et al.*'s work have been outlined – their five guidelines for disputed child placement, encompassing: one overall guideline, the 'least detrimental alternative'; three component guidelines (concerning continuity, sense of time, and the law's incapacity); and a guideline on legal representation; and then their seven grounds where compulsory intervention between parent and child would be justified (parental requests, bonds with a psychological but non-biological parent, disappearance etc. of the parents, conviction of a sexual offence, serious injury, failure to authorise life-saving medical care, and need for legal assistance).

Some difficulties may be found with the overall placement guideline, that is, the 'least detrimental alternative'. It may be thought just as potentially subjective as the 'best interests' test and just as problematic in terms of interpretation. The first three component guidelines are meant to feed into and give substance to this general guideline. The first guideline, the emphasis on the child's sense of time, would seem to be helpful and well-founded. The second, 'continuity' guideline seems, however, virtually to elevate continuity above all other values. As Freeman (1983b) comments: 'At the very least the breaking of ties cannot be "invariably detrimental" [i.e. as Goldstein *et al.* claim]. If that were the case no state intervention into the family could ever be justified' (p. 72). The third guideline, the law's incapacity in the field of parent–child relationships may be recognised as valid; it is only one possible response to that problem, however, to recommend that as far as possible the law should withdraw. Another is to advocate an improvement in the functioning of the law and state machinery, for example, through more sophisticated systems for assessment and substitute care.

Greater difficulties arise with the recommendations in the second work (1980). The main problem with the seven grounds for compulsory intervention is their narrowness and inflexibility. With the first ground, where the parent asks the state to intervene, no such intervention is seen as justified where parents come to an agreement about the child's care; thus divorce or separation are not sufficient grounds for intervention in themselves (this being effectively the position now in England and Wales under the Children Act 1989, it may be noted). Yet it may be argued that the machinery of the state should (as it does under some jurisdictions) satisfy itself as to the nature of arrangements for children in these cases even where parents are in agreement.

The time limits laid down in the second, psychological bonding ground, after which a substitute caretaker who wished to have parental rights over the child could be granted them, are inevitably arbitrary – a point which Goldstein *et al.* concede themselves. Specific time periods are seen as the least intrusive modes of intervention, giving advance warning to the parents. Objections to this approach, however, arise because of the rigidities of such a clear cut-off point in time, and because of fears that parents who are aware of the time limit may remove their child – when it is perhaps not appropriate to do so – just before the time limit expires. Furthermore, such fixed time limits take no account of *why* the child has been in another's care for so long.

With the third ground, the death or disappearance of the parent, it should be noted that if the parent has provided for the child's care by delegating it to another, for example, through a will, Goldstein *et al.* take the view that the parent's wishes should be respected. This allows parents a high degree of autonomy to make private arrangements for their children (as in divorce and separation cases in England since the Children Act 1989). With the fourth ground, the sexual offence against the child, the insistence upon conviction (or acquittal by reason of 'insanity') may be objected to. The high standard of proof required in obtaining a conviction means that no compulsory intervention would be possible in many cases of alleged or suspected abuse, and that therefore the child could remain in the alleged offender's care, a situation where there are at least grounds for regarding the child's welfare as being at risk. Goldstein *et al.* take the view, however, that the justification for removing the child is best left to the criminal law with its high standards of proof; thus: 'the authority to assume the risks of intervention, including the termination of parental rights, arises only after the parent–child relationship has been severed by the *criminal process*' (1980:65, my italics). Many would regard this position as not going far enough to protect the child in cases where there is suspicion, or indeed clear evidence, of sexual abuse. The criminal law can also be a clumsy instrument; it also tends to involve delays. And not all abused children wish for their parent to be criminalised (they wish for the abuse to stop – which is different).

The fifth ground is serious bodily injury inflicted by the parent, or repeated failure to prevent the child suffering such injury. Goldstein *et al.* are clear that seriously injured children should be removed; yet no such provision is made for less serious injury or emotional injury. Parents, as they see it, should be protected from unwarranted intrusions arising from undefined terms such as 'denial of proper care', 'emotional damage' or the 'unfit home'. There is no consensus about these concepts, they say, which are too imprecise to ensure fair warning to parents. Again, it may be argued that the proposed ground does not extend far enough to provide adequate protection for the child. Severe physical punishment would occasion no state action, nor behaviour which might reasonably be regarded as physical and/or mental cruelty but which inflicts no actual injury. There is also an apparent inconsistency in the authors' argument. Serious bodily injury, they argue, has the effect of psychological harm – the destruction of the child's trust in the parents and his or her feeling of safety with them. Yet surely less serious injury and neglect may be argued to produce the same psychological results.

The sixth ground relates to the failure to authorise life-saving medical care but only where such care would give the child a chance of normal development or a 'life worth living'. Goldstein *et al.* argue that when death is not a likely consequence of exercising a medical choice, there would be no justification for government intrusion; courts and doctors must not impose their preferences in medical care. In cases in which there can be disagreement about whether life after treatment will be 'normal' or 'worth living', the parents should be left free to decide; parents 'must have the right to act on their belief within the privacy of their family' (1980:95). The authors acknowledge that the ground would allow parents to decide 'whether their congenitally malformed newborn with an ascertainable neurological deficiency and highly predictable mental retardation should be provided with treatment which might avoid death, yet which offered no chance of cure' (pp. 96–7). 'Families' (i.e. parents) know their own values here and have to live with the consequences; they may feel the euthanasia option is in fact forced upon them. If their autonomy here is not respected, then the state must take on itself the burden of providing the resources that the child needs.

Goldstein *et al.*'s comments make it plain that treatment could be withheld from disabled children on the ground that they could never have a normal life or a life worth living, and Freeman's (1983b) discussion of the case of Philip Becker, a child with Down's Syndrome, in the light of Goldstein *et al.*'s guideline, underlines this point, highlighting dramatically what the Goldstein model of parental autonomy might imply if the sixth guideline were rigidly applied. Philip Becker was an 11-year-old American child with Down's Syndrome who also had a heart defect which could be corrected by surgery, although with the risk of post-operative complications. Without surgery he would positively deteriorate and probably die; with it, if successful, he would develop into a healthy, although never 'normal' adult. Although his parents were not caring for him and were in only intermittent contact, they refused to consent to surgery, and the courts upheld their decision. The parents' refusal of consent was based partly on the grounds that the child's life was not worth living and should not therefore be prolonged by surgery (Freeman, 1983b). While Goldstein *et al.* have not commented specifically on this case, it does highlight the narrowness of permissible state intervention under their sixth ground.

The seventh ground for compulsory intervention is the child's need for legal assistance. This has already been discussed in the context of Goldstein *et al.*'s tendency not to differentiate the child as a separate person and to identify child and parental interests to a high degree. Again the narrowness of this ground, and the emphasis given to parental choice, may be noted. *Only* where one of the other grounds has been established may the child have separate legal representation regardless of parental wishes. It may be objected here that it is not at this late stage that the child needs a lawyer.

Besides the narrow and clearcut nature of the grounds for state intervention in Goldstein's work, there is the further characteristic of somewhat draconian intervention when the grounds *are* proved. While in cases of problematic child care which stop short of the grounds, *no* intervention (certainly no compulsory intervention – and only minor reference is made to voluntary intervention) is seen as justified. However, where the grounds *do* apply, state intervention would usually be sweeping, with the original parent–child bonds being severed and new ones created. The approach is essentially black and white. The scope for prevention of family break-up is overlooked, and in this the Goldstein position differs sharply from the third value perspective to be discussed in Chapter 4, the pro-parent perspective. As Katkin *et al.* (1974) comment, Goldstein *et al.*: 'while obviously concerned about the effects of separation on children, seem uninterested in how separation occurs initially' (p. 678). Freeman (1983b) makes a similar point with respect to the second, 'psychological bonding' ground for intervention, that it is strange 'that the reason why a child is in care should count for absolutely nothing' (p. 80).

It is clear that the authors do not adopt a totally *laissez-faire* approach, as drastic intervention by force of law is permitted in certain extreme cases. They also do not apparently object to compulsory education or legal restrictions on child labour. These powers exercised by the state also limit parental freedom but are seen as unproblematic. Like other thinkers on child care policy, Goldstein *et al.* do see the need to draw a line somewhere, bounding parental autonomy. But it may be argued, with Freeman (1983b), that they 'have drawn the line in the wrong place ... too close to the parents' interests and too far from the children's' (p. 91).

Some similar problems arise with Morris *et al.*'s (1980) and Taylor *et al.*'s (1979) recommendations for child care policy. Morris *et al.*'s grounds for compulsory intervention are self-confessedly narrow. These grounds make a distinction 'between situations in which harm or neglect has actually occurred and situations of possible future risk, and also between physical and emotional harm' (p. 132). *Possible* abuse is excluded because of the difficulty of predicting accurately, and emotional harm because of the subjectivity and unreliability of such judgements. The authors favour 'concern with conduct based on identifiable and objective criteria' (p. 133). So, for example, child abuse registers should only include those children about whom a court has made a specific finding, not those merely 'at risk'. The authors concede: 'We accept that such a narrowing of criteria may entail risks' (p. 133). While Taylor *et al.*'s grounds for intervention are broader in some ways, in that emotional injury and the likelihood of injury are included, abandonment, for example, is overlooked. Both groups of authors, however, do not anticipate the rather draconian severance from the family of origin – together with integration into a new family – envisaged by Goldstein *et al.* as a necessary consequence of intervention; on the contrary, Morris *et al.* argue for the disposition which does least to sever children's bonds with their families, while Taylor *et al.* clearly wish to reduce the number of children in care.

Problems of rationale and underlying values

Further objections may be put to some of the ideas underpinning the Goldstein minimalist approach. First, the notion of 'psychological parenthood' may be seen to have much validity; but the degree of emphasis put upon it by Goldstein *et al.* may understate the importance of biological and genetic ties, or even deny their existence. Biological ties *per se* may still be of importance to people. For example, the fact that some individuals, adopted or otherwise separated from their genetic relatives, have attempted to trace their original family suggests that pure biology without a psychological link can be important (see, for example, Bean and Melville 1989, Howe, Sawbridge and Hinings 1992). The present author in a paper on surrogate motherhood (Harding 1987) suggested two points here; that:

> while childhood carers are of crucial importance, the people with whom one shares part of one's *genetic* make-up – not only parents but also siblings, grandparents, aunts, uncles, cousins – do tend to resemble oneself in certain respects. This resemblance can form a basis for affinity, fascination, curiosity, insight into self, and relationship – even when one has not known these people early in life. The second point is that, Goldstein, Freud and Solnit notwithstanding, society still tends to define families largely in biological terms – so unseen relatives may still be socially construed as relatives regardless of the lack of a close interactional link – and their absence may be acutely felt.
>
> (Harding 1987:57)

This paper also makes the point that the Goldstein argument seems to ring most true when applied to very young children who do not understand the psychological–biological distinction themselves. A further point is made by Katkin *et al.* (1974): 'psychology does not offer the same guarantee of clear-cut issues as biology' (p. 678), and it therefore leaves more scope for judicial discretion.

Secondly, criticisms may be put of the argument that true psychological parenthood can only be achieved when there is minimum intervention from outside in the parent–child bond. Goldstein *et al.*'s position – that there should be only two psychological parents, or, if the two are separated, only one, functioning in an autonomous way – overlooks the possibility that children can relate happily to a number of parent figures who are not co-resident, and can benefit psychologically from doing so. This point will be referred to further in discussing the third, pro-birth parent perspective, which takes a far less exclusive view of parental roles towards children. It may be noted here that there is evidence that, for example, children may benefit from contact with their birth parents, notwithstanding that they are cared for on a long-term basis by foster parents, or benefit from contact with a non-resident parent after separation/divorce. Holman (1975a), for example, argued that the 'inclusive' type of foster care, where contact with the natural parent is favoured, is positively related to fostering success (absence of fostering breakdown and of child problems), while Benians (1982) identified five ways in which a non-custodial parent's access can contribute to the child's well-being. There is considerable literature suggesting that in general contact with both separated parents is beneficial (for example, Wallerstein and Kelly 1980, Hetherington, Cox and Cox 1982, Richards 1986, Cockett and Tripp 1994). Children may perhaps also benefit from their relationships with part-time caretakers, teachers, social workers and other adults. Goldstein *et al.*'s insistence that, in effect, the basis of emotional health is exclusive parental possession of the child is, to say the least, questionable.

To deal with Goldstein *et al.*'s political philosophical rationale briefly: this rationale is not set out in the same detail as the psychological rationale, but appears to bias their work in a particular direction and to lead them to make certain assumptions. One is a rather poor opinion of the abilities of legislators, judges and professionals, in their work in the field of child care; and another the apparent dismissal of any benefits in institutional care. The authors emphasise at many points in their writings the dangers arising from an over-intrusive state. Their ideal state acts in a narrow, legalistic way. Various arguments may be put against this extremely restricted view. With reference to children, the most obvious are that the vulnerability of children requires strong state protection (associated most clearly with the second value perspective, to be described in Chapter 3, the paternalist perspective) and that there is a social responsibility to care for all children and therefore to help parents in their role (more likely to be put by proponents of the third, pro-parent value perspective described in Chapter 4). Wider arguments concerning the welfare role of the state relate to notions of collective responsibility, social rights, the meeting of needs and the creation of greater equality, arguments which will not be explored here. Perhaps the main point to note is that these *laissez-faire* proponents do not, on the whole, see state intervention as benign. Yet it may be argued powerfully that the state in its welfare role, for all its obvious faults, has achieved much, particularly for dependent groups. Furthermore, it may do much to protect such groups from the exercise of the 'individual freedom' which Goldstein *et al.* appear to find so appealing. As Freeman (1983b) puts it: 'in a world of basic structural inequalities individual freedom can be so exercised as to undermine not only the freedom of others but also their human dignity. The parent–child relationship is a microcosm of this imbalance' (p. 72). Finally, the suspicion of a hidden economic rationale here has been mentioned. The general advocacy of a reduced welfare role for government has much to do with support for a reduced level of public expenditure (and lower taxes).

The various other arguments put by Goldstein *et al.* may be conceded in principle. Yes, the law is a blunt instrument; standards can be vague and may involve personal and class prejudices; professional discretion is a potential threat to liberty; prediction is difficult; and the momentum generated by a labelling process may result in unfairness to individuals; while it is conceded that the state child care machinery is often ineffective (as cases of children abused and killed while under state supervision make tragically clear). As has already been said, an alternative response to Goldstein's to this state of affairs is to seek to improve the response of the law and the child care agencies rather than to curtail it. Further, as Freeman (1983b) also concedes, what is engaged in here is a line-

drawing exercise; some boundaries *should* be drawn round state power –
but Goldstein *et al.* have drawn their line in the wrong place.

The underlying values and rationale of the two other groups of
authors identified as belonging in the modern *laissez-faire* camp are not
so well-developed, although some of the same themes are identifiable.
These include the limits of knowledge and prediction, the unsatisfactory nature of much substitute care, and the problems of excessive
discretion. However, while anxious to see a shrinking of the state's role
in compulsory intervention, Morris *et al.* (1980) envisage both a concentration (rather than a reduction) of resources, and the provision of
extensive services on a voluntary basis. Taylor *et al.* (1979) stress both
natural justice and children's rights, here having much in common with
the third (pro-parent) and fourth (children's rights) value perspectives,
but do not want their book to be regarded as a plea for legalism. They
are acutely aware of the lack of state resources which causes the need
for substitute care to arise.

A final critical point to be made here relates to the overlooking of the
child as a separate entity with rights of her own. A few issues may be
mentioned. The first is the absence of emphasis on the child's own
wishes, which may be seen as a serious shortcoming in the Goldstein
minimalist school. Perhaps it is assumed that children do not have
wishes, or that, if they do, these do not accord with their 'best interests'
and can therefore be disregarded. It may be objected that in the real
world children may have strong views and feelings about, for example,
whom they should live with; that children vary; and that, while their
wishes may not always be consonant with what psychoanalytic theory
would prescribe for them, perhaps this should call into question psychoanalytic theory as much as it does the validity of the child's viewpoint.
A second issue is that of independent legal representation for the child,
which has already been discussed. A third is the notion of the child's
right to proper care, somewhat overlooked in the Goldstein approach,
which assumes a higher value for continuity, 'psychological parenthood', and being a 'wanted child'. It is interesting in the light of these
concerns to note the contrast with some versions of the children's rights
school, which would see child placement decisions as resting *with the
child* – thus, presumably, largely obviating the need for guidelines and
formal grounds for intervention to guide adults in their decisions.

The perspective in practice

The main elements in this value perspective, the work of some authors
associated with it, the underlying rationale, and some problems found,
have been discussed. A brief account will now be given of some patterns in nineteenth-century English child care law which illustrate the
workings of the perspective in practice. The account is intended to give
some idea of what the value perspective may mean when translated

into law, policy and decision-making. A note will be added on the slow apparent decline of patriarchy and recent attempts at its revival.

A striking illustration of an early and extreme form of *laissez-faire* is afforded by the situation of children and child care in England in the nineteenth century, particularly the earlier part of the century. Only gradually was the common law presumption that the rights of fathers were virtually absolute, eroded by various statutes which first gave some rights to mothers and, later, some protection to children. (It is worth remembering that animals gained statutory protection from cruelty well before children did.) Even early in the century, however, some interventions in paternal rights were allowed for, in what were then regarded as extreme cases: for example in 1817 the poet Shelley's atheism and intention to bring up his children without religion were regarded as sufficiently serious to constitute grounds for depriving him of custody (Shelley v. Westbrooke 1817, Jac. 266n). On the other hand, even much later in the century, and in the face of some movement to give higher priority to child welfare, a strongly *laissez-faire* viewpoint could still be demonstrated in judgements in court cases where the custody or upbringing of children was at issue.

A well-known example was the case of the Agar-Ellis family, regarding whom there were a number of court hearings under the wardship jurisdiction in the 1870s and 1880s (In re Agar-Ellis 1878 10 Ch.D. p. 49; In re Agar-Ellis 1883 24 Ch.D. p. 317). This was an English upper-class family where there was a dispute between the estranged parents about the religious upbringing of the three daughters, aged 12, 11 and 9 at the time of the first proceedings in 1878. The Protestant father, having initially promised his wife that their children would be brought up as Roman Catholics, changed his mind and, in the face of resistance by the children to being brought up as Anglicans, started an action to have them made wards of court, with a summons in the action concerning their religious education. The mother then petitioned with a view to the children being brought up as Roman Catholics. Her petition was initially dismissed by the first court to hear the case, and on appeal by her, the father's rights to decide were again upheld, although the judgement hinted that it might be for the children's welfare to remain Catholics. Of interest here are the fact that the court refused to examine the children, who were well past infancy, and some of the comments made by the judges concerning paternal rights. The Vice-Chancellor in the first judgement, for example (1878, above), criticised the mother for having forgotten 'that by the laws of *England*, by the laws of Christianity, and by the constitution of society, when there is a difference of opinion between husband and wife, it is the duty of the wife to submit to the husband' (p. 55), later going on to say that the court never interfered between a father and his children, except when the father brought them up irreligiously (quoting the Shelley v. Westbrooke case), or where there was immoral conduct (quoting Wellesley v. Wellesley 2 Bli. (N.S.) 124), or where the father had been guilty of the abandonment of parental duty. In the appeal case, while the mother's lawyers argued that the interests of the children should be considered when the children were wards of court (In re Agar-Ellis 1878), the judges made comments like the following:

> The right of the father to the custody and control of his child is one of the most sacred of rights. No doubt the law may take away from him this right or may interfere with his exercise of it, just as it may take away his life or his property or interfere with his liberty, but it must be for some sufficient cause known to the law.   (In re Agar-Ellis 1878:71–2)

The perception of paternal rights as comparable to other basic civil liberties is symptomatic of a marked *laissez-faire* position.

In 1883 the Agar-Ellis family returned to court with their dispute; this time the problem concerned restrictions put by the father on the mother's access to the second daughter, now aged 16 (In re Agar-Ellis 1883 24 Ch.D.:317). A petition had been presented by mother and daughter asking that the daughter be allowed to spend her vacation with her mother and that the mother be allowed free access and communication in the future. Although the children were still wards of court, the courts refused to interfere with the exercise of the father's rights and dismissed the petition. Again, the mother's lawyers argued for the child's benefit to be considered; again, the courts came down on the side of paternal authority. It is of interest that economic arguments came into this case. The father's lawyers stated that the father, if he were not allowed to bring up his children in his own way, would consider himself discharged from all legal and moral obligation to maintain them (and that no offer to maintain had been made by the mother's side, while only a small fund was available to the court). A reciprocal link was made between maintenance and the right to control, in other words. The court refused to see the daughter, and the judges made similar comments to those made in the 1878 case, such as: 'The rights of a father are sacred rights because his duties are sacred duties' (p. 329) and: 'It is not in our power to go into the question as to what we think is for the benefit of this ward' (p. 334). It was said that the court could not bring up a child as successfully as a father 'even if the father was exercising his discretion as regards the child in a way which critics might condemn' (p. 335). There are strong similarities with the Goldstein *et al.* emphasis on parental autonomy here.

Another way in which nineteenth century *laissez-faire* can be illustrated, however, is by looking at those changes in the law which in fact moved away from *laissez-faire,* and the debates which these changes stimulated. The fact that specific measures were introduced to protect the rights of women and children – and that the measures were opposed – is an indicator of what *laissez-faire* had meant, and its strength. Two strands may be identified in the legislative changes. At various points during the century, legislation eroded the near-absolute common law paternal rights by granting some restricted rights to married women in relation to their children. For example, in 1839 an Infants' Custody Act introduced into the Commons by Sir Thomas Talfourd gave married mothers restricted custody and access rights in relation to young children in cases of marital separation. Interestingly, the Bill was argued against in terms of its propensity to undermine marriage by reducing the woman's incentive to remain in her marriage. Nevertheless, it passed, and later legislation extended maternal custody, access and guardianship rights further. By 1886 (that is, after the Agar-Ellis cases) the mother had the right to apply for custody of, or access to, a minor child up to the age of 21, and had rights to appoint a testamentary guardian and act jointly with one appointed by the father. Even so, maternal rights were not yet equal to paternal ones.

The second strand in legislative change concerned greater protection for children. As is widely known, child labour in much of the nineteenth century was still extensively exploited under harsh conditions, and education was for most children rudimentary (as was the case in previous centuries); there was also no specific statutory protection against cruelty by adults (until 1889) and child criminals over the age of seven still tended to be treated in a similar way to adult offenders. Pinchbeck and Hewitt (1969) point out that the statutory protection of children only became a subject of serious concern in the nineteenth century, and even then there was a long struggle to bring it into being, requiring: 'a revolution in contemporary attitudes to social responsibility' (p. 347), attitudes in which ignorance and religious views were both a factor. Also, to undermine parental responsibility was, it was feared, to undermine family stability and therefore the stability of society itself. Interestingly, both laws restricting child labour and those introducing compulsory education were opposed on the grounds that they constituted an unacceptable intrusion by the state into family responsibility and parental rights. So control of the working hours of children (and women) could be argued against on the grounds that their care and protection was a *family* responsibility which state intervention would tend to break down. A related argument was that parents had the right to do what they liked with the labour of their children as long as they provided adequate support. Similar arguments were advanced against the growth of state education; education could be seen as a family responsibility, which would be damaged should the state intervene. Compulsory education could also be seen as an abrogation of the parental right to the child's services. The factory reformer Shaftesbury saw it as an infringement of parents' rights to bring up their children as they saw fit, and as encouraging undesirable dependence on the state (Pinchbeck and Hewitt 1969).

By the 1880s effective campaigns were mounted against child cruelty within the family. The concept of the father's absolute right to custody had to be challenged; these campaigns, it may be noted, were being conducted around the same time as the Agar-Ellis judgements discussed earlier. A Prevention of Cruelty to, and Protection of, Children Act was passed in 1889; prior to this cruelty to children was not a specific criminal offence, and the only recourse at law was for minors or their 'next friend' to sue the parent or for the Poor Law authorities to prosecute, where they were responsible for the child. Behlmer (1982) attributes the slowness of change in this field largely to the persistence of the idea that parent–child relations were immune to government regulation. In fact, the 1889 Act made only restricted interventions possible. Even so, as Hendrick (1994) says, it 'marked a turning point in legal and social attitudes towards children' (p. 54). Hendrick sees the emergence of a distinctive notion of 'the child' and childhood from the 1870s onwards, so that by the turn of the century a recognisably 'modern' concept of childhood was being put in place. But the reformers' view of children was an essentially middle-class one based on patriarchal and domestic ideals.

In conclusion, it should be remembered that the *laissez-faire* of nineteenth-century England was different in significant ways from the modern form of *laissez-faire* which has been the main focus of this chapter. In particular, it concentrated on the *blood tie* to the *father* (rather than, as Goldstein *et al.* do, on an *emotional* tie to a *psychological parent*); did not – even nominally – give first priority to the child's interests; and allowed for a narrower scope for state intervention in more extreme cases. Nevertheless, it had certain points in common with modern *laissez-faire* and illustrates where the logic of *laissez-faire* might lead. Both positions see state intervention as inherently undesirable and only reluctantly accepted when extreme circumstances justify it. Both positions see the child's interests – in the vast majority of cases – as really lying in remaining with the parent and under parental control. Compare, for example, the following two statements a century apart, one made by a judge in one of the Agar-Ellis cases in 1883, and the other by Goldstein, Freud and Solnit in 1980:

When, by birth, a child is subject to a father, it is for the general interest of families, and for the general interest of children, and really for the interest of the particular infant, that the Court should not, except in very extreme cases, interfere with the discretion of the father, but leave to him the responsibility of exercising that power which nature has given him by the birth of the child.

(In re Agar-Ellis 1883:334)

We believe that a child's need for continuity of care by autonomous parents requires acknowledging that parents should generally be entitled to raise their children as they think best, free of state interference. This conviction finds expression in our preference for *minimum state intervention* and prompts restraint in defining justifications for coercively intruding on family relationships.

(Goldstein *et al.* 1980:4)

The rationales and the language might be different, but the central themes regarding state policy are much the same.

Note on the decline and defence of patriarchy

The value perspective outlined in this chapter has been dubbed '*laissez-faire* and patriarchy'. So far, most direct attention has been paid to the principle of *laissez-faire*, but is it worth saying something more about patriarchy in its own right. As has been said, *laissez-faire* tends to support patriarchy where men already have greater power than women in the family. Since the nineteenth century, however, specific inroads have been made into the formal patriarchal power of men within families by means of statutes affording some rights to women and some protection to children. Some of the English legislation of the nineteenth century giving mothers certain custody, access and guardianship rights over their children has been referred to. In addition there were Acts in the 1870s and 1880s granting married women greater rights to control their own property. The situation was still far from legal equality, however. In the twentieth century, English legislation moved towards establishing at least a formal equality for women both in the family and outside it; the 1925 Guardianship of Minors Act, for example, began: 'Whereas Parliament by the Sex Disqualification (Removal) Act, 1919, and various other enactments, had sought to establish equality in law between the sexes, and it is expedient that this principle should obtain with respect to the guardianship of infants and the rights and responsibilities conferred thereby:', then stating in Section 1 that in custody and related proceedings the court was to regard the child's welfare as the first and paramount consideration, and was not to consider: 'whether from any other point of view the claim of the father, or any right at common law possessed by the father ... is superior to that of the mother, or the claim of the mother is superior to that of the father'. Later legislation, in the 1970s, equalised maternal and paternal rights in general, that is before custody or other disputes arose, and thus carried the 1925 principle further; and other legislation such as the Equal Pay Act 1970 and the Sex Discrimination Act 1975 has moved towards establishing formal equality for women in the public sphere. The Children Act 1989 abolished the formal notion of custody and favoured arrangements worked out between parents themselves, but there was still a presumption of equality in parental claims.

In a situation of formal equality for women, is it fair to associate the modern form of *laissez-faire* with patriarchy? It might be thought, as Goldstein *et al.*'s wording suggests, that the discussion is only about parents and in no sense favours the power of fathers over that of mothers. Indeed, in a context where women as primary caretakers are more likely to be construed as the main 'psychological parent', and certainly in practice are more likely to gain care of the child on divorce, it might be thought that *laissez-faire* entails matriarchy rather than patriarchy. Single parents were by the 1990s a sizeable minority among families (1.3 million families in Britain in 1992 or 21 per cent of families – OPCS 1992), and most single parents are mothers (over 90 per cent in Britain – Garnham and Knights 1994). As well as divorced motherhood, it may be noted, unmarried motherhood has been becoming more common. In Britain in 1992, for example, 32 per cent of births were outside marriage (Central Statistical Office 1994). In an increasing number of cases, then, the parent who has sole day-to-day care of the child is the mother. Parental autonomy would then mean maternal autonomy – the right of mothers to conduct their family life in their own way, without interference from either child care agencies or other adults – including, among these other adults, non-resident fathers, if the Goldstein model is followed.

The point may be conceded to a degree with regard to single parents; although single parent mothers remain vulnerable to the forces of patriarchy in the wider society (see Walby 1990, for the shift from private to public patriarchy) and indeed to pressure and attempts to control from the supposedly absent father (see, for example, Clarke, Glendinning and Craig 1994) who still usually has parental responsibility under the Children Act. Where there are two co-resident parents, however, it may be argued that males still have greater *de facto* power, for example, economic power, and the power of violence; and there is a considerable body of feminist work which supports the notion that husbands/fathers remain the superordinate party within marriage and the family (see, particularly, Delphy and Leonard 1992). Parental autonomy could then mean greater autonomy for fathers than mothers. Offsetting this, mothers may have much scope for day-to-day control and minor decisions. 'Parental autonomy' thus needs deconstructing – *whose* autonomy is in fact likely to be more strongly present?

Before leaving the first value perspective, a modern connection between *laissez-faire* and patriarchy should be commented on. There is a school of thought which would like to see both a reduction in the welfare and therapeutic interventions of the state, and a reassertion of male authority within the family (and this school also tends to be deeply antagonistic to single-parent families). Berger and Berger (1983) have characterised this school of thought as a 'neotraditionalist' perspective on the family, and as essentially a backlash phenomenon. It contains strands of anti-permissiveness, anti-feminism, and a moral anxiety about the breakdown of the family and the wider moral order (see also Parton 1981, 1985a, 1985b). It favours traditional role divisions within the family and permanent marriage. In the British context, a pressure group called the Conservative Family Campaign, formed in 1986, numbered among its aims: 'to put father back at the head of the family table' (Conservative Family Campaign 1986), although it was vague about how this might actually be achieved. Other bodies with this type of objective have also appeared (for the 'moral lobby' in general in Britain, see Durham 1991; for other writing on the right and the 'pro-family' position, see, for example, Abbott and Wallace 1992). The right-wing Institute of Economic Affairs issued a publication on the family (Anderson and Dawson 1986), which spoke of: 'the normal family … the husband being the principal if not the only breadwinner' (p. 9), lamenting a perceived transfer of power and responsibility from family to state. Further publications from the same body subsequently appeared thick and fast in the 1990s. These were of a 'neotraditionalist', 'pro-family' or 'family values' kind, and also sometimes explicitly anti-feminist. For example, *Families without Fatherhood* by Dennis and Erdos (1992) saw crime and a breakdown of the social order as linked with absent fatherhood. Other publications focused on crime again (Dennis 1993), a critique of state policy for families which was seen as favouring single parents over married couples (Morgan 1994), and the shortcomings of feminism and the need to 'liberate' women from it (Quest 1992, 1994). The particular theme of interest here is the wish to reinstate a form of private patriarchy, the controlling presence of the father in the family. Without this presence, a major social control problem is seen to occur, particularly affecting young males.

As mentioned earlier, support for patriarchy is not confined to the political right. Two academic examples may be cited (see also Barrett and McIntosh 1991, for these authors). Lasch (1977) deplored the decline of the patriarchal family over the last century, seeing state control over the family and child rearing as having been extended in an undesirable way, while paternal authority had been weakened by capitalism, consumerism and market forces. Donzelot (1980) saw family authority as no longer endorsed and supported by the state but 'colonised' in a patriarchy of the state, through the interventions of various 'experts'. These therapeutic interventions, working through mothers specifically, are distrusted as apparatuses of control. It appears that the reduction of paternal power is regretted. The support for patriarchy is more subtle in these authors' work, but is nevertheless arguably present. Certainly patriarchy is seen as being weakened as the welfare role of the state has expanded – and both trends are apparently lamented.

CHAPTER 3

State paternalism and child protection

Introduction

The term *state paternalism and child protection* is taken to indicate the school of thought which favours extensive state intervention to protect children from poor parental care. Where parental care is inadequate, finding the child a new permanent home where good quality care will be provided, is favoured. The rights and liberties of parents are given a low priority; the child is paramount.

The main elements of the perspective

In striking contrast to the *laissez-faire* school of thought, the second perspective envisages a very considerable role for the state in intervening (coercively if need be) in families, in order to protect children from cruelty or inadequate care. The approach may be seen as rooted in a stronger awareness that (birth) parental care is not always good, indeed may be intensely damaging; higher standards would be set for appropriate care than in the *laissez-faire* perspective, norms of child rearing would be more likely to be defined and imposed, and there is a tendency to be more punitive towards parents who fall short of particular norms and standards. The paternalist/protectionist orientation to parental care is complemented by the view that children should have a high priority in society, that they have rights to a good standard of care, and should at all costs be protected, using the force of the law where necessary, from ill-treatment. Thus parental rights are not valued highly in this approach; it is the parental *duty* to care properly for the child which is prominent, and where this duty is not met, the state may well be justified in removing the child permanently to other caretakers. The child's well-being is paramount, and adult needs, interests and rights must if necessary be sacrificed to this end. There is thus a strong sense of identification with the suffering child.

While in a sense the state paternalist perspective emphasises children's rights, it focuses on the child's right to adequate nurturance and care rather than to self-determination, in contrast to the fourth, 'children's rights', perspective. That is, the child is seen as essentially dependent, vulnerable, and with needs which are different from those of the adult; children's rights are, in effect, to the presence of caring adults who will then meet their needs – and are thus different from adult rights. As children are not perceived as responsible for themselves in the way adults are, their welfare is largely imputed to them by adults, in this case usually the agents of the state, and possibly the substitute parental caretakers. There is not the same assumption as in the minimalist school that the birth parents generally know and do what is best for the child – but it seems that other adults are expected to do so.

Somewhat overlooked in the second value perspective is the possible strength of the child's bonds with the original parent even when this parent is deemed to be unsatisfactory. Proponents of this school share with Goldstein, Freud and Solnit (1979, 1980) an emphasis on psychological rather than biological bonds; but their attitude to continuity with the original biological and psychological parent seems to differ. Goldstein *et al.* would see value in a child remaining with an unsatisfactory parent who has nevertheless psychologically parented the child; the threshold of mistreatment at which, in their view, removal would be justified, is relatively high. With the state paternalist perspective, removal, or at least some form of intervention, could take place at a much lower threshold of problematic care, with the child's welfare more readily seen as lying with other, better caretakers, with whom psychological bonds could then be formed. Continuity *per se* is not so highly valued, nor is the original family's integrity and autonomy.

The concept of the state in this approach also stands in marked contrast to the first value position. Much greater faith is placed in the value of beneficent state action to protect children's welfare. The state not only has the duty to intervene where there is inadequate care or suspicion of it, but also the capacity to provide something better for the child. The state decision-makers – courts and social workers – are seen as able to make sound and valid assessments of what would be best for the child. Substitute care through adoption and (secure) fostering is also positively valued, and in particular adoption tends to be seen as an extremely favourable solution for the care of the child whose original parents are found to be wanting. There is a lack of emphasis on the possible negative aspects of state intervention, and a highly favourable image of the 'rescue' of suffering children to other, better homes. There is neglect of the insidious class element in state care where, broadly speaking, middle-class decision-makers pass judgement on working-class parents and, again broadly, children from deprived homes are placed in somewhat better-off ones. Also overlooked are the difficulties of arriving at a judgement of what is best for the child's future welfare; and the problems and stresses attendant upon the substitute care provided by the state. The concept of adoption and foster care is perhaps over-idealised, with the problems of relationships within adoptive and foster families, of lost biological and early psychological ties, of children being removed from their cultural origins, being played down.

Furthermore, the emphasis is on good quality child care as judged by professionals and experts. Such a judgement may in reality be experienced as oppressive and intrusive, and both the parent's and the child's viewpoint as to the most preferable option may be under-valued here (although one variant of the view would give some emphasis to the child's own wishes). The state in the paternalist perspective is construed as neutral and wise, taking the best course of action for children. Yet the controlling aspect of the state's role is perhaps not fully acknowledged. The implied role of the state is one of extensive surveillance of, and intervention in, child rearing; but the civil liberties implications of such a role may be disregarded, as may the possibility of misjudgements of abuse and the unnecessary – and traumatic – separation of parent and child. Parents would be highly accountable to the state – a notion in conflict with the traditional one of (relatively) autonomous and private family units. The child protection machinery of the state takes on a potentially authoritarian character in this perspective. What perhaps is under-estimated is the degree of resistance by individuals to what is perceived by them as excessively heavy-handed state action. Nor is the essentially political nature of the state sufficiently recognised, it seems. The state is not seen as a political creation defending particular interests and systems, as an institution which may have undeclared political reasons for taking the actions it does; the state is perceived more as a 'good parent', acting wisely to protect the weak, and blind to divisions of class, ethnicity and gender. Another way in which the viewpoint may be described as apolitical lies in the way that apparently 'bad' parenting is construed. This is largely seen as stemming from personal pathology rather than from structural factors such as oppression and deprivation.

In summary, in the paternalist and child protection value perspective, those birth parents who do not bring up their children 'well' cannot expect to keep them. When they fail, state power should be readily and extensively used to provide something better for the children. This would usually be an adoptive or secure long-term foster home. (It might also be a residential home, although residential care is not on the whole favoured in this perspective.) The original unsatisfactory parents would then tend to be excluded from the child's life and would lose their rights. The state in this perspective has a much broader role than in the *laissez-faire* view and would act authoritatively at a much lower threshold of parental mistreatment. The focus is very much on the child as a separate individual rather than the parents or the (birth) family as a unit. Other possible terms for this position are the *child salvationist* or *child rescue* approach.

Some authors associated with the perspective

A considerable number of authors have, broadly speaking, supported strong state intervention in child care matters, and favoured adoption and fostering as alternative methods of child care to the birth family. This viewpoint was particularly prominent in the 1970s and early 1980s. The first example to be discussed is Mia Kellmer Pringle, who in *The Needs of Children* (1975a) was extremely critical of a societal emphasis on biological parenthood which she saw as detrimental to the child. In her view society over-valued children's ties with their birth parents and was too slow to cut them permanently. Society suffered from a misplaced faith in the blood tie and an over-romanticised picture of parenthood. Pringle identified an idea that children belong to their parents like their other possessions, over which they may experience exclusive rights; she saw this as a view which had no factual foundation and should be rejected. Children should be seen rather as only on temporary loan to their parents. Pringle argued for a concept of responsible and informed parenthood, and a recognition that the ability and willingness to undertake the responsibilities of parenthood are not dependent on, nor necessarily a consequence of, biological parenthood.

The stress on psychological parenthood is in line with that of Goldstein *et al.* (1979, 1980). Where Pringle parts company with them sharply, however, is on the preferred role of society, acting presumably largely through the state, in intervening between parent and child. She suggested that we go too far in asserting that the way parents bring up their children is solely their own concern. In law and policy we often act as though the over-valued blood tie ensured satisfactory parenting, with the result that the child's well-being is sacrificed; for example, abused children were returned to parents when there was a high risk of their being abused again, while thousands of children were condemned to remain in care without permanent substitute parents, in the hope that biological parental interest might be reawakened. Pringle might be deemed to be punitive towards parents and too prepared to prejudge them in a rather rigid way. For example, she commented: 'Those who have been deprived of adequate parental care ... have little chance of becoming in turn responsible parents themselves' (p. 157), and argued that it was a myth that the maternal role will be fulfilling to a single young woman who has herself been rejected in childhood; in the argument that the young woman should keep the child and will be helped by this to maturity, the child's welfare is sacrificed to the adult's.

Pringle's comments on (then) existing law and policy must be seen in the context in which she wrote, the early 1970s in Britain. In a later publication in 1980 (Pringle 1980) she put greater emphasis on prevention of poor child care through wide-ranging support services to families, thus falling into line more with the third value perspective to be discussed, the pro-birth parent view; although the child's rights to loving care, and the parental duty to provide it, were still stressed.

The theme of support services occurs elsewhere in Pringle's writing (see, for example, Pringle 1978) but the 1975 publication remains an interesting example of the protectionist approach.

Like other authors associated with this perspective, Pringle is keenly aware of the problems of inadequate child care and failure to meet children's needs. Some authors of the 1970s and 1980s whose particular preoccupation is child abuse see a need to make child welfare an overriding social priority and therefore to have strong state intervention in child care. Dingwall, Eekelaar and Murray (1983) quote one example, A. W. Franklin (1982), who says:

> What is needed is for all countries, including our own, to accept the overwhelming importance of the growth and development of children to their full potential and of the need to make this a conscious goal. Each country should then accept certain responsibilities – to examine the ways in which this goal can be achieved, to examine those attitudes and practices which hinder the achievement of this goal and to renew, in the context of their own society and culture, the priority to be given to the achievement of this goal.
>
> (Franklin 1982:16, Dingwall *et al.* 1983a:211)

Dingwall *et al.* comment: 'The heavy-handed paternalism and religiosity of these sentiments are characteristic of many of the best-known writers on child mistreatment. It is argued that child welfare should and must be an absolute social priority. Anyone failing to accept this whole-heartedly may then be justly criticised' (p. 211). The analysis favoured by Dingwall *et al.*, however, 'depicts agencies as balancing several partially conflicting objectives and points to the real disadvantages of an unreflective pursuit of child protection as an overriding goal' (p. 211). The failures of child care agencies then are 'not necessarily ignoble' (p. 211). This point will be taken up later.

Another example of an author concerned with child abuse is Howells (1974) who in an anecdotal book *Remember Maria* – a reference to the Colwell case of 1973 – argues against giving excessive weight to biological parent–child bonds, stating that 'We are forced to conclude that the parent–child bond is not mystical, nor is it ever-present' (p. 30), and that 'The capacity to relate does not depend upon gender role, legal status, mental status etc., but upon the relating experience of that person in his own preceding family' (p. 60). Separation from the birth family may be beneficial to the child, leading to loving care elsewhere. The implication of this is presumably that such separation must sometimes be enforced or forcibly maintained. However, Howells favours non-coercive therapeutic work with families as well as greater surveillance and coercive action in some circumstances.

The type of approach advocated by some child abuse authors is characterised by Dingwall *et al.* (1983a) as a 'strict liability' approach (p. 36). Such an approach regards all injuries or disorders in children as unequivocal evidence of neglect or abuse, and of deficiency in the parents. That is, the emphasis is on clinical rather than social evidence, and the approach is particularly associated with the medical profession.

It may also be linked with a strict moral code and absolute standards; departures from the ideal in this approach would indicate psychopathology. Dingwall *et al.* in fact in their research found the approach to be a minority one; most of their informants took the view that clinical evidence must be supplemented by considerations of the child's general state and social environment in identifying abuse.

An overweening concern with abuse may also give rise to definitions which broaden the concept of abuse, and therefore the grounds on which society may be deemed justified in intervening. For example, Gil (1975) puts forward a 'value-based definition' (p. 119) of child abuse as follows: 'any act of commission or omission by individuals, institutions, or society as a whole, and any conditions resulting from such acts or inaction, which deprive children of equal rights and liberties, and/or interfere with their optimal development, constitute, by definition, abusive or neglectful acts or conditions' (p. 120). Such a broad definition of abuse contrasts sharply with the *laissez-faire* attempt to restrict the definition. Perhaps a logical conclusion of extremely pronounced concern about child abuse is the concept of licensing for parenthood. As early as 1974 Lord and Weisfeld suggested that this had already been advocated or predicted, with a similar rationale as for licensing people to drive. They commented: 'Perhaps in the 21st or 22nd centuries such legislation and licensing programs may end – or diminish – child abuse, battering, and neglect. In the meantime ...?' (Lord and Weisfeld 1974:80). The absolute goal of elimination of child cruelty is here linked with stringent limitations on the liberties of adults.

Strict liability, a broader concept of abuse, and licensing for parenthood – all indicate where concern about child abuse may lead taken to its logical conclusion. A less extreme position can also be taken, however, which might also be argued to lie broadly within the state paternalist camp. Although Dingwall *et al.* (1983a), as shown, are somewhat critical of the position of some of the child abuse-centred authors, they occupy at least a moderate state paternalist/protectionist position themselves, stating in an article (Dingwall, Eekelaar and Murray, 1983b) that in their view 'children are not the property of their parents. Parents are trustees for their children's interests: as with any trust, if they fail in the duties involved, they should be discharged. The only body with the legitimacy to monitor and enforce such duties is the state' (p. 19). To reiterate an earlier point, Dingwall *et al.*'s research in the early 1980s showed that in practice social workers preferred the least stigmatising interpretation of what had happened to a child and the least coercive form of intervention. They erred, in other words, on the side of using power too little. Dingwall *et al.*, writing in the early 1980s, did not seek a sweeping extension of state power, although they recommended, among other changes, a power to make *parental* supervision orders which would give local authorities more power in child protection cases where children were not actually taken into care. The proper alternative to removing a child, they contend, is a power to supervise parents – the existing supervision orders only conferred power to direct the *child's* conduct, an absurdity in protection cases. A parental supervision order would give authorities the power to direct parents in the discharge of their duties, which might include presenting children for medical inspection or bringing them regularly to a nursery, for example. Staff would also have a right of entry to the home and an emergency power to remove children for a short time. However, because of the sweeping nature of the parental supervision powers, the order should be limited to one year (and not be renewable) with parents able to apply for revocation after three months. Dingwall *et al.* also advocated some legal provision to cover children *at risk* of abuse, without having to wait until the damage had actually been inflicted. To some extent their concerns were later reflected in the Children Act 1989, under which there were greater powers to act on suspicion of abuse or on likely future abuse, and powers to direct a parent to present a child for a medical examination, for example.

Dingwall *et al.* are aware that child protection walks a 'delicate tightrope' (1983b:19) between libertarian critics on the one hand and authoritarian critics on the other; in fact, they saw the existing balance in English child care as about right, albeit 'maybe even excessively respectful of the non-interventionist case' (1983b:19). In their main publication (1983a) the authors say that while their 'personal conclusion might be that agency staff are over-respectful of parental liberties and that "justice for children" may require more rather than less state intervention' (p. 207), they see the deficiencies arising, not so much from the failings of the agencies, as from the limitations of 'the licences and charters which we, as citizens, have granted to them' (p. 207). They explain the dilemma facing the liberal society and state within which child care agencies operate, a state which is different in concept from the 'absolutist "paternal" state' (p. 211) advocated by the more extreme of the child abuse-centred authors. In the liberal state the family is seen as an important check on state power, yet childhood is a critical point in moral socialization. The problem for the liberal is how to make child rearing into a matter of public rather than purely private concern, without destroying the ideal of the autonomous family as a counterweight to state power. While the liberal model of society outlined here would seem to be compatible with Goldstein *et al.*'s *laissez-faire* approach, Dingwall *et al.* in fact identify a 'liberal compromise' (p. 218) which has occurred in the society they are studying, namely Britain. The result of this compromise 'is a system which is fully effective neither in preventing mistreatment nor in respecting family privacy but which lurches unevenly between these two poles' (p. 219). There is a need for state surveillance of the well-being of future citizens, but the state: 'will always remain vulnerable to criticism from Utopian libertarians whose ideals break on the brute physical reality of children's dependence on adults' (p. 220). Dingwall *et al.* discuss the liberal state and society sympathetically, but perhaps

the wording of this comment, as well as the actual policy recommendations that they make, illustrates the distance they stand both from
laissez-faire and, as will be shown, the children's rights school. In a
later edition of their book (1995) they comment: 'although the institutions may have changed, the practical problems and moral dilemmas of
child protection work have not' (p. 245).

Other authors whose research work may be associated with the state
paternalist/protectionist school of thought will be considered briefly.
Tizard (1977) put a case for greater readiness to terminate parental
rights and place children for adoption, based on her study which compared children in institutional care in early life who were subsequently
adopted, with similar children who were instead restored to their
natural parent. The findings led Tizard to conclude that the adopted
children were the more fortunate group – they had fewer problems than
the restored children (although this was related to social class). With
reference to the natural mothers whose children had been restored to
them, she commented: 'The blood tie by no means implied a love tie'
(p. 233), and that the adoptive mothers were warmer and more affectionate on the whole than the natural mothers. In Tizard's view,
fostering did not offer the security of adoption; the uncertainty disturbed the children and contacts with the natural parents aroused
anxiety in them. Her study suggested that social work decisions (at that
time – the research was done in the late 1960s and early 1970s) were
influenced by a number of assumptions including the primacy of the
blood tie and the primacy of natural parental possession; it was
accepted that children should be put in care while parents made up their
minds whether to relinquish them finally or not. Parental contact,
though irregular, prevented the child from forming an alternative
parent–child relationship. Tizard argued that her study, together with
others, suggested that attempts to restore children to their birth families
may not be in their best interests. In this view, children need someone
who is unconditionally and permanently committed to them; it is difficult to see why a parent who takes no responsibility for a child's care
has a right to prevent someone else from doing so. There is some
resemblance here to Goldstein *et al.* (1979, 1980). However, Tizard did
acknowledge that the issue was complicated by social inequality; in
some cases, parents would have been able to keep the child if minimal
material assistance had been available.

Other research also appeared to show favourable outcomes for the
adoption of children, particularly when adoption was compared to leaving a child in what might be thought to be a deprived original home.
For example, Lambert and Streather (1980) using data gathered for the
National Child Development Study, studied illegitimate children who
were adopted, those who were not adopted, and legitimate children
(also not adopted), all at the age of 11. The illegitimate children who
had not been adopted were on the whole disadvantaged in unfavourable
circumstances, compared with both those who had been adopted and

the legitimate, although the authors emphasise the effects of favourable environments here rather than adoption *per se*. There has also been evidence that adoption was preferable to fostering because of its greater security; Tizard (1977), as indicated, argued this, and Wolkind (1984), for example, stated that there was overwhelming evidence that adoption was more successful than foster care. However, in the 1980s and 1990s there has been a trend to greater openness in adoption, which has perhaps made it resemble fostering more closely (see, for example, Triseliotis 1995). There has also been a trend towards the adoption of older children rather than babies, which may well make a difference to outcomes (see, for example, Howe 1995).

Another study used to defend a state paternalist/protectionist position was an investigation influential in child care policy in Britain in the 1970s – that by Rowe and Lambert (1973) on children in long-term care, *Children Who Wait*. This broadly supported the view that permanent substitute parents should be found for these children. It was found that decisions about placements were often long delayed while efforts were made to solve the (birth) family's problems, yet rehabilitation back with the family was only expected for about a quarter of the children studied, and there was little actual contact with the birth parents. Most of the children judged by their social workers to need placement, needed a permanent rather than a temporary substitute family. Rowe and Lambert believed that social workers should be more committed to placements in permanent homes, and *Children Who Wait* had some influence on policy and practice at the time. The view would be that children should either be speedily returned to their own family or they should be securely established in a substitute one.

Finally, the publications of the organisation British Agencies for Adoption and Fostering (BAAF) in the 1970s and 1980s should be mentioned. BAAF is an organisation linking adoption and fostering agencies, most notably local authorities functioning in this role, which publishes a journal and pamphlets, sponsors research, conducts conferences, and generally links together and informs various professionals in this field. BAAF may be broadly associated with the child protectionist position. Although it claimed in the 1980s that it was aware of the vital role of birth parents (see, for example, *Adoption and Fostering*, Adcock 1983), the tenor of most of its publications particularly in the late 1970s was in favour of permanence in good substitute care – adoptive and foster homes – as an alternative to poor parental care, with involuntary termination of parental rights accepted more readily than in some other quarters.

The approach was illustrated by two practice guides to the 1975 Children Act produced by the then Association of British Adoption and Fostering Agencies (ABAFA) in 1976 and 1977. These guides dealt with the 1975 Act in general (ABAFA 1976), and with the assumption of parental rights over children in the then 'voluntary care' (ABAFA

1977), respectively. They aimed to help social workers understand the Act, making use of case histories and similar exercises. The emphasis was on the termination of parental rights in favour of long-term fostering and adoption. One commentator, Tunstill (1977), pointed out that in three out of four case histories in the guide to the assumption of parental rights, the only possibility of a 'happy ending' was by means of such steps. Children were seen as needing long-term substitute families if their own parents could not meet all their needs – if, for example, there was no consistent or affectionate relationship with the parent, or if contact was only sporadic.

A slightly later ABAFA publication, *Terminating Parental Contact* (ABAFA 1979), a collection of papers by various authors, considered whether, and in what circumstances, a parent might be prevented from having contact with a child in care. It stressed the need to make plans for children based on a realistic assessment of whether or not rehabilitation with the birth parents was possible, and to consider the purpose of parental contact and its effects on the child. The starting point in assessing the value of contact should be: is it of benefit to the child, and if so, how? Contact might strengthen bonds with a parent who was unlikely to resume care, and then constitute an obstacle to finding an appropriate placement. Uncertainty and lack of continuity made it hard for the substitute parents to make a strong commitment to the child *and* include the birth parent. The concluding chapter went on to say that since 'there is an assumption in our society that the blood-tie or relationship with the parent is the ideal, then any alternative is seen as a failure rather than as something in the child's best interest' (p. 51). This attack on society's over-valuation of the blood tie resembles Pringle's (1975a). The tendency to see alternatives as second best, the ABAFA pamphlet argued, inhibited decisions. If decisions were not made, then:

foster parents and natural parents often make them for us by making things happen. This can be very damaging for the child. The consequences of not making a decision must be recognised. Too often we may receive a child into care and then do nothing. Yet it is at this crucial time that the child will be forming attachments to substitute caretakers, and parents will begin to deal with their pain and loss by becoming more detached.   (ABAFA 1979:51)

Forward planning and positive decision-making were emphasised – preferably at an early stage of entry to substitute care. As a later BAAF publication (Adcock, White and Rowlands 1983) noted: 'A child in care cannot have a permanent home' (p. 14). State intervention is favoured; but as a means to hasten movement through care to permanence. It has to be stressed, however, that later publications by BAAF leaned rather more towards a preference for permanence with the original family. For example, an article in *Adoption and Fostering* by Smith (1995) stated: 'no one would dispute that for the great majority of children permanence is best achieved within their family of origin' (p. 11).

Rationale and underlying values

The first point to note about the rationale and underlying values here is that *the child* is differentiated from the parents and family, and the focus on the child's welfare is paramount. A number of justifications may be found for this. First, there is the moral duty to relieve suffering, especially when inflicted on those who are too weak to defend themselves. Secondly, there is the liberal argument that children are in a different category from adults in that they do not enter into contracts freely. The parent–child relationship is not one which the child chose, and therefore the state has a special duty to protect the child from mistreatment suffered in that relationship. Commenting on this 'classic liberal exemption of children' (p. 18) from full individual responsibility, Dingwall *et al.* (1983b) say, in their article already cited: 'Although conservative intellectuals have argued for the deregulation of marriage, as a private contract between freely consenting adults, parenthood is different. Children do not enter the relationship freely. As such the state has a duty to protect them until they are capable of making rational judgements about their participation in this contract' (pp. 18–19). Thirdly, there is the more instrumental argument that children represent the society of the future, and therefore society and in particular its organised expression, the state, has an interest in their socialisation. It is widely believed that abused and neglected children are more likely to become delinquent or disturbed adult individuals, that, specifically, there is a link between being ill-treated as a child and ill-treating one's own children. For example, some types of child abuse theories have posited that abusing parents were themselves abused as children (Wasserman 1967, cited in Parton 1985a, Strauss *et al.* 1980, cited in Elliot 1996). There is a perceived social investment in treating children well, in attempting to ensure that they receive the type of upbringing that will enhance their development and produce well-socialised adults. As suggested earlier, this does raise the more fundamental question of what sort of upbringing will do this, as well as what sort of adult it is thought socially desirable to produce. There is also the danger of excessive determinism in, for example, assuming that individuals who were abused and neglected as children will necessarily abuse and neglect children themselves. Nevertheless, it is widely accepted that childhood experience does affect later development.

Children in this perspective are seen as essentially vulnerable, dependent and in need of protection. Their psychological needs are construed as somewhat different from those of adults. Mia Kellmer Pringle, whose most relevant work here is in fact entitled *The Needs of Children* (1975a), outlined children's psycho-social needs in a four-fold classification: the need for love and security, for new experiences, for praise and recognition, and for responsibility. If these needs are not met, there is the possibility of long-term damage; indeed Pringle comments: 'If one of the basic needs remains unmet, or is inadequately met, then development may become stunted or distorted. The consequences can be disastrous (and costly) later on, both for the individual and for society' (p. 152). Thus it seems children are different from adults in their vulnerability to the frustration of their needs, while again, childhood experience affects adult personality.

A knowledge, or perhaps a particular view, of child psychology, underlies this value perspective as it does the first, but the emphasis is far less strongly on the child's bond with the original parental caretaker(s). Goldstein *et al.* (1979, 1980), for example, would recognise the biological parents as also the psychological parents in most cases. The proponents of the second perspective are, by and large, more prepared to discount this when the standard of parenting is poor and the relationship does not seem to the social worker to be good. C. Cooper (1979) admits that early attachment may exist in the face of some cruelty and neglect, but 'in this situation it may be relatively easily replaced by a stronger attachment to a warmer and more nurturing maternal figure' (p. 26).

The emphasis on children as psychologically different from adults means that their rights are also different from adult rights. Freeman, an author who will be considered further in discussing the fourth, children's rights perspective, summarises the perception of these rights in a protectionist perspective (1983a). This category of children's rights, he suggests, is overtly concerned with protection, stressing the vulnerability of children. He says that:

When rights are spoken of in this context, it is to inject more responsibility into the parental role. This approach to children's rights is the oldest and the most firmly entrenched. It is the concept which is to the fore every time a tragedy occurs and a child dies or is seriously injured as a result of parental ill-treatment.
(Freeman 1983a:43)

Freeman further suggests that when rights are spoken of in the protection framework the attention is on certain freedoms that we believe children should have – freedom from abuse and neglect. But this perspective is based on: 'the premise that children are unable to care for themselves and so need adult protection, care and guidance' (p. 43). As Freeman points out, claims to protection are very different from claims to autonomy. The notion of protection rights constitutes: 'a highly paternalistic notion. We do not ask children whether they wish to be protected' (p. 44).

A second element of the underlying rationale concerns how parenthood is seen. There are some important differences in the concept of parenthood from the almost sacrosanct notion largely held by those who subscribe to the *laissez-faire* position. Parenthood is seen here more as a conditional trust which, if abused, can and should be removed. The status of socially recognised parenthood is, or should be, dependent upon the provision of good quality child care; being a parent *per se* confers no special rights. Any rights contingent on parenthood are dependent on the appropriate exercise of duties; and thus adult freedoms are rightly limited by the presence of children. Pringle (1975b) carried this further than many were prepared to go by at one stage arguing that motherhood should necessarily be seen as a full-time job. This could be construed as a denial of the rights and freedoms of women. This point will be taken up later. Dingwall *et al.* (1983a) say that it seems meaningful to talk in terms of children's rights 'which justify placing appropriate duties on their caretakers' (p. 223). Although such duties exist within a context which also ascribes certain rights to parents (and these rights, Dingwall *et al.* correctly point out, have a longer history of recognition than rights ascribed to children), the rights of parents are different from rights over property. Dingwall *et al.*'s characterisation of parents as trustees has already been mentioned. In their book they maintain that parental rights: 'must be exercised for the child's benefit. In this respect the rights of parents also have some of the characteristics of duties' (p. 224). Trustees' rights must be used in the interests of the beneficiaries; in the case of parents, the trustees must promote the child's welfare. Where trustees prove deficient the beneficiaries have a ground for legal action in respect of the negligent discharge of their trustees' duties. But as many mistreated children are unable to initiate their own remedies, others must be licensed to do it for them. As Eekelaar (1973) argued, parents' rights are duty-rights which parents are not free to abandon. This approach to parenthood has some echoes in the construction of 'parental responsibility' in child and family policy in Britain in the 1990s, as embodied particularly in the Children Act 1989 and the Child Support Act 1991 (see Fox Harding 1994).

Another way in which the child protectionist school tends to characterise parenthood is its construction of poor parenting as being largely due to individual psychopathology and history, with larger structural determinants of parenting styles tending to be de-emphasised. In this, as will be shown, it parts company with the third pro-parent value position. Pringle (1975a), as indicated, saw those who had been deprived of adequate parental care themselves as having little chance of becoming responsible parents. Individual characteristics of abusing parents were a focus of interest for early writers on child abuse (for example, Helfer and Kempe 1968; see also Allen 1978, Parton 1985a for critical comment), and it has been widely held, as an article by C. Cooper (1985) puts it, that:

> A harsh, neglectful or otherwise unsatisfactory upbringing ... makes it hard for parents, in many ways, to empathise with their children and to show the necessary awareness, patience and tenderness, and the ability to put the child's needs before their own. Most abusing and neglectful parents ... lacked adequate affection, interest and concern when young and they are now swamped by their excessive need for these supports in adult life.   (p. 64)

A comment in an article by Loney (1987) is of interest here; noting the key role of medical practitioners in concern about child abuse in the 1970s and 1980s, he suggests: 'This may help to explain the overwhelming focus on the pathology of the individual abuser or his or her family ... there is a danger that the equally important social and cultural factors which contribute to abuse will be omitted' (p. 20). A focus on child death cases, with a legal rather than a medical emphasis, may tend in the same individualistic direction. For instance, Parton (1991) comments in relation to the inquiry report on the death of the abused child Jasmine Beckford (London Borough of Brent 1985) that: 'The "cycle of violence" whereby parents who abuse their children were themselves abused in childhood was accepted as received wisdom' (p. 60).

A third strand underlying the protectionist position concerns its view of the state. The state is seen as capable of beneficent, competent and unbiased action in removing children from inadequate homes and providing them with alternatives, not as an unwarranted threat to civil liberties, or as acting differentially towards parents of different social groups. In fact, the class element in child care is not perceived as significant, whereas other perspectives may see a class pattern both in parenting styles and problems, and in the actions of the state towards parents. In the protectionist perspective there is a relatively high degree of faith in the professional servants of the state, although this may be implied rather than explicit. When social workers and other professionals are criticised, it is characteristically for respecting the birth parent–child bond too much. There is a belief that the state can indeed arrange a better future for the child.

The implied view of the state in this perspective accords neither with a right-wing or classically liberal concept, nor with a more left-wing radical critique. It is a view of a heavily paternal state which presumably devotes considerable resources to the searching out of, and response to, child mistreatment. Substitute care represents a cost to the state, as does investigation and supervision of children in their own homes. On the other hand, foster family care, which is generally preferred to care in residential homes, is also usually cheaper than residential care, while adoption, after it has been accomplished, may represent no definable cost at all (exceptions to this being post-adoption support and the payment of allowances to adopters). While the notion of large-scale supportive services to families is not completely overlooked by the proponents of this perspective, it is emphasised much less than the interventionist response to particular families where there are clear child care problems. The notion of the state here is perhaps less of a broad-based welfare state than of a more narrowly focused family policing state. The existing economic and political system is often taken as given, and the state's focus in child care matters is resricted (or, from a critical viewpoint, blinkered). This point will be taken up again in considering criticisms of this perspective. It may be noted here that while some subscribers to the paternalist and protectionist viewpoint might present their position as apolitical, rather as though child care matters arose in a political and social vacuum, critics might see their perspective as politically naive. It may be seen as ill-founded, for example, to view state child welfare agencies and courts, and the principles by which they operate, as independent of the forces of class and political power.

Criticisms of state paternalism and child protection

Empirical support

In general, the second, state paternalist value perspective seems better supported than the first, *laissez-faire* one by empirical studies relating to children and the state's child care system. Two major aspects of the empirical support for this perspective will be critically examined here: studies relating to adoption, and a study relating to children in care which was influential in the development of the paternalist viewpoint in the 1970s. In addition, brief reference will be made to the role of individual cases of extreme child abuse as support for the protectionist position.

Tizard's and Lambert and Streather's studies have been referred to. Tizard (1977) found that the adopted children in her study compared favourably with those who were restored to their natural mothers. She gave a positive picture of the effects of adoption on the child's development and the creation of an affectionate family unit, as compared with both restoration and long-term fostering. In her concluding chapter Tizard states:

> The findings of this study suggest that of the children who came into residential nurseries as infants for long-term care, the most fortunate were those who were subsequently adopted. Of course, not all the adoptions had a happy outcome; ... Yet as a group the children were in a more stable situation, had fewer emotional problems, and were intellectually and academically superior to the fostered, institutional and restored children.   (Tizard 1977:232)

Lambert and Streather's (1980) data from the National Child Development Study showed that illegitimate adopted children compared favourably with the illegitimate non-adopted. Earlier data from the NCDS showed a similar trend. For example, it was found that at the age of seven, despite their poor start in life, the adopted children did as well as or better than others in various aspects of ability and attainment, and better than others in general knowledge and oral ability. Conversely, the illegitimate children who remained with their own mothers did relatively badly, and this was so even when they grew up in a middle-class home (Seglow, Pringle and Wedge 1972, Pringle 1972).

Criticisms of this type of empirical support for the child protection perspective revolve first around the degree of significance to be afforded to the dimension of social class. Clearly the observed beneficial effects of adoption have stemmed in part from the tendency of adoption to move children to a somewhat higher social class than that of the family of origin. Holman (1978), in an article analysing the class nature of adoption, noted the gross under-representation found in studies of adoption of Classes IV and V among adoptive parents. (However, the exclusion of many lower-class would-be adopters by agencies, practised in the early post-war decades, would be a less strong factor by the 1990s – Triseliotis 1995.) The adoption studies themselves acknowledge the class factor. Tizard (1977) was aware of the social differences between the two groups of families studied, although she also cautions: 'much more than social class differentiated the natural and adoptive parents' (p. 233). Lambert and Streather (1980) emphasised the powerful effects of environment, stating: 'Some children were fortunate and lived in an exceptionally favourable environment, and many of the adopted children were among this group' (p. 141). In a later era, Triseliotis (1995) comments that in adoption: 'younger and healthier children still go to predominantly middle class families' (p. 39). If class, and the advantages/disadvantages arising from the class position of parents, are the key to adoption success, then adoption *per se* is not necessarily the beneficial strategy for deprived children that the paternalist school of thought claims. Another, quite different strategy, might be proposed: to equalise the class advantages of all parents! This goal might of course be dismissed as utopian and of no immediate help to children in need. Furthermore, there is a strong argument that other, not immediately class-related, characteristics make the adoptive home superior (Tizard 1977); Burghes (1994), having reviewed some evidence on this, comments: 'Children who are born "illegitimately" and subsequently adopted often outstrip the achievement of children born into and remaining in their two parent family *even after allowing for social class.*' (p. 23, italics added). Even so, the class character of adoption arouses some unease about the benefits claimed for it as a method of care.

Another type of reservation concerns the long-term effects of adoption, which may damage personality and identity. It has been suggested (Fox 1982, Smith 1984) that many studies of adoption have not been sufficiently long-term to demonstrate these effects. Cervi (1994), writing about adoption breakdowns, indicates that: 'Hidden problems [arising from the child's history] may not materialise until many years later' (p. 15). There is some evidence that adopted children make greater use of the psychiatric services than the general population, though this could also be due to class factors (Pringle 1967, Smith 1984). In general, it is more difficult to trace adoption placement difficulties or breakdown than foster home breakdown, as the families concerned will not necessarily return to the agencies involved in the original placement. There has also been a lack of post-adoption support. So again, it can be argued that adoption is in fact a less successful aspect of child care policy than it appears. The trend in the 1980s and 1990s towards adoptions of older children is also a factor producing more difficult placements; while in an era of high divorce rates, the marriages of adoptive parents may break down, causing further disruption (see Garvey 1992). And instances in the 1980s and 1990s both of adopted adults seeking out their birth family, and mothers who gave up children for adoption years before seeking out those children when adult, suggest a somewhat less rosy and more compli- cated side to adoption than had been apparent in earlier years (see, for example, Howe, Sawbridge and Hinings 1992, Wells 1993). This is not to suggest that where contact with birth relatives is sought later, the adoptive placement *itself* was necessarily unhappy or a failure. But it does seem that a certain number of individuals feel the absence of close genetic relatives from their lives as a loss.

Another type of research which may be used to support the child pro- tectionist position consists of studies of children in care, most notably Rowe and Lambert's *Children Who Wait* (1973), which has already been referred to. Investigating children in care whose social workers wanted to find homes with substitute families for them, the study found that 22 per cent of the whole group of 2,812 children studied – who had all been in care for six months or more – were thought to need a substi- tute family; permanent substitute families were being sought for three quarters of these. Forty per cent of the children needing placement were considered to need permanent foster homes, 6 per cent direct adoption, and 26 per cent a foster home with a view to adoption. However, these judgements were only the social workers' assessments – the research team did not themselves make a decision as to which children ought to be placed in what type of placement. Rehabilitation was only expected for about 25 per cent of the children studied; 61 per cent, a clear major- ity, were expected to remain in care until they were 18. Most of the children had been in care for the greater parts of their lives. Contact with the birth parents was limited – only 5 per cent of the children saw their parents as often as once a month; while 18 per cent saw *one* parent at least once a month, 35 per cent saw one or both parents occasionally, and 41 per cent had no parental contact. The longer the children stayed in care the less parental contact they had. But children in residential establishments were more likely to be in touch with their parents and return to them than children in foster homes.

In the 1970s the Rowe and Lambert study was widely taken to sup- port a policy of permanence in good substitute homes when children had been in care for some time, but other interpretations of their data are possible. First, the social workers' judgements were presumably not the only ones that could have been made of the preferred future for the child. Taking the social workers' views as the object of study inevitably carries this sort of limitation. Secondly, on the issue of parental contact specifically, it may be argued that absence of contact did not necessarily indicate parental indifference, that parents may find many obstacles in the way of remaining in touch with their children in care (see, for example, Millham *et al.* 1985, Millham *et al.* 1986), and that social workers could and should have done more to facilitate an active parent–child relationship while the child was in care (this is now emphasised more in social work practice following the 1989 Children Act). A study by Thorpe (1974) of long-term foster children also found little parental contact, but a quite different conclusion was drawn from the findings. The point here is that Rowe and Lambert's data are open to a number of interpretations.

Finally, on this question of empirical support, individual cases of extreme child abuse, particularly abuse leading to the child's death, lend considerable emotive power and apparent empirical support to the child protection position. Such is the compelling horror of these cases that it is tempting to conclude that any disadvantages arising from the protectionist position would be tolerable if a protectionist policy prevented such cases from occurring again. The obvious reservations are the relative rarity of such extreme cases, the assumption that in principle they could be stopped, and the weighting of the prevention of such child deaths as against other values and objectives.

Problems with the implications for policy

The clearest and simplest policy implication of the paternalist position would seem to be that the state, acting chiefly through courts and local authorities, should have more power to intervene between parent and child and should use those legal powers which it does have more readily and extensively. This value perspective, then, could imply widening of the legal grounds for coercive intervention by the state – for example, in the English context, of the grounds for care or emergency protection proceedings, or for dispensing with parental agreement to adoption. Greater powers could also be given to block parental contact with children in care where it was thought that parents would never care satisfactorily for their children again. Foster and prospective adoptive parents could be given more rights to achieve legal security and control of the child.

Many of the policy preferences of the modern paternalist school of thought found expression in the English legislative and policy changes of the 1970s. The way in which this occurred will be shown in discussing the value perspective in practice. It should, however, be noted that detailed blueprints for change do not emerge from the authors in this school in the same clearcut way as they do from the writings of Goldstein *et al.* (1979, 1980), although some detailed recommendations are made. The discussion here will focus on three general aspects of the policy implications which seem most problematic: the resources aspect, the civil liberties aspect, and the potential clash with women's aspirations and feminism.

To deal briefly with the resources aspect first: it is clear that the paternalist position, if effectively implemented, has considerable implications for societal resources. Such resources could be drawn from voluntary child care agencies but would probably mostly come from the state (which may also partly fund voluntary bodies). The extensive surveillance of children and families thought to be at risk of various types of maltreatment, the initiation and following through of registrations, case conferences and court proceedings, the finding and supervision of substitute placements, the investigation of prospective adoptive homes – all carry staff and management costs. The provision of residential homes is notoriously expensive, and although this form of care is not favoured by the child protection school, it is likely to be needed in the short-term for some cases. Foster homes are much cheaper, but in the case of some children who are recognised as difficult to care for, a larger than usual allowance can be paid to the foster parent(s), approximating more closely to a salary. While adoption may signal the end of the agency's involvement, it is also possible in Britain for local authorities to pay an allowance to adopters in some cases (under the Children Act 1975, Section 32), and there may also be a need for post-adoption support.

Paternalism without adequate resources is likely to result in poor planning and decision-taking and inadequate substitute care. The case of Dennis O'Neill, removed from his parental home for neglect in England in the mid-1940s, but killed in his supposedly supervised foster-home, is a tragic reminder of an earlier form of state paternalism which was unsophisticated and under-resourced (Monckton 1945). There have, however, been other child deaths in foster homes since that time (for example, Shirley Woodcock in 1982, Jason Plischkowsky in 1986, Gavin Mabey in 1987). Substitute care may in general tend to be unsatisfactory, with unhappy and disrupted placements. A Department of Health document (1991a) comments: 'Research ... shows how difficult it is to provide a stable and positive experience for children or young people who are being looked after by local authoritites for more than a brief period' (p. 18). A sufficiently skilled and resourced child care service is needed to prevent the interventions of the state making an unsatisfactory situation worse.

The second problematic aspect of the implications for policy concerns the threat to civil liberties. Intensive surveillance of children and families to safeguard against abuse or unsatisfactory care carries consequences for such liberties – for example, where professionals visit the home, where records are kept on families, and where there is a stigmatising labelling process at work. Concern may be expressed at the keeping of registers of children thought to be at risk of abuse, and about adequate mechanisms for removing children and families from these lists. The exclusion of parents from reports, reviews, case conferences and meetings where serious charges may be laid against them, which they have no opportunity to answer, also gives rise to this type of civil liberties concern. However, the Children Act 1989, with its emphasis on greater partnership between professionals and parents, might be thought to ameliorate some of these concerns, and in the 1990s parents were more often included in these meetings. The power to remove parental rights over children in care merely by a *resolution* of a public body (a local authority committee), in existence in Britain for a century until abolished by the Children Act 1989, long aroused opposition because of its 'behind closed doors' nature (see, for example, Fox 1986, Harding 1989).

Although resolutions could only be passed on specific grounds, and were basically intended to protect children whose parents seemed unlikely ever to care for them again, the fact that the decision was taken not in court but in a *committee* (to which – until 1984 – the parent was unable to make representations) where the local authority acted as judge in its own case, was seen to be a denial of natural justice (see National Council for One Parent Families 1982). It was no surprise that the 1989 Act abolished these resolutions, requiring care proceedings instead.

Even the relatively modest proposal of Dingwall *et al.* (1983a) for parental supervision orders may be objected to in civil liberties terms. The local authority could acquire express power to direct parents in the discharge of their duties; so parents might be required, for example, to bring the child for regular medical inspection, to comply with pre-scribed treatment, or to participate in a particular remedial programme. There would be a right of entry to the home and an emergency power to remove the child for a short period (eight days), with this period being extended if the case were being prepared for a full care order. Such powers would occupy an intermediate area between full-scale removal of the child, and leaving parents to bring up the child as they see fit or only offering supportive, non-coercive help. While the parental super-vision order was never enacted, the Children Act 1989 did contain a child assessment order which requires the parent to produce the child for assessment (as well as an emergency protection order for short-term removals). A dangerous erosion of civil liberties may be thought to be implied in this rather 'grey' approach, which contrasts with the more clear-cut specifications of the *laissez-faire* school. The child is neither wholly removed nor left under parental control, but kept under some kind of shadowy state control in her or his own family home. Civil lib-erties protagonists might see another area of dangerous 'greyness' in provisions that would enable legal action in cases of *likely* harm, as is now the case under the 1989 Act (for example, Section 31). The ill-defined nature of such a specification, it might be thought, leaves scope for oppression of, and injustice to, parents. The threat of such action is also a form of control, with the authoritarian possibilities which accom-pany such power.

There is, in other words, a head-on clash here, between parental civil liberties in relation to the state and the wish to protect children via the mechanisms of the state, highlighted dramatically in well-known cases of alleged sex abuse and organised abuse such as the incidents in Cleveland in 1987, and Orkney in 1991, where numbers of children were removed compulsorily from home and kept away for some time on suspicion of abuse (see, for example, Secretary of State for Social

Services 1988, Clyde 1992, Asquith 1993). It is the awareness of this conflict which leads the *laissez-faire* school to attempt to restrict the state's room for manoeuvre. There are also deep reservations about the adequacy of the law itself as an instrument of child welfare (see King and Piper 1990, King and Trowell 1992).

There is another more general sense in which adult liberties are restricted by the policy implications of the child protectionist school. The ideal of parenthood which it promotes gives a low priority to adult freedoms. Pringle (in 1974 edn of *Needs of Children*) proposes as one of the basic features of parental love that constraints imposed on parental freedom are accepted without resentment. That is, the ideal is of unrealistically high standards which could be experienced as oppressive. The ideal of parenthood is an unreasonably self-sacrificing one. To the extent that such an ideal is imposed via child care policy, parental liberties will be firmly limited and parental anxiety and insecurity raised.

This brings us to the question of women's liberties in particular and the extent to which the policy implications of the protectionist school may be construed as anti-feminist. Pringle (1975a), notably, appears to be explicitly so in some respects. For example, she argued that:

women should no longer be subjected to the twin social pressures to marry and have children, yet to feel they are 'wasting their education' or are otherwise 'unfulfilled' if they devote themselves full-time to child-care. While it was the destiny of yesterday's woman to raise a family, today it can be her choice. Henceforth only those willing to devote some years to this task should contemplate it; and they should then receive recognition for undertaking one of the most crucial tasks for society's future.   (Pringle 1975a:70)

This of course assumes that a mother does indeed have a choice about participation in the paid labour market, in particular that some other form of maintenance is available for her and her child. At a later point Pringle suggests that the rights of children, particularly the very young, are 'subtly but insistently and dangerously, being undermined by the women's movement, aided and abetted by the media' (p. 160), adding: 'While a woman certainly should have the right not to become a mother, the current dogma that "a baby should not be allowed to make any difference to a woman's life" is not only double-think but also ignores the basic needs of young children' (pp. 160–61). Pringle does suggest the possibility of sufficiently generous allowances to enable a parent to look after young children full-time, and investigation of 'how many mothers (or fathers) would wish during these earliest years to exercise this option in preference to an outside paid job?' (p. 161). This proposal does at least seek to diminish the economic dependence on men which feminists might find an objectionable concomitant of full-time motherhood; and in fairness to Pringle she also emphasises the role of fathers and the sharing of parenting between the genders. It must also be remembered that she was writing as far back as the mid-1970s. But through much of her work there appears to run the assumption that it is usually mothers who are the primary parenting figures in the early years. Furthermore, the implications of Pringle's 'Ten Commandments' for child care might alarm feminists concerned about women's well-being and interests, about women as ends in themselves rather than means to serve the ends of others; for example:

1. Give continuous, consistent, loving care ...
2. Give generously of your time and understanding ...
3. Provide new experiences and bathe your child in language ...

and:

10. Don't expect gratitude; your child did not ask to be born – the choice was yours. (p. 159)

The impression is conveyed that the parent – chiefly the mother – is the means to the end of the child's well-being; there seems little room for female self-determination here.

Problems of rationale and underlying values

A first objection to the rationale and underlying values of this perspective is shared with the criticisms of the *laissez-faire* school, and concerns psychological parenthood. This is emphasised over and above biological parenthood, and a (perceived) over-valuation of biological ties is criticised by proponents of this perspective. The converse problems of over-emphasising psychological bonds in parent–child relationships, to the near-exclusion of birth and genetic links, have been discussed in the previous chapter and will not be reiterated here. It should be remembered that supporters of the protectionist school are more prepared on the whole than the *laissez-faire* protagonists to break existing biological *and* psychological links in order to establish new psychological ties in a more caring substitute home.

A second problem is also common to both the first and second perspectives, and concerns the devaluation of children's rights in the sense of rights to self-determination, and the overlooking, to a degree, of the child's own wishes and viewpoint. The psychological differentiation of children in this perspective, as shown, leads to the conclusion that their rights are different from those of adults. Their rights are essentially to better standards of care, not to freedom in the sense of the freedom to choose, to be independent, or to care for oneself. It is consistent with this emphasis that Dingwall *et al.* (1983a) are sceptical about separate representation for the child in court. They see protective care proceedings as essentially an adversarial dispute between parents and state agencies over the appropriate care of a child. Parents therefore should be full parties to the proceedings with access to legal aid; but as far as separate representation for the child is concerned: 'the arguments in favour are so weak that such provision ought to be regarded as an extravagance in the present economic climate' (p. 241). Dingwall *et al.* see an element of unreality in the concept of independent representation of the child's interests, as if these 'were an objectively discoverable entity which only awaited a mouthpiece' (p. 241). They elaborate their argument fully and convincingly; but the basic problem remains: children as separate individuals, with a view of their own, are generally excluded.

Another problem with the child protectionist school is partly political and partly psychological; this is its implicit (or explicit!) authoritarianism. The potential threat to civil liberties from the type of policy preferences which tend to emerge from this perspective, has already been examined in the previous section. The power of professionals and courts militates against parental autonomy, and over-idealised notions of standards of parental care may be experienced as oppressive, particularly for women. The general authoritarianism of the protectionist position is found in its characterisation of the state as benign and class-neutral. Criticisms of this view are essentially that the power of the state can worsen situations as well as improve them, even in terms of the child's welfare; that the state acts differentially towards different groups, for example, it may discriminate against the lower socio-economic classes, ethnic minorities, and 'deviant' family forms; that the state may impose judgements of child rearing practices which are not universally shared – and this again would tend particularly to penalise minorities; that state intervention may be resented, however well-intentioned. Furthermore, the coercive actions of the state in protecting children may be seen as missing the point. It may be argued that unsatisfactory child care arises largely from conditions of deprivation, conditions in the labour market, the inadequate provision of daytime child care, the low social status and lack of support accorded to parenting, and so on, and that the child protectionist standpoint is merely concerned with reacting to the symptoms of wider social divisions which cause child rearing problems to arise. It is an authoritarian response because it gives a high profile to individual culpability, overlooking those social factors over which families have no control, and because it seeks to replace supposedly unsatisfactory parents rather than assisting them. As King and Piper (1990) say of the law as an institution: 'the individualised brand of welfare dispensed by the courts ... ignores wider social and economic factors' (p. 13). Thus the most powerless groups in society are punished for their powerlessness by the break-up of their family life. This type of criticism of child protection policies is characteristic of the third, pro-kinship perspective.

The psychological dimension of the authoritarianism of the paternalist/protectionist viewpoint is revealed in its somewhat exacting approach to standards of parenting. It is perhaps illuminating that Pringle (1975a) chooses a 'Ten Commandments' format for her advice on child care. The ten commandments of the Old Testament were absolutes and were delivered by God. There is a greater tendency in this second value perspective than in the others to lay down what parenting ought to be like. Parents who themselves received 'bad' parenting tend to come badly out of this. They tend to be represented as so damaged that they are unlikely to reach satisfactory standards of care for their own children. Pringle is particularly cautious about very young parents, and recommends a social climate 'in which it is considered irresponsible to have children before, say, the age of twenty-two or twenty-three' (p. 157). She also lays stress on conscious preparation for parenthood, which again may be construed as a somewhat authoritarian approach. Furthermore, the interpretation of who is likely to make a good parent may be seen as over-deterministic. The uncertainties about inter-generational continuities in behaviour are overlooked (see Quinton and Rutter 1988). It may be argued that predictions in individual cases cannot be made with any certainty even from general trends. But it sometimes seems that for the child protectionists, certain potential parents are written off in advance.

A final general aspect of the rationale for this second value perspective which may be criticised is the single-mindedness of its preoccupation with child welfare. This can lead to a crusading, almost messianic tone in some of the writing. Dingwall *et al.* (1983a) (here defined as only moderate paternalists) bring this out well with their quotation from Franklin (1982) already referred to, pointing out the religiosity of the sentiments and the emphasis on child welfare as an absolute priority. While not all the authors completely overlook the needs of other groups, there is a general tendency in this perspective to value childhood far above other states and stages of life. It is rather as though children were a separate race with highly privileged claims, rather than ordinary individuals in the process of becoming. The obvious criticism is one of lack of balance. Child care policy is only one area of social policy, and other needs represented by other policy areas also clamour for attention. Children's welfare is also significantly affected by other, more general social policies, particularly those affecting poverty, education and health. To split children off, in effect, from the rest of society may be seen as ill-founded. Furthermore, the approach, by focusing on the child in isolation, disregards the importance of the (original) family as a unit. The family, rather than the individual child, may be seen as the proper object of policy.

Also, an implied perception of parents as merely means to the satisfaction of their children's needs not only diminishes the parents as people, but may be counterproductive. As some authors who deal with the treatment of child abuse in fact recognise, parents may need to have *their* needs met before they can satisfactorily respond to the needs of their child. It may also be that setting excessively high standards for parenthood will lead people to reject it. It is interesting that a century of, generally, greater focus on the needs of the child and higher expectations of parental care, has also been one of striking decline in fertility – although no simple causal connection can be made between these factors.

The perspective in practice

As in the previous chapter, the discussion has covered the main elements of the value perspective, some authors associated with it, the underlying rationale, and some problems and criticisms. Again, the value perspective will be illustrated by reference to actual policy developments – in this case, in England in the 1970s.

In the 1970s, in response to well-publicised cases of child abuse, and the 'rediscovery' of child abuse in the late 1960s, paternalism emerged in its modern form. The child abuse scandals produced a greater emphasis, as compared with the immediately preceding decades, on protecting children from their families, and on the use of substitute care. Greater use was made of local authorities' powers of compulsion with respect to children, and it became more likely that unsatisfactory parents would lose their children against their will. More was seen of the controlling state; the family oriented support work which had been present in the 1950s and 1960s (and which will be discussed in Chapter 4) was giving way to a greater readiness to focus on children as separate individuals and to act, coercively if need be, on their behalf. Meanwhile foster care (as opposed to residential care) dropped, and then revived in popularity (Packman 1981, Central Statistical Office 1987, Department of Health and Social Security, various years, including 1987a); concern developed about its legal security, and legislation in 1975 in fact strengthened this. The tendency to emphasise security and permanence for the child in care was linked with a greater readiness to use legal powers against parents. And adoption was viewed increasingly favourably, although fewer of the traditional type of adopted children – illegitimate babies – became available. But older children with a history of being in care were more readily considered for adoption. At the same time, the proportion of all children in care rose (Department of Health and Social Security, various years).

As the fate of the child Maria Colwell was so influential in this decade, and is so often referred to when the recent history of child care policy is discussed, a few details of this case will be given to illustrate the roots of the 1970s child abuse 'panic' (see Secretary of State for Social Services 1974, Howells 1974). Maria, born in 1965, was fostered from an early age (about six months) with an aunt and uncle, initially on a private and voluntary basis and later (after a short period with her mother) under a fit person order (precursor of the care order). Altogether she was fostered for about six years, but with the long-term plan being to return her to her mother. Contact with her mother continued irregularly, and her mother increasingly pressed to have her back. Maria, however, had a close relationship with her foster parents, whom she called Mum and Dad, and she began to be distressed by contact with her birth mother and to fear a permanent return to her. Her mother was by 1970 living with a new partner and had a number of children by him. Contact was increased, as the local authority Social Services Department long-term plan was still for integration of Maria into her mother's family. Increasingly, though, Maria resisted the visits and showed signs of trauma as a result of them; in June 1971 she was diagnosed as depressed. Yet the Social Services Department decided not to oppose the mother's intended application for a revocation of the fit person order, despite the evident undesirability of moving Maria full-time to her mother's home at that stage. She *was* moved full-time to her mother's in October 1971 and never saw her foster parents again.

In November 1971 the mother's application to discharge the fit person order was heard, and was not opposed by the local authority, although a supervision order was recommended; the court granted both the discharge of the fit person order and the making of a supervision order. In the ensuing period (1972), despite the local authority's supervisory role, there was abundant evidence of neglect and abuse of Maria, including reports from neighbours and observations by teachers; but not all the relevant information was passed on, and the social worker supervising only saw Maria infrequently and failed to pick up the severity of the signs of ill-treatment. What seemed to be lacking was a comprehensive overview of the case, taking in all the available evidence. Howells (1974) notes that: 'In the last nine months of her life, 30 complaints were made by 17 people or groups of people about the way she was cared for by her natural mother and stepfather. The complaints referred to loss of weight, neglect, injuries, scape-goating, and excessive physical demands' (p. 11). Yet Maria remained where she was. In January 1973 Maria was taken to hospital by her 'parents' where she was found to be dead. She was found to be brain-damaged, severely bruised with internal injuries and severely underweight. Her mother's partner, the 'stepfather', was convicted of her manslaughter.

The history of Maria thus highlighted a number of crucial child care issues: the attachment of a child to long-term foster parents; the absence of a bond with the biological mother; the problems surrounding a 'stepfather' figure; the inadequate response of the agencies to signs of abuse; and the overlooking of a child's clearly expressed preferences (it had been obvious from Maria's behaviour that she did not wish to live with her mother). The Inquiry report emphasised the role of the failure of the system in the case, particularly a failure of communication, but also implicated child care *policy*. The media, broadly, blamed the individual social worker involved.

A rapid outcome of the Colwell case was a proliferation of procedures and safeguards to ensure the early detection of, and action on, child abuse. The inquiry report had highlighted poor communication and co-ordination between the different professional groups involved. Corby (1987) comments that the result 'was a swift reaction on the part of the Department of Health and Social Security which by means of a series of circulars issued between 1974 and 1976 established the framework of the administrative system for detecting, investigating and processing child abuse cases that currently exists' (p. 5). The main features of the system were area review committees, drawn from the higher levels of the agencies, which were to be involved with policy decisions; case conferences, bringing together front-line practitioners to assess and make decisions about individual cases; registers to record children deemed to be at risk of abuse or further abuse, so that previous instances of recorded abuse were not overlooked; and manuals providing guidelines for cases of child abuse allegations. Corby sees this response as largely a managerial one. Other well-publicised child abuse cases and subsequent inquiries added to the emphasis on protectionist responses.

In line with the protectionist trend was the major piece of child care legislation of the 1970s, the 1975 Children Act, which was influenced by the Colwell case, as well as by cases of long-term foster children reclaimed by birth parents who had retained their rights. Most of the Act followed the recommendations of the Houghton Committee Report 1972 (Home Office/Scottish Education Department 1972). Broadly, it extended the powers of local authorities and foster parents over children in care and brought in certain measures which made adoption easier. Many of its provisions were changed by the subsequent 1989 Children Act, it should be noted.

To take the most significant changes in the order in which they occurred in the Act: under Section 1 local authorities were obliged to establish an adoption agency service, and under Section 3 the welfare of the child became the first consideration in all decisions relating to adoption; adoption was accordingly construed more definitely as a child welfare service. Section 12 widened the grounds for dispensing with parental consent (now termed agreement) to adoption. Section 14 introduced a new procedure for 'freeing' a child for adoption before a specific placement was found; it was thought that this would facilitate the adoption of some children. Section 26 contained an emphasis on genetic ties not found elsewhere in the Act in enabling adults adopted as children to obtain their original birth certificate, and therefore information about their parent(s) of origin. Under Section 29, those who had cared for a child for five years (less with parental agreement) could apply to adopt, and the child could not be removed from them before the court hearing. Section 32 permitted the payment of allowances to adopters under approved schemes. Sections 33–55 of the Act set out a new form of guardianship termed 'custodianship'; substitute parents could apply for this status if they had cared for a child for three years (less with parental agreement), and again the child could not be removed before the court hearing. (It was some time before these latter provisions were implemented, and in fact the new legal category of custodianship was short-lived.)

Other sections dealt with children in care. Section 56, for example, enabled the local authority, if a child had been in voluntary care for six months, to require the parent to give 28 days notice of reclaim of the child. (During that period, parental rights might be assumed; voluntary care would thus become compulsory and parental removal be prevented.) Section 57 widened the grounds for assumptions of parental rights – most significantly, they could be passed solely on the grounds that the child had been in voluntary care for three years. (These provisions did not survive the 1989 Act.) Section 59 applied the 'welfare principle' to decisions on children in care, that is, the child's welfare was the first consideration. In both Sections 3 and 59, it may be noted, the wishes and feelings of the child were to be ascertained where practicable. Sections 64–66 are worthy of note: they acknowledged the possibility of conflict of interest between parent and child and thus allowed for their separate representation in court in certain cases and under certain conditions. This could occur, for example, where the parent applied for a discharge of a care order and the local authority was not opposed to this step (which had been the situation in the Maria Colwell case). These provisions were extended in the 1989 Act. These sections, like the 'wishes and feelings' provisions in Sections 3 and 59, reflect more of a children's rights perspective; it is recognised here that children may have a viewpoint of their own.

The Act, it should be noted, was implemented by stages in the late 1970s and 1980s.

The Children Act, like several statutes before it, was described as a 'children's charter'; it was also hailed as 'anti-mother' and 'anti-family' (Samuels 1976:5). The latter epithets are too extreme but it is true that a significant extension of the powers of foster parents and local authorities took place. Hendrick (1994) describes it as: 'a signpost marking the end of the rehabilitative ideal; it signalled a loss of faith in the natural family, usually that of the poor' (p. 241).

As well as acquiring new powers, it seemed that local authority social services departments were also using the powers they had more widely. For example, the power to assume parental rights was more commonly used in the late 1970s: 13.6 per cent of children in care were subject to these assumptions in 1972; 18.2 per cent by 1979 (Department of Health and Social Security, various years). There was apparently an increased use of place of safety orders, for example, figures from Hallett and Stevenson (1980), also quoted by Parton (1981), show the number of place of safety orders increasing from 204 in March 1972, to 353 in March 1974, to 759 in March 1976. Parton (1981) also claimed an increase in children taken into care at birth. Furthermore, the percentage of the under-18 population in care increased over the 1970s, from 0.65 per cent in 1971 to 0.75 per cent in 1976 to 0.77 per cent in 1980 (Department of Health and Social Security, various years). The numbers and proportions of those who were in care under care orders also increased (Department of Health and Social Security, various years including 1978, 1987). The use of wardship proceedings, another form of compulsory care, also rose sharply in the 1970s (Lowe and White 1979). Packman (1993) comments that by the end of the 1970s, at least a quarter of children entering care did so via place of safety orders (citing Packman, Randall and Jacques 1985). The use of voluntary care declined proportionately. It may convincingly be argued that local authorities had greater resort to their legal powers in the child protectionist 1970s, although debate may arise about the significance of the figures. Practice became more defensive in response to anxiety about child abuse. Parton (1985a) comments: 'It is evident that the panic and subsequent procedures and practices developed to "manage" the problem of child abuse, have had far more wide ranging implications than simply work with children in physical danger. The more alert, anxious and decisive approach has been applied to children of all ages and very different circumstances' (p. 122). The 1970s, broadly, saw local authorities increasingly seeking permanence for children either through rapid return to the family of origin, or through a substitute home placement secured by means of, for example, the assumption of parental rights or adoption.

It is of interest that in the 1970s the family as an institution experienced a certain loss of status. Critical views of the family emerged from at least two sources: early 'second wave' feminism, which saw the family as particularly disadvantaging, indeed oppressive, to women, locking them into powerless and dependent positions (see, for example, Firestone 1971, Greer 1971, Mitchell 1971, Millett 1971); and the 'anti-psychiatry' movement associated with R. D. Laing, which construed many parent–child relationships in the nuclear family as damaging to the child, and as implicated in much apparent psychopathology (see, for example, Esterson and Laing 1970, D. Cooper 1971, Laing 1976; also see Fletcher 1988 for both these sources of criticism of conventional family life). In some quarters there was a quest for alternatives to the conventional family. Particular types of family also came under attack. The politician Keith Joseph identified a 'cycle of deprivation' in which maladaptive behaviour forms were supposedly passed on in certain families (Joseph 1972). There were other anxieties about the state of the family on the political right. Parton (1981, 1985a) saw the preoccupation with child abuse and readiness to use legal powers as stemming from a deeper moral anxiety about the decline of the family as a socialising agent; this was linked with wider fears about the social order. Traditional values were felt to be under attack; violence and permissiveness were feared. There was objective change in the family: an increase in marital break-up, a falling birth rate, and an increased movement of married women into the labour market (see, for example, Fox Harding 1996 for family change at this time).

It may be helpful to see child care developments in this context. The family's uncertain status may have contributed as a background factor to a greater willingness to break families up. On the other hand, it was with substitute *families* that children were, ideally, to be placed. It is thus hard to link state paternalism unequivocally with a rejection of the nuclear family form as such.

The changes in child care policy in the 1970s also took place against a background of increasing tough-mindedness towards certain groups and towards welfare policies in general. Within the field of juvenile justice, attitudes to offenders hardened somewhat; the 'treatment' or 'welfare' philosophy probably reached its peak at the end of the 1960s and thereafter declined, with magistrates seeking the power to send offenders away from home for specific periods, and a demand for more severe sentences. Welfare spending was begining to be cut back, and a 'crisis' in the legitimacy of the Welfare State was identified, ending years of apparent consensus when a major role for a high-spending Welfare State was widely accepted (see, for example, Mishra 1984, Loney 1986, Wicks 1987, Hill 1993). The social climate was becoming more utilitarian and less generous towards deprivation. Hence a search for cheaper solutions, in child care perhaps as in other areas of social policy. Parton (1991) comments: 'In the context of a deteriorating economy, the research [on child care] seemed to suggest that rather than concentrate efforts on time-consuming casework and wide-ranging preventative programmes, it was better to retrench and emphasise "less harm rather than more good"' (p. 201). Growing attention to child abuse, however, made child care provisions difficult to ignore.

A number of general themes, then, may be drawn out of child care developments in the 1970s. Child abuse was a preoccupation; more positive child protection was the response. This took the form of new procedures, wider powers, more extensive use of the powers, more use of adoption and secure fostering for children in care, and generally a philosophy well represented by the publications of BAAF in this era. Permanence was favoured; expensive 'preventive work', complex arrangements where children belonged to more than one family, or extensive efforts to rehabilitate them or keep original family contacts alive, less and less so. Packman (1993) summarises as follows: 'the positive and idealistic stance of the sixties, in which pride in an improved care service did not dampen optimism about the help that could be offered to families in their own homes, had been superseded by a gloomier analysis, leading to tougher interventions' (p. 230). The standing of parents *qua* birth parents was at a low ebb, and the family itself seemed almost under seige. Cuts in welfare services in response to public expenditure policies began to bite in these years, although they were not as extreme as in the decade which followed.

CHAPTER 4

The modern defence of the birth family and parents' rights

Introduction

The third, pro-birth family perspective encapsulates the idea that birth or biological families are important both for children and parents, and should be maintained wherever possible; where families have to be separated, links should usually be kept up. The role of the state is seen as, ideally, neither paternalist nor *laissez-faire*, but supportive of families, providing various services that they need to remain together. Class, poverty and deprivation are seen as important elements in child care, explaining much of what occurs in the child care field.

The main elements of the perspective

Two preliminary points should be made about this value perspective. First, it is clearly distinguished from the state paternalist viewpoint just described. The latter, paternalist position, as shown, focuses strongly on children as entities distinct from their parents, seeing parenthood in terms of its service to the children's welfare. Parental duties or responsibilities are valued, not parental rights. Where high standards of parental care are not met, a strong role is envisaged for the state in transferring children, where necessary, to other adults who will parent them better. Early parent–child bonds are – relatively – de-emphasised. And much faith is placed in the power of the state and its agencies. On all these points – the emphasis on the *child* as a separate entity, the devaluing of the original *parents*, the faith in the role of the state – the second and third perspectives part company sharply, as will become apparent.

Secondly, and perhaps less obviously, the third perspective should also be firmly distinguished from the first, *laissez-faire*, position. It might seem that as both the first and third perspectives resist coercive state intervention and wish to keep families intact wherever possible, there is little to differentiate them. The proponents of both perspectives emphasise, broadly, the right of birth parents to care for their own children, and the right of children to live with their own parents. Nevertheless, important differences open up; again this will become more apparent as the third perspective is discussed. These differences are partly to do with concepts of the preferred role of the state and the nature of the state child care system; they also reflect differences over the relative importance of biological and psychological bonds between adults and children, and over the basis of effective parenthood.

To take the biological–psychological issue first, the modern defence of the birth family stresses the value of both psychological and biological bonds for individuals. The original, biological family is perceived as being of unique value and as being, for the vast majority of children, the optimum context for their growth, upbringing and development. Biological bonds are usually emotional ones as well, but even if they are not, knowledge of, and contact with, one's family of origin are thought to be important. It is not altogether clear to what degree the proponents of this perspective would want to maintain a link with biological parents who are in no sense the psychological parents as well – that is, how much they value the blood tie as such. It seems that in supporting the birth family they have mostly in mind cases where the original parents are or were also the psychological parents, albeit inadequate ones. Yet some value is seen in the birth tie and genetic links *per se*. Biological bonds are also emphasised from the parents' point of view; there is great sensitivity in this perspective to the needs of parents for their children, and to the sense of loss of parents whose children pass into the care of the state and to substitute families. There is an emphasis on the rights of parents as people in their own right; and alongside this an explanation of poor quality child care which is sympathetic to parental difficulties. Where parents fail to parent their children satisfactorily, this is often because they are oppressed by circumstances outside their control. Bad parenting is firmly linked with social deprivation and its concomitant pressures on families. The remedies focus on reducing deprivation and its pressures through measures such as increased daytime care for children and better financial and other kinds of support for parents. The basis for effective parenting is thus both biological and material (rather than, say, rooted in individual psychological history) – birth parents are (mostly) the best providers of care, but they need support from a materially favourable environment.

This point leads on to the issue of the child care role of the state in this perspective. The perspective prefers an extensive role for the state, not in separating children from parents or providing substitute care, but in providing support for families so that children do not *need* substitute care. This may take the form of intensive help directed to those families on the verge of breaking up, or of broader social policies to support all families with children. This, it should be noted, is very different from a 'minimalist' position on the role of the state. The state should be active in helping families. But actually putting children in substitute care is seen as generally (though not invariably) undesirable.

Where children do, almost as a last resort, have to come into state care, considerable intervention should be devoted to helping their families and maintaining links so that the children can return home again.

This may mean the child relating to a number of parent figures at once. While the first two perspectives seem preoccupied with the necessity for certainty, permanence, security, and a stable bond with a single set of parent figures, defenders of the birth family find more acceptable a situation where, say, a child may maintain an active relationship with the birth parent(s) while living with foster parents. Indeed, the type of foster care which is preferred in this perspective is of the 'inclusive' or open kind where the birth parents remain positively involved in the child's life. 'Exclusive' fostering, where the foster parents tend to treat children rather as though they were their own or they had adopted them, is thought to be damaging to the child's identity, as well as hindering restoration to the birth parents (Holman 1975b, 1982). Ideas of 'open' adoption have also developed in the 1980s and 1990s (Mullender 1991, Ryburn 1994a, Adcock, Kaniuk and White 1994).

State policies on child care tend in this perspective to be viewed critically for their insufficient emphasis on the prevention of children entering state care or on work to reunite families separated in this way. There is also scepticism about the adequacy of courts and social service agencies as decision-makers on child placements and the child's interests, and about the quality and value of substitute care. Removing a child from an unsatisfactory home is no magic answer but may be damaging, resulting in, for example, placement in a series of unsuitable foster homes, and a cumulative experience of rejection and failure. Substitute care may be worse than care in the birth family. The extreme is represented by child deaths in supposedly supervised foster homes (see Chapter 3), and serious, systematic and prolonged abuse in residential care (see, for example, Levy and Kahan 1991).

It is also stressed that findings which apparently indicate the beneficial effects of adoption may have their root in a class effect whereby adoption transfers children to a higher class (see Chapter 3). The birth parent perspective sees parents whose children come into contact with state child care agencies as in a weak power position, this being related to factors of social disadvantage, primarily social class. This perspective is thus much more conscious than the first two of the class element in state child care. It is pointed out that social workers, magistrates and judges – the state decision-makers in child care – are middle-class, while the child care interventions of the state are not uniformly distrubuted among parents in society but are concentrated on those parents who come from particularly poor and disadvantaged groups – single parents, the unskilled, the unemployed, those from ethnic minorities and in poor housing and deprived neighbourhoods. The causes of their poor parenting, as already noted, are seen as lying largely in these external factors; yet the state, it is said, offers little tangible help, punishes them by too readily removing their children, and makes it extremely difficult for them to get the children back. This perspective is highly conscious of this injustice; it does also value child welfare, but sees the child's interests as lying in remaining with the birth parents in the vast majority of cases.

To summarise, this viewpoint favours extensive state intervention but not of the coercive kind. Birth families should be supported in their caring role; children should not enter substitute care except as a last resort or on a 'shared care' basis; having entered care, most of them should be kept in touch with their original family and should wherever possible return to it. The state in its child care role pays insufficient attention to upholding birth families; it also operates in a discriminatory way on the basis of social class. Most of the child care problems to which the state responds are attributable to poverty and deprivation.

Some authors associated with the perspective

The most notable author associated with this position is Holman, who has argued consistently for the defence of the natural or birth family. For example, in a pamphlet entitled *Inequality in Child Care* (Holman 1980a) he argues that a good deal of the apparent need for substitute care for children is produced by social deprivation and its attendant pressures on families, rather than parental inadequacy or culpability. The ties between parents and children are strong; parents may be forced into, rather than willingly accepting of, separation from their children through substitute care; once separated, they may not want to make the final break via adoption. The response of the social services to poor standards of parenting should be the provision of more supportive services to enable birth families to cope better, rather than facilitating the removal of children to substitute care and the ultimate separation of adoption. Holman thus sees the major child care policy need as being a broad one: to provide the necessary environmental supports to prevent families breaking up because of poor child care, and to enable separated families to live together again. Prevention, at the broadest level, involves the amelioration of wider conditions that cause deprivation; this involves more general questions about how best to care for all children.

A major plank in Holman's argument is that the need for children to enter care is strongly associated with – indeed caused by – various forms of deprivation. Drawing on research, he identifies five features associated with social deprivation as conditions linked with children's admission to care. These five are: lone parenthood, large families, parents who are unskilled manual workers, low income, and inadequate housing. Generally there is evidence of a relationship between poverty and admission to care. Children coming into care also come disproportionately from geographical areas of social deprivation. Holman suggests that social deprivation has two relevant effects: first, it affects parenting behaviour and child rearing methods, and secondly, it leads to a lack of child care resources in the home. So certain families among the socially deprived find it difficult to attain the child care standards set by societal norms (norms which they may share). A life of deprivation makes children vulnerable to separation through coming into care.

Parents who lose their children to public care are thus disproportionately poor and lower class. (The inference is that inadequate
middle-class parents suffer less visibility and have a wider range of
child care options open to them.) Class, then, is significant in the child
care actions of the state – a variable which is conspicuous by its
absence in the first two perspectives discussed. Holman also carried a
class analysis into the field of adoption (Holman 1978), noting the
gross under-representation of Classes IV and V among adoptive
parents. In other words, adoption had been perhaps moving children
up the social scale, or redistributing children from the worse off to the
better off.

Holman speaks emotively in *Inequality in Child Care* of parents
'losing' their children, which suggests that he regards the wishes and
feelings of parents as being of not insignificant importance alongside
the needs of children. Identifying emotionally with the parents, and
calling on his readers to do likewise, Holman seeks help for parents
which would directly or indirectly benefit their children also. Parents
are subjects to be considered; indeed, in an earlier article on unmarried
mothers and child separation (Holman 1975a), he specifically stated
that the wishes of the mothers should be taken into consideration more
strongly in the legislation concerning the future of the children.

In his pamphlet Holman is particularly critical of the 1975 Children
Act for taking no cognizance of the link between child separation and
poverty and for facilitating the placement of children in other, permanent homes while doing nothing to help parents struggling in the face
of material difficulties. The 1975 Act as shown in Chapter 3 contained
various provisions to limit parental rights, the effects of which were to
increase the likelihood of parents losing touch with their children and
to encourage quasi-adoptive fostering, while no extra resources were
provided to prevent children having to leave their parents at all. The
Act, in other words, encouraged permanence in the secure foster home
or adoptive home but militated against prevention and rehabilitation.

In Holman's view social work practice at that time (the 1970s)
tended not to encourage contact between parents and their children in
care, or the reunification of separated families. In support of this he
quotes research done by, for example, Thorpe (1974), who found in a
study of long-term foster children that only 27 per cent had contact
with their parents every six months or more frequently, and that over
60 per cent of the parents did not know where their children were living, with only 21 per cent feeling encouraged by their social worker to
maintain contact. In only 5 per cent of cases was rehabilitation considered by the social worker to be a possibility and in no cases at all was
there any definite plan for rehabilitation. Holman stresses that lack of
contact did not necessarily reflect parental wishes (in fact nearly a half
of the parents wanted their children back) but parents felt they were
being tacitly excluded by the agency. Holman's conclusion from findings of this type is not – as supporters of the child protection
perspective might infer – that the children should therefore be found

secure substitute homes, but that more effort should be put into maintaining children's links with their original parents. This seems an equally defensible conclusion. Thoburn's research (Thoburn 1980), for example, has shown that persistent social work can in fact bring about the return of children to birth parents who previously could not cope, while work by Millham *et al.* (1986) confirmed that absence of contact between children in care and their parents was due more to various structural barriers experienced by both children and parents, such as changes in the parents' situation and limited social work support, rather than just to parental unwillingness or indifference. Millham *et al.* comment that the majority of parents initially do seek access to their children, and it says something for the resilience of the blood tie that the majority of children and parents do manage to remain in contact. The Department of Health (1991a) noted the disadvantage affecting parents over access, referring to Thoburn's (1990) and Berridge and Cleaver's (1987) research which showed that family links were too often not maintained.

In an article, Holman (1980b) reiterated his arguments. He suggested that the drop in children available for adoption in the 1970s had led adoption pressure groups to advocate a form of fostering which was closer to adoption, with the birth parents being less involved in the foster placement. Holman saw a link here with Goldstein *et al.* (1979, 1980) whose doctrine, as shown in Chapter 2, stressed psychological rather than biological ties and the difficulty of children relating to more than one set of parent figures. In contrast, Holman finds the more desirable form of fostering to be that of the 'inclusive' kind where parents are actively included in the placement and therefore do not lose contact (Holman 1975a). Children having more than one set of parent figures – living with foster parents while continuing to relate to birth parents – is not seen as problematic.

A later book by Holman (1988) *Putting Families First. Prevention and Child Care* restates the position, while giving considerable space to the role of voluntary bodies in preventive child care work. Reviewing the history of child care policy, Holman notes the case for prevention which was put in the 1950s and 1960s. This was partly an argument about costs – keeping children in local authority care was expensive; partly there was concern about foster home breakdown; then there was the theory (derived from Bowlby) that separation from the original parents, especially the mother, was damaging. So 'the conviction gained ground that a child's own family was, in most cases, the best place for him to be' (Holman 1988:39). There was also research evidence that many admissions to care could have been avoided by earlier intervention. Holman broadly sees the 1960s as strongly preventionist, the 1970s as dominated by fear of child abuse and the permanency movement, and the 1980s, it seems, as mixed, with a further drive for prevention but also pressures against it, including the recession and financial curbs on services.

In his last chapter Holman (1988) restates the case for prevention. The essential themes here are: that prolonged separations are likely to impair child development; that care placements are unstable, with many changes; that residential care in particular is damaging and does not prevent delinquency; and that separation has a negative impact on parents as well. Being in care is also stigmatised. Thus, the trauma of separation and entry to care should be prevented whenever possible. Holman next argues that the case for prevention depends on the place of the family in society. The family of parents and children remains a major institution held in high esteem; here Holman refers to the family's functions – basically socialisation and the provision of individuals with an identity. And the fact of birth constitutes a powerful and special bond. The point here is that if children are taken from their families, they are deprived of 'what is considered the normal and rightful lot of most children' (p. 203). Holman brings in his personal experiences as a wartime evacuee and child care worker, from which he draws five lessons, two relating to the family, two to care, and one, interestingly and significantly, to neighbourhoods. In the order that Holman gives them, these points are that:

the family is the basic unit of our society;
children and families may relate closely to their neighbourhoods;
families rarely wish to be broken up;
public care produces complications and sufferings;
some admissions to care and custody could have been avoided.

Again, Holman's central themes of the importance of origins, and the dubious value of being in care, are present. Referring to his Christian and Socialist beliefs, Holman acknowledges his debt to R. H. Tawney. Holman briefly addresses the role of the state, referring to the right-wing *laissez-faire* writer Mount (1982), with whom, predictably, he disagrees. Mount sees all forms of state welfare as threatening to the family by removing its privacy and self-responsibility. To refute this position, Holman refers back to Victorian times, when many families were destroyed by huge deprivation in a society where there was little collective welfare provision.

Later writing by Holman (1993) on social welfare in a more general sense reflects on the influence of the New Right on policy and suggests 'mutuality' as an alternative basis. By this he means a concept adapted from 'fraternity', a concept associated with the work of Tawney. Mutuality involves the recognition of obligation based on common human kinship and expressed in joint action directed towards more equitable sharing. Within the personal social services: 'the aim should be to modify the devastating effects of social inequalities which now ruin the lives of so many' (p. 71). He envisages an expansion of supportive, publicly provided services.

Holman, then, has consistently backed the integrity of the nuclear family and an extensive supportive role for the state. The title of his work *Putting Families First* (1988) may be usefully contrasted with that of a volume published in honour of Kellmer Pringle, who has been identified with the child protectionist stance: *Putting Children First* (Vallender and Fogelman 1987). The titles neatly summarise the difference in emphasis. Finally, two quotations from Holman's writings highlight his perspective:

> By failing to tackle social deprivations, by refusing to strengthen effective preventive work and by legislation only for the separation of families, the government ... casts the parents in the role of those who are not to be helped but are to be punished.

> the fact of living with parents who conceived the child does usually create an affinity and should be the foundation on which socialisation and domestic life is based. The present social system appears to accept this premise for most families but its inequalities inhibit a minority of families from enjoying normal family life. (Holman 1988:32, 36)

Putting Families First ends with a vision of the 'preventative neighbourhood' (not to be used as an excuse for avoiding structural reforms), which might lead to 'the reality of a society where far fewer children have to leave their homes and neighbourhoods, where few are subject to neglect and abuse, where all families are prevented from suffering gross social disadvantages, and where all parents are enabled to develop their parenting capacities to the fullest' (p. 224).

Considerable space has been devoted to Holman as perhaps the most explicit proponent of this value perspective. Other writers who have put similar arguments may be referred to more briefly. Walton and Heywood (1975), noted a general social trend to separation and disengagement in relationships, and foresaw a strong tendency in society to minimise the importance of the blood tie and kin relationships. Like Holman, they argued for better community provision and for policies that would prevent families breaking up, rather than the provision of more substitute care. Tunstill (1977), as mentioned in Chapter 3, attacked practice guides for social workers issued by the then ABAFA (later BAAF) for emphasising the removal of parental rights and placement of children for adoption and long-term fostering, suggesting that the guides took a hardline criterion against the birth parents which did not take account of social workers' failure to encourage regular contact between parents and children in care. In a later article (Tunstill 1985) Tunstill analysed the extent to which the 1975 Children Act resembled elements of the old Poor Law legislation. Emphasising the link between poverty and entry to care, Tunstill was critical of the 1975 Act for doing nothing to alleviate poverty or facilitate preventive work.

Andrews (1980) is another author who may be identified with the birth parent school. He argued that in general the blood tie was not a bad presumption for child care legislation; the birth family provides security, consistency of care and attachment. But for the family to work, the parents need to feel protected and free from undue interference; parental rights provide a framework for the responsible exercise of parental obligations. Andrews maintained that the assumption that a parent knows what is in the interests of his [sic] child is a reasonable one and holds for the vast majority of families. The arguments take place around the exceptions to the general rule. Andrews noted that the 1963 Children and Young Persons Act revived the blood tie philosophy, assuming that the long-term interests of children could best be secured within their own families, and that the 1969 CYPA similarly interpreted children's welfare in terms of their own families. However, the 1970s witnessed a move away from the blood tie philosophy, and the 1975 Children Act incorporated this shift, in the provisions giving additional powers to local authorities and foster parents. Andrews noted that the Act was passed in the wake of the Maria Colwell outcry and 'tug-of-love' incidents (involving birth parents and foster parents), which led to a search for greater security for those providing substitute care.

An account of the development of child care policy by MacLeod (1982) also broadly took a preventionist, pro-birth parent stance. MacLeod charted the movement in policy towards, and then away from, family based child care, seeing social work as being directed to the support of the family in the 1950s and 1960s, but moving away from family care in the 1970s. It is clear that MacLeod is critical of the latter move and broadly in favour of the former supportive policy. She is also aware of the financial disadvantages experienced by many parents of children in care, and of their difficulties in staying in touch with their children. Interestingly, MacLeod commented on the changing view of the family in child care policy, that: 'It is as though the relationship aspects of family life now take second place to the caring/nursing aspects and the family is valued for its caring capacity, rather than being seen as a grouping of individuals linked by a network of relationships which locate and provide status for individuals in a complex society' (p. 56). Sceptical about the value of fostering and about changes in the 1970s which pushed social workers 'to look energetically for new homes rather than spend a great deal of energy enabling natural families to live together' (p. 57), MacLeod favoured general supportive services for families.

The House of Commons Social Services Committee Second Report *Children in Care* (House of Commons 1984) shared to an extent this broadly preventive and rehabilitative emphasis. For example, under the heading 'Prevention' (p. xvii) the Report recommended, *inter alia*, that the (then) long-term rate of supplementary benefit be paid to unemployed families with children; that local authorities compare preventive expenditure under Section 1 with the actual cost of keeping a child in care, 'in order to judge the potential effectiveness of a more constructive use of cash payments or loans' (p. xxii); and that there be every effort by local authorities to improve cooperation between housing and social services departments to avert the reception of children into care because of homelessness. Under its 'Conclusions' the Report again has a section headed 'Prevention' which favours closer cooperation between social services departments and social security offices, easier access to day care for pre-school children, more effort in the prevention of child abuse, and a coordinated approach to non-school attendance. Another section headed 'Rehabilitation' comments that the extension of the then duty to seek rehabilitation to all children in 'care' as it then was (that is, whatever their legal status) might be effective, and referred this idea to the proposed review of child care law (Department of Health and Social Security 1985). The Report was aware of the significance of social deprivation, and its Introduction had commented that it was often the adults concerned and not the children who most needed help. However, the Committee also thought that there was a danger of over-stating the potential for preventive strategies, and that the idea of 'preventing' care gave an unduly negative picture of it.

A more radical approach is taken by Parton in his writings in the 1980s (Parton 1981, 1985a). Locating child abuse in its social and political context, Parton saw – and regretted – a growth in coercive interventions by social workers in the late 1970s and early 1980s, based on a social anxiety about the decline of the family, as well as on the assumption that child abuse is rooted in individual pathology rather than in social inequality or social divisions. It is difficult to do justice to the sophistication of Parton's extensive work on this subject in a short résumé, but briefly, Parton (1985a) regarded the 'disease model' of abuse as fundamentally flawed. Abuse cannot be predicted and identified with precision; and the 'disease model', he claimed, had been interpreted in an increasingly conservative way, with a strong emphasis on personal responsibility for abuse and the social control role of social workers. Shifts in child care policy in Britain in the 1970s and 1980s reflected these trends. Parton refers to 'panic' over child abuse, to a 'more alert, anxious and decisive approach' and a 'more resolute approach' (p. 122). Local authorities used their statutory powers more, and were more unhappy about involving parents in child care. Such a 'rescue' approach 'has helped to deflect attention from the more serious deficiencies in welfare provision for all children and families and implies that help is only available in situations of extreme severity or crisis' (p. 175). Parton saw this general trend as in line with the Thatcherite political economy of the 1980s.

By contrast, Parton himself viewed child abuse as strongly related to class, inequality and poverty, and favoured preventive action in the broadest sense, tackling the wider conditions associated with abuse. The terms of the debate needed to be recast, and: 'It is not that we simply need an expanded role for the state but that the social relations which it reflects should be democratic and play an active and supportive role in bringing up children' (p. 186). In a slightly later article (Parton 1986), which critically analysed the inquiry report on the case of the abused and murdered child Jasmine Beckford (London Borough of Brent 1985), Parton elaborated some of the same themes. He was critical of the 'disease model' of abuse adopted in the Report, and its assumptions that social workers should make greater use of statutory power and authority, becoming controlling and more sceptical about how far parents can change. In Parton's view both the disease model and the assumptions about current social work were open to doubt, and the report was in danger of directing attention away from the major issues. In 1989 Parton and Parton discussed the recurring concept of 'dangerousness' in child protection, and supported instead broader notions of prevention which: 'far from being based on residual, individualistic interventions which rely on assessing dangerousness and the use of statutory authority, should be based on universal services which work to support those rearing children and rely on voluntary relationships' (Parton and Parton 1989:73).

The development of Parton's later work is interesting, showing an increased awareness of the reality of abuse for the child. In a chapter in an edited collection (Violence Against Children Study Group 1990), Parton acknowledged that his 1985 work *The Politics of Child Abuse* was inadequate in at least three areas, and that the difficulties: 'reflected a much more fundamental problem with the analysis itself' (p. 10). Parton now sees his own analysis as having: 'underestimated the impact of child abuse on certain children' (p. 12). It also encounters difficulty in explaining both abuse in more affluent families and why only *some* children in deprived families are abused (see the later section here on 'Empirical support'). We need to recognise: 'that child abuse takes many forms and that these need to be analysed in ways that draw upon quite different explanatory concepts' (p. 16). However, while being self-critical, Parton has certainly not departed completely from his earlier structural analysis, stressing: 'the attempt to locate individual experiences in wider social structures and the ability to address causal issues rooted in the wider society' (p. 24).

In his later book (Parton 1991), Parton examined developments in the 1980s and in fact continued to be critical of an emphasis on individualistic and legalistic responses to abuse. Focusing on the theme of social control/regulation and families, Parton investigates the discourses (structures of language and knowledge) of child protection, social work, medicine and law. The growth of social work in the twentieth century has been closely related to the welfare state, and as Parton notes: 'The emergence of "the social" and its central concern with the family was a positive solution to a major problem posed for the liberal state ... how can the state establish the rights of individual children while promoting the family as the natural sphere for raising children' (p. 12). Social work has an ambiguous role, then, and forms part of the compromises of the liberal state. But child abuse has, in Parton's view, increasingly been seen as a socio-legal problem, where it is *legal* expertise that takes pre-eminence. Parton examines two strands in the development of child care policy, under the chapter headings 'Child Care, Prevention and Partnership' and 'Child Abuse, Authority and

Risk' respectively, noting that: 'The mid-1980s witnessed a resurgence of widespread concern about child abuse tragedies' (p. 74). A different type of child abuse scandal, the 'Cleveland affair' (1987), is considered in the subsequent chapter. Having then analysed the Children Act 1989 in terms of how various balances were struck in the new legislative framework, Parton outlines a 'political economy' of child protection, drawing some conclusions from his analysis of recent policy. He asks what forms of social regulation have emerged, and sees *legalism* as predominant, with social workers having become more accountable to the courts. This recent emergence of legalism may: 'be interpreted as evidence of the collapse of the political consensus upon which the institutional fabric of the welfare state was so dependent' (p. 195). Criticisms of social work tended towards emphasising greater reliance on individual rights, along with increased interest in 'dangerousness' and an enlarged influence for right-wing attitudes to the state in which the role of the law is primary. The law provides the framework for contracts and an explicit rationale for state intervention, with clear family–state boundaries. Nevertheless, despite this emphasis on the law and legalism, Parton believes that in child protection, social work and its discourse still have the central role.

Other authors relevant to this camp, Frost and Stein (1989), also present a structural analysis of child care issues, arguing that child welfare can only be fully understood as a political process reflecting social divisions. Their basic premise is that child welfare cannot be understood in isolation from broader social forces; and they argue that the fundamental theme of inequality provides an explanatory framework for child welfare. Inequality is manifest in class, gender, ethnicity, disability and generation differences. While wary of the dangers of idealising 'the family', and aware that children and young people have a separate identity and set of interests distinct from their parents, Frost and Stein share with Holman and other proponents of the birth parent school an emphasis on the link between class/poverty/deprivation and child care, and quote some of the relevant evidence; they also point to the increasing isolation of working-class families; and to the overrepresentation of black and mixed race children in care, which seems to be due not just to social deprivation but to 'Eurocentric' assumptions imposed on these families by white social workers. Seeking a response to child welfare which is firmly located in its social context, Frost and Stein favour policies of 'structural prevention', and a child welfare practice responsive to divisions of class, ethnicity, and gender. Progressive child welfare practice should embrace the key theme of empowerment of children and young people, and challenge models which are based only on individual and family pathology. However, Frost and Stein distance themselves from the more extreme manifestations of the children's rights approach (to be discussed in Chapter 5). Although sympathetic to the notion of empowerment of children, they say: 'we do have some serious reservations about the form that the current children's rights lobby takes' (p. 135). Day care for children under five is seen as crucial, the struggle for this being 'a struggle over the definition of the public and the private, the dispute over whether parents should be left to care for their children, a struggle over the construction of gender and of whether child care is properly a public concern' (p. 150).

Another group of authors who may be mentioned here are Beresford, Kemmis and Tunstill (1987) who in *In Care in North Battersea* reported on a study of children in care, and pointed to the relationship between the socio-economic structure and the percentage of children in care. Beresford *et al.* found a high proportion of black and mixed race children in care, that single parents and those dependent on state benefits were most likely to have their children in care, and that a high proportion of children in care had unemployed parents. Generally, there was evidence for an association between reception into care and social deprivation. The authors emphasise the importance of prevention, and the lack of it in practice; the need to give special attention to the needs of black families; and the need for resources to combat poverty, unemployment and poor housing. Relevant also to the over-representation of children from certain groups in care is a study by Bebbington and Miles (1989) which found that children entering care came disproportionately from certain groups: families on income support; where both parents were not present; where the family lived in rented housing, were overcrowded, and living in 'poor' neighbourhoods; where mothers were young, and parents of different races. The parents tended to be deprived on a variety of dimensions, and deprivation was found to be *more* closely associated with coming into care than in an earlier study by Packman (Packman 1968). However, 'broken family' was the factor most strongly associated with coming into care, rather than unemployment, as in the earlier study.

A marked example of identification with, and sympathy for, vulnerable parents is Booth and Booth's (1994) *Parenting Under Pressure*. This study focused on parents with learning difficulties from a pro-parent point of view, and argued for effective support for them. The authors speak of rights to parenthood as a part of normalised, ordinary living, and comment: 'Much remains to be learned in this field, not least about how to achieve a balance between the welfare of children and the rights of parents. The evidence of our research suggests that too often this balance is unfairly tipped against parents' (p. 144), advising: 'Never seek permanently to remove a child from home for reasons of neglect, inadequate care or abuse by omission before every effort has been made to equip parents with the skills they need to cope' (p. 147).

Mention may also be made of the Department of Health's (1991a) *Patterns and Outcomes in Child Placement*, which presents various research findings from a largely pro-birth parent viewpoint, and of a recent author, Utting (1995), in a report for the Joseph Rowntree Foundation. Utting draws on a programme of research to review family change, identify family problems, and formulate policy and practice responses relating to parenting and family support, arguing for greater priority to be given to problems of parenting in a wide range of families. The approach is clearly preventive: Utting's last two chapters argue that 'a wide range of family based initiatives focused on helping parents and children to lead happier, healthier lives can confidently be expected to yield dividends for society as a whole as well as the individual families' (p. 54). Under 'The Case for Prevention' Utting proposes that: 'The requirement is for a wide range of support services, extending from those which should be available to every family in the land to the kind of intensive support that only becomes appropriate at times of crisis' (p. 75).

Looking at relevant organisations, mention must be made of the pressure group, the Family Rights Group, which has worked with numerous parents who have felt unfairly deprived of care of, or contact with, their children by local authority social services departments; this group has issued publications arguing the value of the birth family, and contact with it, for the child. For example, *Fostering Parental Contact* (Family Rights Group 1982) in a series of papers put forward arguments for preserving contact between children in care and the birth family. A later pamphlet (Family Rights Group 1984) questioned the trend at that time to the severing of contact between children in care and their families, rather than encouraging and enabling families to share in their children's care. Concerns of this kind subsequently fed into the 1989 Children Act's emphasis on local authorities shifting their approach and working more in partnership with parents. Later, training materials linked to the Children Act 1989 were produced by the Family Rights Group, on the theme of social workers working in partnership with families (for example, Family Rights Group 1991).

The National Council for One Parent Families (or One Parent Families) has taken a similar approach to the Family Rights Group, defending birth parents and arguing in particular (NCOPF 1982) that the use of the then local authority power to assume parental rights by resolution could constitute a breach of natural justice. There is also evidence that single parents are more likely than others to lose their children to local authority care (see, for example, Parker 1977, Beresford *et al.* 1987, Bebbington and Miles 1989). These parents are seen as being in a weak power position vis-à-vis the state, finding difficulty in defending their rights. In a small study of 40 (nearly all single) parents who had had their parental rights removed by means of a resolution, the NCOPF (1982) found that:

The majority of the parents were poor, on Supplementary Benefit and under emotional stress. Voluntary care was often the only immediate solution to their problems because other alternatives and resources did not exist. But the act of accepting this solution was often later interpreted as evidence of a parent's weakness and failure ... many were deeply shocked where resolutions were taken or access curtailed.   (NCOPF 1982:24)

The loss of their child became more permanent than the parents had anticipated.

Rationale and underlying values

In the first two perspectives on child care policy, one element of the underlying rationale which was identified was the emphasis on psychological rather than biological parenthood. For both the *laissez-faire* school of the Goldstein *et al.* (1979, 1980) type, and the state paternalists, the psychological bonds formed between children and their primary caretakers are overwhelmingly more important than any notion of a blood tie, a bond which is based on genetic and birth links alone. But for the proponents of the third perspective, the pro-birth family or pro-birth parent view, links with original biological parents *are* crucial. Being a biological parent or child means something.

Yet the rationale for taking this position is somewhat ambiguous. In so far as these links are important because birth parents cared for children in the early stages of their lives, the third perspective does not part company very sharply with the first two. Here the third perspective can draw on the work of authorities such as Bowlby (1951, 1953), who showed that separation in the early years from a maternal figure (not necessarily the biological mother) to whom the child had become attached, or deprivation of loving, continuous maternal care, could be extremely damaging. Holman (1988) in fact invokes Bowlby's work, referring, for example, under 'The Case for Prevention', to Bowlby's conclusions that normal development required an intimate, continuous relationship with a mother or permanent mother substitute, that separation could have permanent adverse effects, and that adoptions needed to start in the child's first two months to facilitate success. Here the emphasis seems to be mainly on early psychological bonds. There is also the point that children, it is thought, suffer particularly if there is secrecy about their family of origin, experiencing feelings of shame and inferiority. They may also experience feelings of disloyalty if they become too fond of foster parents, or may develop an idealisation of an absent parent. Children, then, may retain a sense of identification with their origins.

However, it seems that proponents of this perspective do, at least, implicitly, go beyond this to support the importance of biological bonds *per se*. It would seem, for example, that Holman values knowledge of, as well as contact with, the birth family as a source of the individual's identity. Andrews (1980) explicitly defends the blood tie. The field of socio-biology might provide one legitimating theory to support the view that individuals feel a deep bond with those who share some of their genes, even in the absence of a history of interaction. However, Holman and the other authors cited here do not explore this. Another possible way of thinking about the issue, mentioned in Chapter 2, is to point out that families are socially defined, but that society defines them in biological terms. Therefore to have lost some of one's nearest biological relatives is to be socially defined as having something missing. And as Holman (1988) says, 'in a society where living at home with natural parents is the norm ,stigma against those who do otherwise is very deeply entrenched' (p. 200). Holman is here supporting biological ties because they are defined as normal.

Another point that may be mentioned here is the importance of ethnic origins and identity for individuals, raising particular issues for children with ethnically different substitute parents. In the late 1970s, 1980s and 1990s there was greater awareness of the need to place children with, in particular, adoptive parents of similar ethnic origin to themselves. Placements with parents of a different ethnic group (most obviously white, when the children are in some sense black) have been thought to raise a number of problems (for criticism of transracial adoption and fostering, see, for example, ABSWAP 1983, Stubbs 1987). Partly the argument concerns the need for black children to learn from black parent figures how to deal with a racist society. But partly it focuses around the idea of a cultural inheritance linked with being born with a particular genetic inheritance. For example, it is argued that genetically African-Caribbean children need to know about African-Caribbean culture and history, and to connect with the African-Caribbean community. Placing such children in a family context where they are cut off from this is seen as damaging and a loss; being brought up by a white family does not make the child white. This line of argument is also, clearly, based on an acknowledgement that society does treat different ethnic groups differently, and that different groups do have different cultures – biological inheritance means something because it is socially constructed in a particular way. It is not so much being black, as being seen to be black, which may cause the black child in a white foster or adoptive family to experience problems of cultural identity and social location. Thus, there have been increasing reservations in some quarters about transracial foster and adoptive placements. In acknowledgment of these concerns, the Children Act 1989 requires the child's ethnic origins to be taken into account in decisions (Section 22). (Other sources on this debate include Gill and Jackson 1983, Dale 1987, Commission for Racial Equality 1990, Small 1991, Rhodes 1992.)

Further support for the view of birth ties as important is found in the evidence that some individuals do strenuously seek information about, and possibly meetings with, biological parents or other relatives who have always been strangers to them. The main categories here are people adopted early in life and those who never knew their biological father (including some conceived by artificial insemination). Of interest here is Section 26 of the 1975 Children Act which made it possible for adopted adults to gain access to their original birth certificate, and therefore possibly to trace their original parents. Only a minority of those eligible have taken up this opportunity, however (see Triseliotis 1970, Melville 1983, Department of Health and Social Security 1984a, Jennings 1992). Nevertheless, it is clear from anecdotal and autobiographical evidence that some individuals do become involved in a passionate quest for a totally unknown biological parent, and other

relatives as well. One supporter of the pro-birth parent school interviewed by Fox (1982) did speak of children: 'having intense feelings
for their own parents even if they've never seen them' (p. 281). And
the Department of Health (1991a) comments: 'The powerful psychological influence of the "hidden", internalised parent has been known
for many decades' (p. 22). While Keppel (1991), in an article on birth
parents and negotiated adoption agreements, notes: 'Research, clinical
practice and the stories of those involved in the "search and reunion"
movement are conclusive in their findings that the secrecy and severance of family ties have not been in the interests of significant numbers
of adoptees and birth parents' (p. 83).

What is also clearly an underlying value in this third child care perspective is the importance to parents of having conceived and given
birth to a child. Unlike the second perspective, the third does not disregard parents' needs and interests or treat parents only as a means to the
end of child welfare. The emotional importance to a parent of a biological bond is identified and given some weight in its own right. And there
is considerable sympathy for the vulnerable parent – for example, the
parent who is poor, single, living in adverse conditions – who may lose
a child about whom they do care.

This concern for parents links with two other elements in the underlying values supporting the third perspective – a focus on the family
unit rather than the child as a separate individual, and a particular view
of society and social problems. To take the first point, the focus on the
family unit, it is clear that in this perspective the interests of parents
and children are seen as (in the vast majority of cases) a relatively
undifferentiated area, so that help to the parents, broadly, equals help to
the family, equals help to the children. The family of parents and children is perceived as an interacting unit whose members' welfare is
closely linked and interdependent. Proponents of this perspective might
convincingly argue (along the lines of the Seebohm Committee Report
of 1968) that different family members' problems, symptoms or
stresses interact with each other in a complex and inseparable way. For
example, mental or physical illness in a parent may have severe implications for the standard of child care. Conversely, extra demands
generated by a child's illness or disability may create great stress for
the parent. Abuse or neglect may be seen as a problem of *family* circumstances or relationships rather than abusing/neglectful *individuals*.
Furthermore, problems such as inadequate income or poor or unhealthy
housing conditions affect the whole family. It is artificial to separate
out children's well-being from that of their parents. At the same time,
children positively need their own parents. While the emphasis is
mainly on the nuclear family, wider kinship links beyond the
parent–child unit may also be seen as valuable to the child.

The next point concerns the underlying view of society, social institutions, social problems and policies held by most proponents of this
perspective. As has already been shown, the social institutions which

respond to child care problems are seen as shaped by social class, in that they embody largely middle- (and upper-?) class decision-makers acting against the most deprived members of the working class. Within this framework, the law itself with its simplistic narrow focus may also be seen as a class-based institution unresponsive to wider social needs and factors. (For the law and children, see King and Piper 1990, King and Trowell 1992.) As King and Trowell (1992) indicate, transforming social problems into legal problems may mask the damage to children caused by policies in other areas.

The concept of society is characterised by social divisions and inequalities of resources and power. Part of the reason why the state is able to remove certain children from their parents, to override those parents' rights, and to keep the children away permanently, is to do with the powerlessness of poor people. Middle-class people, it may be argued, are less likely to come under the kinds of surveillance which lead to an identification of poor child care, neglect or abuse; less likely to have their child care actions labelled in these terms; and, should their children in fact be taken from them, are more capable of agitating effectively to get them back. When better off parents do encounter child care problems, they are less likely to involve social workers from public child care agencies, and more likely to use their resources to obtain private forms of help such as nannies, boarding schools, or therapy. An essentially class-bound society produces a particular pattern of child care policy which is strongly influenced by social class. Similarly, an essentially racist society produces racist child care policies independently, it seems, of the factor of social class.

Thus, social problems, including those of poor child care or troublesome child behaviour, are seen as derived from a divided society and its broader policies. There may in fact *be* problematic standards of child care to a greater extent among certain groups, but in so far as this occurs, and in so far as any definitive judgements can be made about standards, it is thought to be due to pressures of social deprivation. While socially deprived families may share generally held child care norms, they find it more difficult to attain them. Hence the child care actions of the state tend to remove their children to a slightly 'higher' class, to homes which do not experience deprivation to the same degree, rather than tackling deprivation as such.

The political assumptions of the third perspective, then, imply a society which is divided by class and power. Child care policies are seen as part of a structure of unequal political and economic relations in which dominant groups control subordinate and, in particular, deviant groups by a range of sanctions. The underlying view of the state in the third perspective is not entirely negative, however. While it might be thought from the preceding arguments that the state acts, and can act, only in a wholly oppressive way towards the most deprived groups, the supporters of the third child care perspective do not on the whole take a Marxist-type view of a capitalist state fundamentally

opposed to the welfare of the working class. They tend to take an optimistic – perhaps a naive? – approach to what can be achieved even by a
capitalist state, acting in a more enlightened way. The preferred
approach is basically more redistribution and an extension of the
'Welfare State'. Tackling social deprivation and doing effective preventive work *are* seen as possible within the framework of the
capitalist state.

So in this perspective an extended role for the state could achieve
much. State intervention, basically, should be supportive rather than
coercive, punitive or intrusive. Even temporary removal of a child
should (in the vast majority of cases) be undertaken with the objective
of return of the child when the family's problems have eased. So while
the state in its more controlling aspect is certainly seen as threatening
to the liberties of poorer families, the state is also seen as potentially
benign if prepared to commit more resources to a more appropriate
form of intervention. Thus the welfare role of the state is strongly supported – a very different position from *laissez-faire* and more
identifiable with a moderately left-wing perspective on the expansion
of state welfare and the reduction of social inequalities in general.

This faith in the potential ability of the state to extend effective help
to poorer parents and children is complemented in Holman's case
(1980) by a faith in voluntary action and in working-class self-help
and self-determination in finding solutions to family problems, for
example through community action by groups of parents.

Finally, it may be noted that in this perspective what is good for
children is again attributed to them by adults. In this respect the third
perspective falls into line with the first two. In the *laissez-faire*
approach, it will be remembered, the child's own viewpoint is not
strongly present. Childen's interests are largely imputed to them by
others. The paternalists of the second perspective see children as fundamentally different from adults, with different needs and rights; children
are unable to care for themselves and need adult protection and guidance. In the third perspective the relevant adults who make decisions
about children are (mostly) their parents. Parents, it may be safely
assumed in the vast majority of cases, care about their children's welfare and are aware of in what it consists. Again, children's autonomy
has a low profile; but the mantle of paternalism is assumed by parents
rather than the state.

Criticisms of the modern defence of the birth family and parents' rights

Empirical support

In general, this value perspective seems relatively well-supported by
empirical data. Holman (1980a, 1988), for example, cites a wealth of
studies on children in care to support his position. However, one major

aspect of the empirical backing for this perspective must be considered critically, and that is the claim that the causes of poor parenting lie largely in material rather than in individual psychological factors. Two subsidiary aspects which will be discussed are the overlooking of the evidence of the extent of child abuse, and the difficulty of comparing the adverse effects of being in care or accommodation with what *would* have happened to the children if not admitted. Lastly, the force of individual cases in supporting this value perspective will be considered briefly, as it was in examining the paternalist perspective.

An important claim of the proponents of the third perspective is that the roots of poor parenting and poor child care, and hence of the need for the state and other agencies to take full-time care of some children, lie largely in social deprivation and its ramifications rather than in the personal and psychological characteristics of parents. There is research work which does not altogether support this claim. For example, a study by Isaac, Minty and Morrison (1986) of families of children in care and parental mental health found a high rate of past and current psychiatric disorder in the sample of parents which appeared to be an important factor influencing children's admissions into, and discharge from, care, concluding that the study confirmed other recent work which had found 'that families of children who enter care are characterised not only by material and social deprivation but also by considerable personal problems in the parents' (p. 338). The other recent work quoted by Isaac is that by Quinton and Rutter (1984) which compared families with children multiply admitted to care with a comparison group from the same area. Nearly two-thirds of the in-care group's mothers had been under psychiatric treatment at some time; two fifths had been in-patients. These proportions were very much higher than for the comparison group. And the rate of current psychiatric disorder was four times that of the comparison group. Certainly the in-care group also had material problems, but Quinton and Rutter concluded that, while 'the parenting difficulties of the families might be interpreted as being either a direct reaction to social disadvantage or secondary to the resulting stress and psychiatric problems experienced by the parents' (p. 226), nevertheless 'it is not possible to conclude that current social disadvantages are a sufficient explanation for the differences between the groups with respect to either parenting problems or psychiatric disorder. Questions remain as to why some disadvantaged families have children taken into care whereas others do not, and on why families come to be in poor social circumstances' (p. 226).

Studies of children in care whose parents' rights have been assumed by resolution have also shown rather high rates of parental psychopathology. The present author (under the name of Fox 1986) found that just over 40 per cent of a small sample of children whose parents' rights had been assumed after three years in care, had at least one parent who had shown marked psychological problems at some stage (although material problems were also common). Lambert and Rowe (1974), studying parental rights assumptions on all grounds, also found a relatively high rate of parental mental illness; while a similar study in Strathclyde (Strathclyde Social Work Department 1980) found that mental ill-health affected the ability of a third of the mothers to care for their children. More strikingly, Adcock *et al.* (1983), also studying parental rights assumptions, found that social workers thought that only 16 per cent of mothers were severely limited in their parenting capacity by housing problems, and only 9 per cent by economic problems, while many of the parents 'were not thought by their social workers to be overwhelmed by material problems' (p. 25). The emphasis was on personal or behaviour problems or parental rejection of the children. In Packman *et al.*'s (1985) study of children seriously considered for care (some of whom were admitted and some not) 30 per cent of mothers were said by social workers to suffer from some form of mental disorder; there were also high levels of family disruption, although low social class, unemployment and low income were also distinguishing features of the families.

Two questions immediately arise, however, in response to findings that parents of children in care tend to have personal and psychological problems as well as material ones. The first concerns the way in which such personal and psychological problems are identified – to what extent, for example, the findings are reliant on the judgements of social workers; and the second, to what extent mental illness and psychopathology are themselves linked with poverty and deprivation.

Two subsidiary aspects of the question of empirical support for this perspective concern the evidence of the extent of child abuse, and the problem of making hypothetical comparisons. On child abuse, according to the first national Department of Health statistics published on this question (Department of Health 1988a), almost 40,000 children were on child protection registers in England, this being three per 1,000 of those under 18. In 1991 the number was up to 45,300 or over four per 1,000 (Department of Health 1991b), although by 1993 it was down to 32,500 or less than three per 1,000 (Department of Health 1993a). It should be remembered that doubts always arise about the meaning of figures for reported cases – the real figures are likely to be higher. While it may be argued that the figures only represent a small proportion of the child population (about 0.3 per cent), nevertheless levels in the tens of thousands suggest a serious problem of abuse and suspected abuse, and undermine idealised pictures of family life. It is suggested here that the pro-birth parent perspective has tended to de-emphasise the extent and seriousness of child abuse as an actual problem, as opposed to a problem of social response or 'moral panic'. For example, Parton (1979, 1981, 1985a), while acknowledging that official figures are under-estimates, concentrates on the process of discovery and definition of child abuse and the link between concern over child abuse and wider social anxiety. The actual abuse of children and its effects are somewhat marginalised. A more recent comment by A. Cooper (1995) is of interest. He notes that it *is* appropriate that child abuse: 'should cause anxiety. Moral panic may obscure the truth and insult the intelligence, but a complete absence of social reaction would be more worrying still' (p. viii). This orientation of the birth family writers is linked with the relative neglect of the need for the state to have some coercive powers, which is discussed below. It is of interest, however, that in a later publication (1990), Parton did acknowledge his previous understating of the actual problem of abuse.

On the question of hypothetical comparisons between entry to care or accommodation and remaining with the birth parent(s) (or, having entered care, remaining there versus return to the birth parent(s)), one argument is that, while being looked after by the local authority may well be an adverse experience for the child, the valid comparison to be made in these cases is *not* between experiences in care and children's experiences in 'normal', unstressed families where their welfare is well-catered for, but between care and the family situations the children *would* actually have been in, had they not entered care. Tizard (1977) makes this point in her work on adoption quoted when discussing the second, paternalist perspective. She asks:

With whom is one to compare the adopted children?
One obvious comparison group would be the natural children of parents of the same social class and general background as the adoptive parents. But, from the viewpoint of social policy, such a comparison would be both unrealistic and irrelevant.   (Tizzard 1977:16)

The alternatives actually available to the adopted children in Tizard's study were institutional care or a return home to birth mothers who were usually living in difficult circumstances. Similarly with children who come into care, or may come into care, the actual alternatives to care may be very unfavourable. It may be that the picture of the birth family life of these cases held by the proponents of the third perspective is idealised and inaccurate. The reality may be more disturbing. Millham *et al.* (1986), for example, have shown that the families of children in care tend to be subject to many changes, with partnerships and households fragmenting and re-forming. Packman *et al.*'s research (1985) found that 26 per cent of children seriously considered for care came from reconstituted families where one parent was 'step', and that the most striking feature of the families studied was the degree to which they were incomplete, disrupted or restructured. The 'family' life which is the alternative to being 'looked after' is, then, for many children, unstable and volatile. The problems of being in care need to be seen in this context.

In discussing the state paternalist perspective, individual cases of horrific child abuse were mentioned as constituting apparent empirical support for the position. Such cases tend to give rise to a feeling that any action must be contemplated, any policy disadvantage born, to prevent such cruelty occurring again. On the other side, the birth parent school of thought also have their catalogue of horror stories: cases of anguished parents who have been apparently maltreated by the authorities and deprived of their children unjustly and against their will, sometimes losing them altogether to adoption. Cases of parents who desperately want their children back but are forcibly deprived of them have been dealt with by pressure groups; some have been highlighted by the media, and a few have reached the European Court of Human Rights (see, for example, Eaton 1986, Fogarty 1986). But a reservation about the strength of this 'empirical support' arises over and above even the reservations held about individual cases of child abuse. There is a sense in which, say, *post-mortem* findings of child injuries and extreme malnutrition have a factual nature; by contrast, the wounds of parents are emotional rather than physical. Parents, when putting their case to an advocate, pressure group or the media, will inevitably give their view of events – or the view they wish to project. This sounds hard on parents, but it is suggested that individual cases cannot be used to provide evidence for this perspective in the way that child abuse cases can (within limits) be used to support the second perspective. An example of the sort of problem of distortion that can arise is the book by the MP Stuart Bell on the Cleveland child sex abuse scandal of 1987, *When Salem came to the Boro'* (Bell 1988). This book has been criticised by Campbell (1988) for only recounting one side of the case (the fathers') – for not mentioning, for example, when dealing sympathetically with the sufferings of the men accused of sexually abusing their children, that the children had indeed made allegations of abuse, or that the wife believed that abuse was in fact taking place.

Problems with the implications for policy

It is clear that the implications for policy of the pro-birth parent position are that the state should do more for parents and children in a supportive sense, but less in a coercive sense. For example, the state in this view should increase family benefits via the social security system, and extend payments to vulnerable families via local authorities to prevent children coming into care or accommodation; and should expand day care provision for children, and other services in kind for children and families, again through local authorities.

An obvious first objection is the cost of such programmes. Depending on how wide the net of supportive programmes is cast, and on the levels of provision, the cost could be moderately high to astronomical. A moderate increase in Child Benefit, for example, because of the large number of recipients of this universal benefit for children, entails a considerable increase of government expenditure of many millions or billions. Day nursery places are also expensive to provide (the Chartered Institute of Public Finance and Accountancy (CIPFA) 1995 gives a figure of gross cost per place of around £7,000 in 1993–94), so again, rather large amounts of public expenditure are involved in even modest increases in provision. The costs of social work and other forms of practical support to families are difficult to quantify and highly variable according to the level of intensity, but could, perhaps, be more expensive than an ordinary foster placement for a child. Intensive social work activity to help rehabilitate a child could also be relatively costly. Tackling all family problems of housing and homelessness, which can cause children to come into care/accommodation, would also be an expensive project to carry out effectively, although it may justly be pointed out that the cost of a local authority house or flat may well be less than maintaining a homeless family in a bed-and-breakfast hotel, as was done increasingly frequently in the 1970s and 1980s.

The detailed costs of such policy proposals are not characteristically worked through by the supporters of the pro-birth parent perspective (although Holman 1980 does give a figure of £11.8 million to provide 12,000 additional day care places at that time). It has to be remembered that state welfare expenditure in Britain, and local authority expenditure in particular, was held under severe restraint from the mid-1970s, initially under the Labour government, and later, with greater stringency, under the 1980s and 1990s Conservative governments in the interests of their wider economic policy of reducing inflation, taxation and public expenditure. Local authority expenditure was kept down by a series of devices, including expenditure limits, withdrawal of government grant, prohibition of supplementary rates, and statutory limits on the amounts that could be raised in rates ('rate capping'), and later the community charge and council tax. Local authorities therefore seemed to have little scope for extending their services to families without cutting back elsewhere, yet in the 1990s the newly established system for community care for dependent adults was making increased demands on their resources.

Notwithstanding apparently greater provision for prevention and family support under the Children Act 1989 (to be discussed further in Chapter 7), there was little support for the kinds of policies favoured by the pro-birth parent supporters at central government level in the 1980s and 1990s. It is true that child benefit did increase marginally under the Major government from 1991 and was then intended to keep pace with price inflation until the next general election after 1992 (see, for example, Lister 1996). Also there was some government support for nursery education, with a new scheme involving universal vouchers to purchase places for four-year-olds being introduced from 1997. But in general Conservative ideology favoured the reduction of state welfare expenditure and provision rather than its expansion; housing subsidies were progressively withdrawn; and in social security the government preferred means-testing or 'targeting' to universal benefits. Child benefit, for example, was significantly reduced in real terms under Thatcher, although as noted above it later revived a little under Major. Better means-tested benefits for families with children might have provided a way of channelling resources to those families most vulnerable to losing their children to substitute care; however, while the effects of British government social security changes in the 1980s were mixed – and often unclear – no significant improvement in the living standards of families on benefits seemed to have occurred by the late 1980s (for the effects of 1980s social security changes, see, for example, Social Security Consortium 1986, Roll 1986a, 1986b, National Association of Citizens Advice Bureaux 1989, and various publications by the Child Poverty Action Group). In the 1990s, due to a combination of factors including eroding wages and benefits for some groups, child poverty in general increased markedly. For example, more than four million children (a third) were in poverty defined as living on below half average national income in 1992–93 (Department of Social Security, 1995).

To be realistic, then, the policy implications of the third pro-family value perspective seemed unlikely to be followed through while local authority expenditure was curtailed, and while central government ideology militated strongly against welfare expenditure and perceived 'dependency' on the Welfare State, and firmly favoured privatised and individual solutions to need. Colton, Drury and Williams (1995), reporting research on the family support provisions of the Children Act, felt that such support could not develop properly in the current socio-economic context, for example. While government may indeed in its rhetoric have strongly supported 'the family', this was done mainly from a *laissez-faire* stance – it was the family's autonomy and internal responsibilities which were stressed, not its claim to state material support. 'Family responsibility' and 'parental responsibility' were strong themes; in particular 'parental responsibility' emerged as a theme of government policy towards children in the 1990s (see Fox Harding 1994). While this might be seen as supportive of family integrity, it is also reminiscent of the paternalist perspective's emphasis on the obligations of parenthood rather than its rights. Furthermore, the hidden agenda might well be that the responsibility of *the state* for families is reduced (see, for example, Edwards and Halpern 1992). The assumption is that families can and will do more.

However, it may be said that the arguments above are only a pragmatic objection to the policy implications of the third perspective, and that the proposals are still worthy of support as ideals (furthermore the political and economic climate is subject to change). Are there then any further objections that would still hold, even should the proposals be capable of early implementation from a government ideological and public expenditure point of view? Three aspects will be explored: the issue of whether the notion of 'prevention' is valid and can be relied upon to work; the neglect in this perspective of the need to use coercive powers when children are at risk; and a rather more specific point about the role of foster care and the difficulties of ensuring the type of foster placement that Holman (1975a), for one, would prefer.

A fundamental objection arises over whether 'prevention' works, about its effectiveness, and indeed its moral appropriateness. A philosophical objection to any kind of broad preventive policy can be derived from Popper. For example, Magee (1973) states that in Popper's work *The Open Society* (Popper 1966) the general guiding principle for public policy is: '"Minimise avoidable suffering".

Characteristically, this has the immediate effect of drawing attention to *problems'* (p. 84). The Popperian approach, Magee argues, instead of encouraging one to think about Utopia: 'makes one seek out, and try to remove, the specific social evils under which human beings are suffering' (p.85). Lait (1979) (see also Brewer and Lait 1980) has applied Popper's views to the personal social services field, arguing that preventative work is based on the dubious proposition that social workers should be involved in making life 'better' rather than making it 'less bad'. Speaking of 'a transformation in my thinking achieved by studying the works of Sir Karl Popper' (p. 24), Lait argues that: 'those who seek to do preventive work have not merely a sense of what constitutes a family so bad that it cannot care for its children, but that they also have a version of a "good" family and their work is focused on helping the family to attain a state of goodness' (p. 25). Preventive work tends to lack clearly defined objectives, and intervention by 'officials' to enhance well-being risks interfering with liberty. 'Since well-being is a quality difficult to define, and highly idiosyncratic in its manifestations, such intervention is in any case unlikely to attain its objectives' (p. 25). The main points of a Popperian objection to a preventive approach in child care would appear to be: that the notion of enhancing well-being and making life in families 'better' for children (as opposed to acting on specific problems) is dubious and based on imprecise objectives; that preventive action does not necessarily have the intended effect; and that it is potentially authoritarian. It is not possible in a short space to do justice to the complexity of Popperian analysis of public policy, or indeed even to the ideas in Lait's brief article; but it seems worth making the point that there are some fundamental reservations about the very concept of policies designed to make life 'better' for children and families with the aim of averting the need for substitute care.

The second aspect of the policy implications where serious doubts arise is the relative neglect of the need for coercive action, that is the use of power backed up by the law, in some cases where children are at risk. It is not being claimed that the supporters of the birth parent position entirely deny the need for local authorities and courts to have some powers to be exercised in some cases. However, where attention is given to the question of legal powers in child care policy, it usually takes the form of criticism of the extent of these powers and the extent of their use. Holman (1980) criticised the 1975 Act from this sort of viewpoint, and Parton (1981) the increasing use of, for example, the then place of safety orders. Parton continued to be critical of legalism in his later work (Parton 1991). Criticisms of the law by King and Piper (1990), and King and Trowell (1992), have already been referred to earlier in this chapter.

Clearly, the supporters of the birth family perspective feel that the implementation of the other measures they favour would reduce the need for the use of statutory powers. Yet there must be some unease about their attack on this important aspect of the state's child care role, and about a possible over-confidence that such compulsory cases could only constitute a small residual minority. This is linked with their relative neglect of the extent of child abuse, referred to earlier. The problem is one of emphasis; it is not that the supporters of the third perspective over-look abuse and the need for legal powers of compulsion altogether. As Holman (1980) says of the 1975 Act: 'It is not disputed that legislation was required to raise the standard of adoption services and to clarify the relationship between substitute parents and the children in their care' (p. 29). Nevertheless, the emphasis on help to families leads the pro-birth parent school to direct their attention away from abuse and the need for legal powers to be held by courts and local authorities.

The final point concerns the feasibility of ensuring the 'inclusive' type of foster placement which the supporters of this perspective would favour as being most conducive to the maintenance of the parent–child link and the eventual return home of the child. In this type of placement the foster parents do not wholly assume the parental role, and the birth parents (and the social worker) remain actively involved in the child's life. It is of interest that one of the supporters of this perspective, Tunstill, herself concluded from a small study of foster parents that:

they appear to be firmly in favour of the 'exclusive' model: ... As a group the foster parents overwhelmingly agreed with the intentions and provisions of the [1975] Act ... they defined that well-being [of the child] in terms of the present security of the child, taking no account of security which might depend on knowledge of, and identification with, natural parents.   (Tunstill 1980:39)

They saw their main task as being to incorporate children in caring families which they could regard as their own. Tunstill also quotes earlier research by, for example, George (1970) and Adamson (1973) which showed that over half of foster parents saw themselves as a natu-ral rather than a foster parent. Rowe (1977), quoted by Tunstill, talks of the gap 'between social work emphasis on the need for foster parents to avoid possessiveness and not become too emotionally involved with the child, and foster parents' persistence in considering themselves as substitute parents' (Tunstill 1980:22). And Kelly (1981), in an article on foster child contact with birth parents, says: 'All the major studies in the UK report that a majority of foster parents prefer to regard the chil-dren as their own and do not see themselves in the role of foster parent but would rather be seen as the child's own or adoptive parent' (p. 8). A decade or more later, however, under the Children Act 1989, it was expected that foster parents work in partnership with birth parents more and encourage their contact with the child, and social work practice was expected to support this.

The problem, then, is that the kind of substitute care seen as prefer-able in this third perspective may not be easily attainable while children are placed in foster homes. In so far as foster parents' motiva-tion is bound up with a desire to 'parent' the child in a full sense, attempts to impose an 'inclusive' model may cause a reduction in the supply of foster homes. Alternatively, foster parents may be explicitly regarded more as 'professionals' than as parents, and paid accordingly, but this is an expensive option. Another alternative is greater use of residential homes, but these are also found undesirable on a number of counts, and have not been in favour in the 1980s and 1990s.

In general, despite the difficulties, greater contact with the original family is supported by the 1989 Children Act's emphasis on parental contact and working in partnership with parents. Worthy of mention here also is the trend towards favouring more openness to original birth family links not just in fostering, but also in adoption, this being expressed in the government's review of adoption law in the 1990s (Department of Health 1992, Department of Health/Welsh Office etc. 1993, see also Ryburn 1994a). If foster parents have been found in the past to be reluctant to include birth parents, are adoptive parents likely to be any more welcoming of the idea? On the face of it, they might be expected to be less so, as adoption involves notions of permanence and legal possession. However, the greater likelihood of adoption of older children since the 1970s has to be remembered; also adoptive parents do not necessarily reject birth family contact and the experience can be positive (see, for example, Ryburn 1994b, Lesley 1996).

Problems of rationale and underlying values

The ambiguity of the rationale given by the proponents of this perspective for supporting birth parent–child links has already been commented on under 'Rationale and underlying values'. It is not clear to what extent these bonds are defended solely because they constitute early psychological links, or to what extent, and why, the blood tie itself is being valued and protected. It is suggested that the way in which this rationale is not fully worked through is a rather serious deficiency in this perspective, and contrasts with Goldstein *et al.*'s (1979, 1980) fuller exposition of why it is that psychological bonds should be respected. A clearer understanding of why the birth family should be important to the child's welfare would at least perhaps enable distinctions to be made between, say, situations where the birth parents have never been known to the child, where there was interaction but there are now no conscious memories, and where the child has conscious memories of the parents. A further distinction which needs to be taken on board, and which is perhaps not entirely faced by the supporters of this position, is between different types of relationship between parents and children, positive and negative experiences, happy and unhappy memories. Not all parent–child relationships are good, and children may reject their parents as well as vice versa. Would it, for example, still be held that the blood tie is good for the child if the child in question denies it? Is it desirable to preserve or revive biological links that are distressing? It may be noted here that adult searches for unknown biological relatives do not always end happily (see, for example, Howe *et al.* 1992).

This leads on to the second point which may be criticised, one which the third perspective shares with the first two, and that is the implicit devaluation, in much of the writing, of the child's right to self-determination. Again, it seems, decisions and judgements are made *for* the child. As was noted in discussing the first and second perspectives, the child's own wishes and viewpoint are overlooked. In the first perspective, children's interests are generally imputed to them by others, and conflict is seen as lying between *parents* and the state. In the second, the psychological differentiation of children led to the conclusion that their rights are different from those of adults: children have rights to proper care, not to freedom to choose. Neither perspective is uniformly supportive of the idea of separate representation for the child in court. With the third perspective, the neglect of children's independent rights arises basically from a high degree of trust in parents' ability to act in their children's interests. The child's voice is therefore effectively unheard. Most proponents of the third perspective tend to be non-committal about the idea of separate representation for the child; they would not throw it out but do not positively support it either. Supporters of the fourth perspective to be discussed, the children's rights school, would be particularly critical of this overlooking of the child's independent view.

A further and related problem with the underlying rationale is a relative lack of differentiation of the interests, feelings and welfare of different family members. For the purposes of this discussion, it is the lack of differentiation of children as separate individuals which is important. Whether or not children's rights to self-determination and autonomy are supported, it is still possible to differentiate children's needs and interests from those of other members of their families. Many proponents of the pro-birth parent perspective tend not to do this. There is a recognition of the family as an interacting system, but less recognition that each individual's life may also be seen as a system in its own right, although linked to other systems (see Zimmerman 1988 for families as social systems). Reference is made to the family as the target of child care (and broader social) policy. Yet the family is a group in which power and resources tend to be distributed unequally. There is simply no guarantee, for example, that an increased child allowance or other income paid to a parent will indeed find its way to benefiting the children. Even in affluent family households, women and/or children may, in fact, be poor (see, for example, Land 1983, Brannen and Wilson 1987, Glendinning and Millar 1987, Pahl 1989). Social work help may come to focus on the parents' needs and problems, and overlook the children's (see London Borough of Brent 1985). To take another example, there is a certain ambiguity in recommending child day care to free a stressed and poverty-stricken single parent to go out to work. It may be reasonable to conflate the parent's and the child's well-being in this situation, but it needs to be made clear that this is what is being done. Some insight into this problem may be gained by translating the parent–child issue into male–female terms. The unacceptability, for many, of such an approach to women would be apparent in a view which neglected to differentiate the two partners to a marriage in terms of needs, interests, feelings and welfare, so that husband and wife were not considered as individuals but conflated, with references persistently made to the need to uphold and support 'the marriage'.

Lastly, a major underpinning value characteristic of the third perspective which must be looked at critically is its broader political viewpoint. It will be remembered that poor child care and the state bodies which respond to it are seen as shaped by social divisions, primarily class; that social inequality is a crucial issue in the approach; and that social problems are accounted for in these terms. Three critical points will be made here. First, the view of the state is inconsistent. Secondly, a related point, if the analysis of a class-divided society is correct, it seems little can be achieved in the child care field without major political structural change. Thirdly, and again a connected point, the Welfare State (whose extension advocates of this perspective broadly support), itself ran into major problems from the late 1970s.

First, the view of the state held in this perspective seems inconsistent. On the one hand its actual interventions in the child care field are seen as excessively authoritarian and intrusive while its public expenditure policies limit the development of a truly preventive strategy; on the other hand the emergence of an effective preventive policy is seen as capable of creation by the same state. Parton (1985a), perhaps, goes some way to recognising that we may be talking about a different kind of state, but in Holman's work the disjuncture is more apparent. However, Holman (1988) does acknowledge that he is envisaging a different kind of *society*, a more equal one, where 'as the cost of public services are [sic] largely raised through central and local government taxation, it is likely that the more affluent sections of society would find their own disposable income somewhat reduced' (p. 209). The power of the more affluent sections to resist, through the state as well as through other institutions, is perhaps overlooked here.

The second objection is that if the class analysis of child care policy is substantially accurate, then child care policy is unlikely to change its fundamental (class-biased) nature unless and until the class nature of society is itself changed. That is, the ending of social deprivation, of a system where middle class decision-makers pass judgement on and punish the poor, and of processes which separate parents and children instead of helping them to remain together, is unlikely – perhaps impossible – while capitalism perpetuates social inequalities and creates victims. The root causes of poor child care – and inappropriately coercive state responses – seem to lie embedded within capitalism, in this perspective. Holman (1988) in fact attempts to side-step the logic of this by saying that the argument is not that no progress can be made without fundamental changes, and that piecemeal gains *can* be achieved; and Parton (1985a) takes a similar position. Holman notes: 'During this present century the state has gradually extended its commitment towards the well-being of socially deprived families and, indeed, the welfare state was brought into existence' (1988:210). Holman here appears to overlook the fact that in the 1980s in Britain there was a serious attempt to reverse such policies and the welfare aspect of welfare capitalism was eroded, albeit not destroyed (for the fate of the Welfare State during this time see, for example, Hills 1991; Holman's later work, 1993, does discuss these developments).

The third critical point, then, is the pragmatic one that, whether or not the expectations held of the state in this perspective are contradictory, whether or not the class nature of society means that a satisfactory (from this perspective) child care policy cannot actually be achieved, the Welfare State which the proponents of this perspective support and require, in fact ran into a serious ideological and fiscal crisis in the late 1970s and 1980s, not only in Britain but in other Western countries. Reference may be made to the extensive literature on this topic (for example Mishra 1984, 1990, Wicks 1987, Johnson 1990, Hill 1993). The point to note here is that a key assumption in the underlying values and rationale of the third perspective is that the Welfare State as it has been known will continue and can expand. This assumption is questionable.

The perspective in practice

Following the model of the previous chapters, the discussion has covered the main elements of the value perspective, some authors associated with it, the rationale and underlying values, and criticisms relating to empirical support, implications for policy, and underlying values. The perspective will now be illustrated by reference to English child care policy in the 1950s and 1960s. This was a period when 'preventive' policies were increasingly favoured.

The atmosphere in child care policy in the early post-Second World War period was one in which there were higher standards for the welfare and care of the child and a greater awareness of the importance of families than in the immediate past (the early twentieth century). Hendrick (1994) sees a shift in perception of children's welfare as compared with what went before: 'In effect it was being officially realised that children required sensitive and sympathetic treatment and understanding' (p. 211). Generally there was a greater interest in the psychological condition of childhood.

Although some general child welfare provisions had appeared in the early years of the century, provisions which might be seen as helping parents to care for their own children appropriately, it was not really until this post-war period that the modern defence of the birth parent perspective became clearly influential, at least in the statutory sector. (It was present earlier in parts of the voluntary sector: for example, the

National Council for the Unmarried Mother and her Child, which in 1973 became the National Council for One Parent Families, from its early days after the First World War worked to enable mother and child to stay together.)

The 1950s and 1960s cannot be fully understood without reference to the late 1940s. The Second World War had engendered much greater awareness of the strength of the bonds between children and their original parents, and sympathy for the family. This was mainly due to two factors. First, the wartime evacuation of children from urban areas served to reveal to many of the middle class just how severe were the conditions experienced by some children (see Titmuss 1950, Heywood 1978). The fact that it was the poorest and most congested areas that had to be evacuated exacerbated the impact. The revelations produced greater support for the family as an institution: while some blamed parents for their children's deprivation, others saw it as aggravated by lack of support for families and particularly mothers, and by policies which had failed to look at underlying problems. Social legislation had mostly focused on the treatment of problems outside the family – individuals tended to be removed from their family background and treated in institutions or substitute homes; and the strength of the family as a social and psychological unit was seemingly not fully appreciated until the wartime disruptions highlighted it. Many families in fact resisted the separation brought about by the evacuation and reunited.

Another factor helping to underline the importance of family ties was the widespread provision of day and residential nurseries, set up mainly to release women into the wartime labour force. Studies of children separated from their families in the nurseries showed the psychological dangers of sudden separation from parent figures, and led to a greater understanding of the need for emotional attachment, security and continuity, and therefore an emphasis on the original parents. It was at this time that Bowlby's work first became influential.

The first major piece of post-war legislation in the child care field, the Children Act 1948, therefore needs to be seen against this background. The specific child care issues which were of concern in the 1950s were mostly linked with the sweeping changes in the organisation of state child care which came about with this Act. The changes included the setting up of local authority children's departments; an emphasis on boarding out or fostering as a method of child care; restoration of children in care to their original family, but also more emphasis on adoption, including the adoption of children in care who could not be so restored; and the involvement of children's departments with young offenders.

The Children Act reflected an entirely new ethos. With the Poor Law, including its child care role, now finally abolished (by the National Assistance Act 1948), the Act set new and higher standards of welfare for children in care. Instead of 'less eligibility' – the Poor Law principle that those cared for and maintained by the state should always be worse off than others – there was a notion of positive discrimination to compensate deprived children for their deprivation. Partly in response to the findings of the Curtis Committee on the care of children (Secretary of State for the Home Department/Minister of Health/ Minister of Education 1946), and partly reflecting the general emphasis on welfare and collectivism of the times, the 1948 Act emphasised the better treatment of children deprived of their home life, stating in Section 12 the local authority's duty to exercise its powers towards the child: 'so as to further his best interests, and to afford him opportunity for the proper development of his character and abilities'.

Most significant organisationally was the setting up, under the Children Act, of separate local authority children's departments to specialise in child care work. These departments were the responsibility of a single local authority committee and a single chief officer, the children's officer. Specialisation was intended to raise standards of care, as was the training and professionalisation of the new occupation of child care officer. The system of public child care now became more sophisticated and demanded greater resources. An important element in this new system was the emphasis on fostering or 'boarding out'. The Curtis Committee had made some disturbing discoveries about institutional care, but had been generally impressed by the system of boarding out. In the years following the 1948 Act boarding out was strongly preferred to the use of residential homes, and the Home Office issued an annual 'league table' showing the percentages of children in care in different local authorities who were in foster homes. Foster care was seen as more in tune with the new individualised and child-centred approach, although the boarding out system itself had a long history. The average boarding out rate rose from, for example, 35 per cent in 1949, to 44 per cent in 1954, to 48 per cent in 1960, with a peak of 52 per cent being reached in 1963, after which there was a decline (Packman 1981).

Perhaps not entirely consonant with the trend to put children in care into foster homes whenever possible was the emphasis, again stemming from the 1948 Act, on restoration of children to their original birth families. Restoration and foster placement might conflict if the foster parents regarded themselves as effectively the child's parents. (Interestingly, the Curtis Committee of 1946, had noted that some foster mothers seemed too possessive.) While the emphasis in the post-1948 child care world was on good quality substitute care, children were to be in care only as long as their welfare required it. The children's department had to strive to discharge children from care to a parent, friend or relative wherever this was consistent with their welfare (Section 1 (3)). This constituted a break with pre-war practice. The official policy was thus now for most children in care to return to their original family, and the children's departments had a duty to help families to resume care. Certainly the ideology of the time emphasised that being in care should not be construed as permanent (even if, in practice, it was).

What was not present in the 1948 Act was a remit to work with children and families to prevent the need for substitute care arising. There *was* some awareness of the problems of children still in their own homes, however. A Women's Group on Public Welfare produced a report on neglected children and the family in 1948 (Women's Group on Public Welfare 1948), and a Home Office circular also in 1948 stressed the importance of prevention, while another in 1950 proposed co-ordinating machinery to prevent entry into care (Home Office 1948, 1950). The 1948 circular stated: 'To keep the family together must be the first aim' (cited in Hendrick 1994:220). However, local authorities' responses to the call for co-ordination were not uniform and there was some difficulty in getting the machinery to work successfully. Feeling also developed in the child care service in the 1950s that its remit was too narrow and its activities were unduly restricted by being confined to children deprived of a normal home life, and thus excluding work with cases where the need for substitute care might have been avoided. While a few local authorities may have informally undertaken 'preventive work' – for example, Oxfordshire appointed a preventive case-worker in the early 1950s (Heywood 1978) – there was no statutory base for spending money in this way, and the authorities were perhaps acting *ultra vires* in doing so. At the same time, emphasis in child care work moved more towards the family and its problems rather than the child taken in isolation. A further factor providing impetus for change at the time was the question of cost: there was concern at the rising expenditure on the child care service, and a belief that extra work undertaken to keep children in their own homes would – in the long term – prove cheaper. Both child neglect and juvenile delinquency were seen as originating in the same type of family, and from a malfunctioning of the family as a socialising agent. The prevention of both problems was seen as involving a focusing on the family rather than the individual child as the target for intervention.

Another element of child care policy in the 1950s, which may, like the emphasis on foster care, be seen as somewhat dissonant with the objective of care by the birth family, was the increased attention given to adoption. This was seen as the best form of care for children who could not be cared for by their own families, and children's departments were given powers to place children in care with prospective adopters and to act as adoption agencies (Adoption Act 1949), while adoption was further regulated and controlled (Children Act 1958). The permanence of adoption, its closeness to the norm of the birth family, constituted an attraction when children faced substitute care for many years. It was also seen as a solution to the problem of illegitimate births. And adoption usually signified the end of the local authority's involvement and thus averted the need for further expenditure. However, the focus on the adoption of children already in care should be seen in relation to the emphasis on rehabilitation of such children with their own families. Adoption was in fact still primarily concerned with placing young babies, rather than older children with a history in care.

A further element in 1950s child care was the involvement of children's departments with young offenders. When the specialist child care service was set up, the groups of children in state care included some young offenders, as well as non-offending children who had been before the courts (under the Children and Young Persons Act 1933). Under the 1948 Act local authorities had a duty to act as fit persons where fit person orders (the predecessors of care orders) were made; they were also empowered to admit to care children released from approved schools; and from 1952 (Children and Young Persons Act 1952) they were empowered to do approved school after-care in the community. Juvenile offending was a field where there had long been work on rehabilitating children with their original family. As indicated, a belief now grew that neglect and juvenile delinquency were rooted in similar causes, factors to do with a malfunctioning of the family. Delinquency was also thought to be due to the 'maternal deprivation' outlined by Bowlby.

Developments in the 1950s also need to be set in their general welfare context. There were enormous legislative changes in the field of welfare in the mid to late 1940s – the Education Act 1944, the Family Allowances Act 1945, the National Health Service Act 1946, the National Assistance Act 1948 – legislation which is generally construed as the foundation stone of the modern Welfare State in Britain. The child care changes thus occurred in a context where there were more generous state provisions for the general health and welfare of the population, including children – universal health care, better social security benefits, an improved education system, and so on. These changes continued to form the background to child care policy in the 1950s. The improved general provisions may be seen as having a broadly preventive role, supporting the family in its care and socialisation functions.

In the 1960s the swing towards favouring 'preventive work' intensified. Indeed, the 1960s may be seen as the high point of the emphasis on prevention and the family, and it is the 1960s rather than the 1950s which best illustrate the birth family perspective. There was greater state activity and involvement with families and children generally. It has been mentioned that in the 1950s the coordinating machinery concerned with child welfare was found wanting; the child care service itself experienced its remit as too narrow; and there was concern about the cost of substitute care. Most importantly, the Ingleby Committee on children and young persons, set up in 1956, reported in 1960 (Secretary of State for the Home Department 1960). It had been felt that there was a need for an inquiry into social services concerned with the family, to look at the issue of child neglect at home and its prevention, and at juvenile delinquency, which was an increasing problem. The Committee's main concerns were the prevention of delinquency, neglect and children entering care; children at risk of these fates and how to provide support for their families; treatment facilities for those who came before the juvenile courts; and the courts themselves. While stressing that parents still had the prime responsibility for their children, which was not to be taken over by the state, the Report emphasised better coordination between agencies, skilled intensive casework with families, and the power to give material aid; and it recommended that local authorities should therefore have a duty to prevent child neglect at home, and powers to give material help to achieve this.

The 1963 Children and Young Persons Act embodied these proposals: the local authorities – in effect their children's departments – were given preventive functions in the duty laid on them by Section 1 to give advice, guidance and assistance in order to diminish the need for reception into care or for bringing a child before a court. Assistance in cash or kind was possible, but cash was only to be given in exceptional circumstances. As a result of this change children's departments now began officially to use resources on preventive work with families, with the child care officer's role becoming more that of a family caseworker; yet the Act had not mentioned extra resources, indeed it was hoped that successful preventive work would save money. Various types of preventive work were undertaken: family casework and family advice work, children's holidays, group and community work, for example, with material assistance being used sparingly at first but growing in scale over the 1960s (see Jackson and Valencia 1979, Packman 1981). Social workers began to have more contact with other agencies, to specialise in 'welfare rights' work more, and to act as advocates on their clients' behalf; they had more dealings with families whose chief or only problems were material rather than psychological. Packman (1993) comments that the Act:

had a profound effect upon the scale and direction of local authority child care services, which became involved in an enormous range of preventive activity, tilting the balance of their work in new directions. By 1967, for example, more than three times as many children were being assisted directly or indirectly through section 1 of the Children and Young Persons Act, as were admitted to local authority care.   (Packman 1993:222–3)

The 1960s, like the 1950s, were marked by a concern for problems at the family level – the 'problem family', or even the 'multi-problem family' was widely discussed. A concern with the less immediate social environment, with the wider social structure and its implications for child deprivation, developed more strongly from the later 1960s and early 1970s, with the appearance of 'radical social work'. This approach stressed the structural origins of many client problems, the inadequacy of other systems within the Welfare State, and a social activist and advocate role for the social worker. More doubt about the effectiveness of preventive programmes also came later; but the early and mid-1960s were a time of relative confidence about what such programmes could achieve (although the proportion of children in care in fact remained stable after the 1963 Act – at approximately 0.5 per cent of the population under 18 – and then began to rise; Home Office, various years). Parton (1985a) speaks of the optimism in child care in the 1950s and 1960s, and the confidence in child care officers, who, it was believed, could bring about change in families through casework and counselling.

Other issues of importance in the 1960s which can be mentioned more briefly include fostering and adoption, and young offenders. Fostering and adoption of deprived children became increasingly linked in child care thinking. Initially, fostering was much favoured, as it had been in the 1950s, and, as mentioned, the highest boarding out rate was achieved in 1963, when it was 52 per cent; by 1970, however, the rate was down to 42 per cent (reaching its lowest point in 1975 – Packman 1981, Department of Health and Social Security, various years). Fostering was becoming less popular as its problems were increasingly appreciated; thinking swung more to seeing an equal balance between the merits of care with foster parents and care in a residential home, and to determining the best solution for each child rather than assuming that foster care was an *a priori* good for all. This might have rendered contact with the birth parent, and eventual return to the parent, easier to achieve. But by the late 1960s, another kind of concern was developing: for the security of foster placements where birth parents retained their rights. This was influential in the deliberations of the Houghton Committee set up in 1969, whose report of 1972 (Home Office/Scottish Education Department, 1972) ultimately led to the Children Act of 1975. These developments reversed the 1950s and 1960s practice of holding open the door to eventual return to the birth family for most children in foster care.

In the field of adoption, the early 1960s saw an increasing number of local authorities making use of their powers to act as adoption agencies, and an increase in adoptions generally. One trend that appeared at the end of the 1960s, however – which intensified later and was influential in developments in the 1970s – was the drop in the number of babies available for adoption. This was due to a number of factors such as more widely available contraception and abortion and a changed social climate with regard to 'illegitimacy' and unmarried motherhood. At the same time there was an increased number of children with particular difficulties and needs, including a long history in care, who were now seen as suitable for adoption. Again, a shift was beginning away from keeping open the option of rehabilitation indefinitely, and this also intensified in the 1970s.

On the question of juvenile offending, the Ingleby Committee's role has already been referred to. The rise in juvenile crime was causing concern, and the Committee addressed itself to the roots of delinquent behaviour and the treatment of delinquency. As with neglect, prevention was seen as involving a focusing on the family, although not to the point of taking over its functions entirely. The Ingleby Report (Secretary of State for the Home Department 1960) commented: 'It is the parents' duty to help their children become effective and law-abiding citizens by example and training and by providing a stable and secure family background in which they can develop satisfactorily' (pp. 5–6, para. 8).

The 1963 Act which followed Ingleby gave the children's departments duties and powers to avert children appearing before the juvenile court, whether as offenders or as in need of protection. The later 1969 Children and Young Persons Act owed much to a family oriented approach and perhaps marked the high point of the 'treatment' model in responding to juvenile crime. Preceded by two White Papers in 1965 and 1968 (Home Office 1965, 1968) (the first of which was more radical than the second), it embodied a further movement away from the concept of punishment of an offence and a conventional criminal justice approach in dealing with young offenders. Children in trouble with the law were to be treated in almost the same way as non-offending children in trouble. Wherever possible offending children were to be kept in their own home, and to be spared the stigma of prosecution and/or punitive sentences. The approved schools were incorporated into the child care system. It should be noted, however, that the Act was never fully implemented, and in the 1970s, this decriminalising trend went into reverse.

1960s child care policy should also be viewed in the general welfare context of the decade. The 1960s were a time when the apparent general consensus on welfare policies continued to hold, and the later 1960s may even be seen as a high point for the Welfare State. Mishra (1984) describes the 'high tide of legitimacy' (p. 1) of the Welfare State, when there was a widespread consensus about social programmes and services. It was a general climate, then, which was favourable to the policy preferences of the pro-birth family perspective for widespread welfare services to support and help families with children generally.

In summarising these two very important decades, certain themes in keeping with the pro-birth parent perspective should first be referred to. Two characteristics of the 1950s were an enhanced emphasis on child welfare and a recognition of the importance of the birth family. The specialisation of the children's service, and the incorporation of knowledge of child psychology, raised standards of substitute care; but the importance of the original family, and of restoration to it, was also a prominent feature of policy and practice. Improved general provisions for child health, welfare and education may be seen as having a broadly preventive function at this time. And the early post-war period was in general a relatively child-centred time, with notions of a more 'permissive' and indulgent style of child upbringing becoming apparent. In the 1960s the concern with birth families and the prevention of children entering substitute care found legislative expression, while towards the end of this decade, a greater awareness developed in social work of the relevance of structural factors and social deprivation to the situations to which social workers had to respond. A generally permissive and child-centred approach to children continued to flourish, although with some signs of retraction towards the end of the period (see Hardyment 1983);

the family was in favour; and the legitimacy of state welfare expenditure remained well-supported.

Other themes of the 1950s and 1960s are not entirely in harmony with the preventive school of thought: the stress on foster care, and later on secure foster care; and the high valuation of adoption and its extension to somewhat older children who had been in care. Nevertheless, in general these two decades, especially the 1960s, provide a good illustration of a broadly preventive, pro-birth family approach at work – more so than any other period in recent British history, notwithstanding the stress on family support in the Children Act 1989.

CHAPTER 5

Children's rights and child liberation

Introduction

The terms 'children's rights' and 'child liberation' are used here for a perspective which emphasises the importance of the child's own viewpoint and wishes, seeing the child as a separate entity with rights to autonomy and freedom, rather like adults. The idea of control of children through the state or by adults individually is called into question, as therefore are notions of custody and parental rights. The strength of children, and their similarity to adults, is emphasised, rather than their vulnerability; but it is not clear how far children would be expected to carry the burdens and duties of adult status as well. A less extreme position would emphasise that children should at least have more say in what happens to them.

The main elements of the perspective

This value perspective may be regarded as having been somewhat more marginal to actual child care law and policy, certainly in its more extreme manifestations. Nevertheless it is of interest for its very different approach from the others; is of relevance to an increasing number of actual developments; and may be more strongly adhered to and expressed in law, policy and practice in the future. The distinguishing characteristic of this perspective, which marks it out from all of the other three, is that the emphasis is on the child's own viewpoint, feelings, wishes, definitions, freedoms and choices; rather than on the attribution by adults of what is best for the child – and therefore, it might be inferred, the very existence of a child care 'system', with the function of making decisions about children, is called into question. Children are seen very much as separate entities in their own right – in this the fourth perspective resembles the second; but the emphasis is on the child's right to autonomy, self-determination, and to do the things that adults do, rather than – as in the second perspective – on the right to proper nurturance and care as this is interpreted by others, be they birth parents, substitute parents, courts or social workers. In the fourth perspective children are seen as *subject* rather than object of others' actions and choices, as actors with the ability to define their situation and arrive at independent decisions. The difference from the *laissez-faire*, paternalist and pro-parent viewpoints is fundamental. *Laissez-faire* basically sees children as appropriately under the control of their parents unless things go badly wrong, when they are put under the control of substitutes; for the paternalists, the state should have more control; while for the birth parent school, parents again should control their children, but with extensive support from the state. The fourth perspective questions the very idea of control itself – or certainly of control that is specifically directed towards the young just because they are young. Such an approach carried to its logical conclusion goes well beyond merely supporting, say, separate representation for the child in court, an issue about which the three other perspectives tend to be unenthusiastic or divided. It embraces a whole field of issues in which, if the implications of this perspective are followed through, children should have a status more like that of adults. The need for any kind of tutelage of children – whether it emanates from state agencies, parents, or adults in general – is fundamentally challenged, even denied. The effects of such an approach are potentially far-reaching.

Underlying this fourth value perspective is a concept of childhood which is radically different from the concepts underlying the other three. The first and third perspectives see children as in great emotional need of their parents, and the second stresses the general vulnerability and dependence of children. But writers who support the children's rights perspective tend to emphasise the competence and strength of children, who are often seen as unfairly treated as inferiors by the adult world. Holt (1975), for example, describes older people's perception of children as 'a mixture of expensive nuisance, slave and super-pet' (p. 15). Holt, as will be shown later, is critical of this, emphasising both the degree of adults' misperception and what children can in fact achieve independently. Indeed, it seems that in diminishing or even denying the idea of the weakness of childhood, the proponents of this perspective are, at least implicitly, denying that childhood is a special developmental state with needs and rights which are important but different from the needs and rights of adulthood. In so far as it is being argued that children should have rights and freedoms similar to those of adults, it seems that there is an underlying assumption that children are not so very different from adults – in terms of behaviour, feelings, ideas, attitudes, competence, knowledge and skills.

But in so far as children should have similar rights to adults, should they also carry similar responsibilities? If their freedom should not be limited specifically because they are children, then it might be thought they should not be granted any special privileges on these grounds either. Such implications are not always fully worked through by the supporters of this perspective, however; similarly, the concept of childhood on which their position rests may be implied rather than explicit. The underlying notion of childhood is crucial, however, for where it is being argued that discrimination on the basis of age constitutes a kind of injustice, what is being implied is that, in certain important respects, age should make no difference.

The basic approach of the children's rights school has considerable implications for the role of the state. The guardian role of the state, even in the residual form which is allowed under *laissez-faire*, is called into question by the insistence on children's liberties. In an extreme version of the perspective, what the state should do is to enable children to gain their freedom from their parents and other adults, by bestowing on them all the normal rights of citizenship, to vote, to work, to live where and with whom they wish, and so on. It thus seems that the protective role of the state to children as individuals in need of special safeguarding and care, would be drastically diminished or even abolished. The state would not distinguish between its citizens on grounds of age, and children would thus be allowed to do whatever adults could legally do. Presumably, neither the state nor individual adults, parents or not, would have significant special rights and powers over children, and there would therefore be no question of formal custody or care, or the legal rights of parents, substitute parents, courts or social work agencies, over children, although there might still be parental *responsibilities*. Such a situation would require certain legal changes by the state, but once these were made, the state's role could be characterised as *laissez-faire* to a far greater extent than in the first perspective. The state – if this perspective is carried to its logical conclusion – would take *no* action to provide for the special needs of children, as this would be to curtail their liberties in a way not done for adults; however, children would have the normal protection of the criminal and civil law like anyone else. Parenthood appears to be reduced to a very subordinate role here, that of enabling children to achieve their goals; parents would have to accept that their children might decide to leave them and live elsewhere.

It is only fair, however, to distinguish between what the proponents of the fourth perspective spell out, and what they do not fully work through but which seems to be logically implied by the direction of their arguments. What they actually say, broadly, is that children should have more freedom from adult authority and control, and a greater degree of self-determination; at the extreme, children should have as much freedom as adults, and possibly even more. Children should not incur particular disadvantages or restrictions just because they are young. These authors see children as affected adversely by the commonly held notion of childhood as a weak, dependent, and less responsible state. Abolition of childhood as generally understood would thus be a liberation. The children's rights authors envisage the benefits of adulthood as being conferred on children, and the more oppressive aspects of adult–child relationships and the social position of children being removed.

Yet adulthood has its disadvantages and childhood as presently construed some privileges. What the authors do not always appear to tackle fully is whether, for example, in the regime they anticipate, child offenders would be treated exactly in the same way as adult offenders; whether children would carry exactly the same responsibilities and liabilities as adults under the civil law; whether they would, when earning, be liable for tax, and for maintaining certain members of their families; whether they would be liable for military service; whether they could expect no special protection or dispensation in any circumstances; and whether, in general, they would be expected to carry the full duties, burdens and responsibilities of citizenship as well as its rights and freedoms. While such notions do seem to be implied by the very libertarian concepts of childhood and adult–child relationships underlying the fourth perspective, it may be that in fact even the more extreme proponents of the perspective would not altogether welcome the prospect of children and young persons being burdened with the full liabilities, and the more negative aspects, of adult citizenship; but would prefer that children should be granted greater power, without necessarily commensurate responsibility. Such a notion carries its own problems, however, which will be referred to again later.

It should also be stressed that a much more moderate version of the perspective can be adopted, which is less aggressively libertarian, while still emphasising children's rights in a rather more limited sense. Broadly consonant with this less extreme children's rights position is the argument that children should, in all spheres, at least have a greater independent say in what happens to them; and that the provisions of the state should allow for this, in child care law and policy, education, health care, and any other relevant areas. Decisions should not (on the whole) be made over the child's head. Thus children's welfare is (at least partly) for children themselves to define.

Some authors associated with the perspective

A fairly colourful exponent of a more extreme version of this perspective is Holt (1975) in *Escape from Childhood. The Needs and Rights of Children*. This book, written in an American context, is said by the author to be about young people and their place or lack of place in modern society; about the ways in which modern childhood is bad for most of those who live within it; and about how it might be changed. Being a child, according to Holt, means 'being wholly subservient and dependent ... being seen by older people as a mixture of expensive nuisance, slave and super-pet' (p. 15), and this situation does harm to most young people. Holt proposes that the rights, privileges, duties and responsibilities of adulthood be made available to any young person who wants to use them, including the right to vote and participate in politics, to work and be financially independent, to receive the state minimum income, live away from home and seek their own choice of guardian, drive, use drugs, control their own sex lives, and generally do what any adult may legally do. He also advocates the 'right' to equal treatment at the hands of the law, and to be legally responsible for one's life and acts. Holt does not propose any lower age limit on these rights, and states that young people should be able to pick and choose which they want to assume.

Holt is critical of the social institution of childhood which he sees as meaning attitudes, feelings, customs and laws which put a great gulf or barrier between the young and their elders, making it difficult for the young to make contact with the larger society or to play an active, responsible part in it. He notes that the concept of childhood evolved with the modern family, but does not work well for many people. Tackling the argument that giving children greater independence could 'weaken the family', Holt argues that 'Any institution that really works is immune to attack, however severe' (p. 37), and that the family was an institution where some people were owned by others – men owned women and children. The family may be seen as a miniature dictatorship – 'a training for slavery' (p. 39). Also, children need a larger network to relate to than the small nuclear family which can be destructive, over-intense and fragile. Children need adult friends other than their parents, as in extended families, so 'we need to allow, encourage, and help young people create extended families of their own' (p. 42). According to Holt, adults resent and dislike children, and bringing them up is an endless worry and emotional and financial burden. Nevertheless the institution of childhood has the function of benefiting adults, giving them someone to boss, someone to 'help', someone to love. Holt is also critical of the notion of 'help' to others, which as he sees it thrives on and creates helplessness. Another argument is that adults grossly under-estimate the competence of the young, and therefore their capacities are not fully used. Children are capable of more than we give them credit for, he believes. A further problem that Holt perceives is the treatment of the child as love object, rather as men use women as sex objects. He comments: 'We treat someone as an object when we use him for our purposes, to achieve our ends, to get things for ourselves, without considering or caring what this does to him or how he feels about it, without asking what he gets out of it or whether he gets anything at all' (pp. 78–9). With children 'We think we have a right, or even a duty, to bestow on them "love" … whenever we want, however we want, and whether they like it or not' (p. 80). This is exploitative, serving adults' needs.

Central to the argument of the children's rights school is the similarity of children to adults, and this is reflected in the title of Holt's Chapter 15, 'What children need, we all need'. Here Holt claims that when we see children's needs as belonging only to children, we trivialise and invalidate them; we also ensure that they will not be met. Seeing childhood as a separate world means that adults decide what is good for children. Commenting on the use of the word 'rights', Holt says that he means by the term what we mean when we speak of the rights of adults. His argument is that the law should guarantee to the young the freedom it grants to adults. Of particular relevance to child care policy is Holt's view of the 'right' to a good home and family. The state cannot guarantee this, he says, in the way it can guarantee an income, but should leave to children the right to decide how good their home is, and to choose something else if they do not like it. The state should not make alternatives compulsory, but should allow children to make other choices.

Holt's ensuing chapters discuss the recommended rights for children one by one: the right to vote, the right to work, the right to own property, the right to travel, the right to choose one's guardian, the right to a guaranteed income, the right to legal and financial responsibility, the right to control one's learning, the right to use drugs, the right to drive, and sexual rights. A few of the arguments which Holt puts forward in defence of these rights will be outlined here.

The right to vote, one of the most important, should not depend on any condition and should extend to people of any age. It is a matter of justice, Holt argues, that those who are affected by laws and decisions should have a say in them, and that 'Given real choices, people will choose for themselves better than others will choose for them' (p. 119). Holt considers that it is particularly unjust to deny the vote to the young, because they will have to live longer with the effects of government decisions. While younger children would probably not want to vote, they should have the right to; childhood ignorance is not a justification for their exclusion, as many adult voters are ill-informed also. On the right to work, it is argued that children need their own money, want to be useful, and find work stimulating. However, working should be children's own choice – not forced upon them. Some dangers in children having wider access to the world of work are conceded. Also beneficial to children would be the right to travel without parental permission – this is an enjoyable way of learning about the world and becoming independent. In defence of the right to choose a guardian, Holt stresses the child's choice and the benefits of voluntarily undertaken relationships, saying: 'There is no *necessary* reason why parents should like their own children best, or like them at all; they might prefer someone else's' (p. 161). There is a denial of both biological and early psychological ties here. Parents would not be free to end their relationship with their children, however, although the child would be free to move about. The right to a guaranteed income is again defended in terms of independence. The rights to travel, seek other guardians, and so on, cannot be meaningful if children cannot get money in their own right. Holt argues that families should not be treated as a single economic unit; in practice this often means that property and income belongs to the head and others have to bargain and beg.

In defending the right to legal and financial responsibility, Holt argues that the law (at the time he wrote) treated children worse than adults, for example, by holding them in 'jails' (that is, institutions) for reasons that would not apply if they were adults. Children should have 'the right to a fair trial, to all the protection of due process, and the right to bring suit' (p. 179). Holt accepts here that children would be account-able to fellow citizens and the law for what they did, and could be sued as well as being able to sue. What Holt has in mind is a means by which children could take a formal step to become independent citizens with full legal responsibility. Children would not have this status automatically, and would also have the right to opt back to 'dependent' status.

The right of children to control their own learning is seen as fundamental because it is a part of freedom of thought; deciding what all young people are to learn is highly authoritarian, and compulsory education a gross violation of civil liberties. On the question of drugs (in the broadest sense) existing prohibitions are seen as counterproductive; driving is seen as ideally dependent on skill, not age; and young people living as independent citizens should have the same sexual rights as anyone else – although Holt is aware of more problems and dilemmas in this field.

Finally, under 'Steps to take', Holt suggests that in the interim adults should treat children as they would want to see them treated in the society here aspired to; that children should take greater financial responsibility, have more adult friends, be freer from dependence generally, acquire work experience, and not be punished more severely than adults. It is symptomatic of Holt's general view that he sees young people without families who currently live as wards of the state, as 'prisoners of the state' (pp. 217–18).

Other authors from the 1970s who may be classed as belonging broadly to the children's rights school of thought, are Foster and Freed (1972), Worsfold (1974) and Farson (1978). Foster and Freed in an article on 'A Bill of Rights for Children' see the status of minority as the last legal relic of feudalism, arguing for checks on adult authority and for children to be seen as persons entitled to assert their individual interests in their own right; paternalism they see as discredited. Foster and Freed do not go quite as far as Holt in arguing that children's rights are or should be like those of adults; some concession is made to the idea of children having special needs and rights, and being vulnerable. Nevertheless, the general tone of their writing is very similar to Holt's. Worsfold (1974) explores a philosophical justification for children's rights. Pointing out that paternalist views do not guarantee the acceptable treatment of children, Worsfold argues that Rawls's theory of justice (Rawls 1972) provides a justification for according children rights to fair treatment. As Worsfold sees it, in Rawls's model children should receive the full protection of the principles of justice because they have the capacity (even if not yet fully developed) for accepting the principle of fairness. Worsfold concludes: 'The justification of children's rights under Rawls's theory has one major emphasis: children have a right to make just claims, and adults must be responsive to those claims' (p. 157). Farson (1978), like Holt, emphasises the child's right to self-determination, saying that the issue of self-determination is at the heart of children's liberation. Farson's 'Bill of Rights' for children contains many of the same ideas as Holt. Farson argues that children should have the right to alternative home environments, to design which is responsive to their needs, to information, to design their own education, to freedom from physical punishment, to sexual freedom, to economic and political power, and justice. These are seen as 'birthrights'. Like Holt, Farson would abolish virtually all age-related disabilities.

A later book, edited by Bob Franklin (1986), *The Rights of Children*, considers children's rights in various different spheres – in the political sphere, at school, in care and the juvenile justice system, at work, and in the area of sexuality. Franklin's introduction to the book shows a clear liberationist orientation. Claiming that the 'irrationality and immorality of systematic and institutionalised discrimination against individuals on the basis of their gender or race has, to some degree, been established' (p. 1), he argues that '*equivalent* discrimination against people on the basis of their age has proven more resilient to change' (p. 1 [my italics]). A consensus that children have suffered and been discriminated against is absent, he says; yet because of their age children are denied rights which adults consider to be basic human rights. Children 'form a large, long-suffering and oppressed grouping in society' (p. 1) with a forgotten and excluded status. For example, they are disenfranchised, economically disadvantaged, are considered to be the property of their parents, are obliged to attend educational institutions, and are subjected to the power and punishment of both teachers and parents. While children are a heterogeneous group, they all suffer political, economic, legal, educational and domestic restrictions.

Franklin goes on to elaborate the problems of the adult, idealised perception of childhood which denies that children are real people. Myths operate about the way adults treat children; an idealised adult concern, Franklin thinks, has informed much legislation relating to children; such legislation can, however, result in further unjust treatment. Because adult–child relationships are idealised, severe cases of child abuse tend to be greeted with incredulity, as an aberration. Another myth is of childhood as a 'golden age', a special time of innocence and happiness. This myth does not correspond to some of the known data about childhood; and Franklin brings forward evidence supporting a more negative view, such as facts concerning child employment, poverty, children in care and child abuse. Acknowledging that the issue of children's rights is complex, Franklin then goes on to consider two aspects in particular: the question of what is a child, and some of the complexities of the term 'rights'.

In brief, he says that childhood is not fixed but a historically shifting cultural construction, subject to wide variations by time and place. The division between childhood and adulthood is arbitrary and incoherent – different rights are allowed at different ages. The diversity found within the 'childhood' age range is clouded by the definition of all young people as 'non-adults'. And the term 'child' specifies a power relationship rather than chronological age as such. Historical evidence of the development of the concept of 'childhood' is cited, this being seen as a European invention of the last few centuries. Prior to this childhood was not seen as a special phase in life. Franklin here refers to the work of Aries (1962) on the history of childhood, work which emphasises the absence of the concept of 'childhood', in the modern sense, in mediaeval times. The progressive differentiation of the child-hood state is related to industrialisation and capitalism. This historical evidence challenges the common sense view of childhood as immutable.

On 'rights', Franklin makes the familiar distinction between legal rights (enforceable by law) and moral rights (based on an appeal to principle); nevertheless the two categories overlap – morality can inform and support law. It can also be a source of criticism of it. Franklin also discusses a four-fold classification of children's rights proposed by Freeman (1983a) which will be discussed below. Franklin puts forward a broader two-fold classification of children's rights termed the 'liberationist versus protectionist orientation' (p. 17), noting that children require an expansion of both kinds of rights: there is not necessarily a tension between self-determination and protection.

As Franklin acknowledges, the chapters in his edited collection express both liberationist and protectionist positions. But his own chapter on the extension of the suffrage to children is, in his own words, 'clearly cast in the liberationist mould' (p. 18), and this chapter will be considered briefly before moving on. Entitled 'Children's political rights', the chapter examines, and finds ultimately unconvincing, the arguments used to exclude the young from political rights. For example, Franklin says that the 'commonsense' exclusion of children from political rights is rooted partly in an uncritical acceptance of paternalism. Franklin next examines paternalism, arguing that it 'offers no cogent grounds upon which to deny young people political rights … but simply provides a justification for political elites' (p. 27). A detailed critique is put forward, of which only a few points will be mentioned here. One concerns individuals' rationality. Interference with an individual's freedom on the grounds of his or her own good (not somebody else's) is often justified, with regard to young people, in terms of their lack of rationality. Yet rationality is a difficult concept to pin down and use as a criterion distinguishing children from adults. Adults themselves are not fully rational, yet do not normally expect or accept the paternalistic interventions of others foisted upon them; indeed, any such paternalistic interveners and decision-makers cannot be considered fully rational either. One aspect of children's supposed lack of rationality is their propensity to make mistakes which are dam-aging to themselves. Again, adults also do this – sometimes horrific mistakes; while children need to make some mistakes as part of their learning process. These criteria do not justify the exclusion of children from political rights, in Franklin's view.

Franklin's solution, which has its root in Holt's work, is that children should have the right to vote when their interest and knowledge are sufficient to motivate them to do so. It is suggested that children have greater political maturity than is generally believed, while younger children who are politically immature would not choose to vote, because they would not be interested. However, political capacities might develop more rapidly if they were acknowledged by the adult world. Franklin further argues that extending the franchise to children would not significantly alter the pattern of voting for particular political parties (an argument which is surely irrelevant). In defending Holt's proposal against likely objections, Franklin goes on to say that ignorance is not and should not be a criterion for the franchise, nor the ability to vote responsibly; the same applies to the tendency to vote for personalities rather than policies; and none of these three factors differentiates children in general from adults in general. Fourthly, there is the question of parental influence and coercion. Broadly, Franklin's response is that while this factor cannot be dismissed in the case of anyone, adult or child, in a society where children had more autonomy in general, parental influence would be less significant. Franklin concludes that the denial of the franchise to the young offends fundamental democratic principles, and that its granting would help to ensure a higher profile for children's interests in various institutional contexts – to a degree that paternalism cannot achieve.

In a later edited collection (1995), *The Handbook of Children's Rights*, Franklin again writes a first chapter, here entitled: 'The case for children's rights: a progress report'. He reiterates some familiar themes, but the tone is perhaps more emphatic. Arguing that 'children's rights' had become a more legitimate notion since the mid-1980s, and citing examples of policy developments (with some retrograde steps), Franklin again examines childhood as a social construct and a state mythologised as a 'golden age'. The abitrary nature of age boundaries, the practice of defining all those under 18 as 'non-adults', and the exclusion of some from the (Western) concept of childhood, are pointed to as problematic. But childhood is essentially characterised by powerlessness. The concept of rights is also addressed, with legal/moral and welfare/liberty rights distinguished. In outlining the debate over children's rights, Franklin again examines arguments relating to children's lack of rationality and proneness to make mistakes, and again finds them wanting. Children have a degree of competence and need to learn by making mistakes, while many adults also lack competence. Self-sufficiency also does not distinguish adults from children. The notion of children *in general* acquiring more competence as they age (though with individual variations) is apparently not embraced by Franklin. The exclusion of children from adult rights is argued to be 'permanent' for children as a social group. And the argument that intervention is justified if the child *when adult* would support the decisions made, as being in her or his long-term interests, also falls, in Franklin's view. This is because 'future consent' is not known, and because upbringing may itself influence what children once grown to adulthood perceive as an appropriate way to bring up children; at the extreme: 'The benchmark of successful brainwashing is that the person violated in this way is happy and confirmed in their new beliefs' (p. 13). Franklin goes on to examine specific practices such as ombudswork with children (that is, the work of Children's Commissioners); the appointment of children's rights officers; the idea of a Minister for Children; and the United Nations Convention on the Rights of the Child (see below: 'The perspective in practice'). In his summary to the chapter, Franklin again firmly nails his liberationist colours to the mast. The responsibility for protecting children's rights belongs: 'Not in the hands of well-meaning but potentially paternalistic adults, but with those who have the greatest interest in ensuring that those rights are not infringed: children themselves' (p. 20).

An author who can be identified with a much more moderate children's rights approach is Freeman (1980, 1983a). First, in an article in 1980 Freeman distanced himself from the more radical of the children's rights spokespersons, seeing their arguments as 'politically naive, philosophically faulty and psychologically wrong' (p. 17). Freeman's view was that it should be obvious that age *is* a relevant differentiating factor in legal status, in a way that race and sex are not. He highlights the inconsistency of Holt (1975) and Farson (1978) in requiring the same freedom for children as adults, while assuming that parents would still have the obligation to nurture and maintain their children, and of bestowing rights on children but not expecting reciprocal responsibilities. Self-determination, in Freeman's view, is a capacity to be developed, rather than a right to be expressed. Freeman is also sceptical of Worsfold's (1974) attempt to justify children's rights with reference to Rawls's theory of justice (1972), though finding Rawls useful in suggesting that decisions in the child's interest should be guided by what the child would rationally want. Freeman offers cautions on the limitations of rights in practice, concluding: 'We need to change childhood but this need not involve ignoring its existence' (p. 23).

Freeman's book *The Rights and Wrongs of Children* (1983a) aims for a more considered insight into the issue of children's rights, reflecting an awareness of its complexity. As early as the Prologue to the book Freeman comments: 'it takes but a moment's reflection to realise that the position of children is not strictly comparable with that of women or blacks' (p. 1). Freeman does much more than the extreme child liberationists to acknowledge the differences between children and adults, although he is concerned with what happens to children and their rights in a broader sense. For example, sentimentality, he says 'is no substitute for the recognition of a child's entitlement to the right to equal concern and respect' (p. 3). Children's capacities should be acknowledged, and they should be given a say in the decision-making process concerning them whenever feasible; their interests should be taken into account in policy-making. But, as Freeman sees it, protecting children and protecting their rights are not incompatible as aims.

Freeman's four-fold classification of children's rights has already been referred to briefly in discussing Franklin's (1986) work. This framework of Freeman's can be found in Chapter 2 of his book, where he elaborates his view of rights (having, in Chapter 1, traced the historical evolution of the concepts of children's rights and, more broadly, childhood). Having examined the importance of rights as a concept, and the nature of legal and moral rights, claims, demands, needs, the 'manifesto' use of the term 'rights', and obligations, Freeman then goes on to set out his four categories of children's rights. The first category consists of 'generalised claims on behalf of all children. They can be described as welfare rights' (p. 40). A clear statement of rights in this sense can be found in the 1959 United Nations Declaration of the Rights of the Child. This includes principles such as adequate nutrition, housing and medical treatment, education and care, love and protection; these can be seen as fundamental human rights, but they are not in general easily enforceable by law, or at least not by courts, and are somewhat vague. These rights are far from those envisaged by the child liberationist school. Freeman's second category is concerned with child protection and stresses child vulnerability and parental and adult responsibility. Freeman says that this is a view 'against which those who espouse children's liberation react with hostility' (p. 43). This protectionist view of rights is broadly in line with the second, state paternalist perspective outlined in this book. A third class of children's rights *does* correspond closely to the preferred scenario of the liberationists. This is where the rights of adults are largely extended to children, either by abolishing age-related disabilities or by proceeding on a case-by-case basis, while any extant age limits should be constantly re-examined. A fourth type of rights is classed as 'rights against parents' (p. 48); again, this is to do with autonomy and would find favour with the child liberation supporters. Children should have the freedom to act independently. At the very least, they should be able to challenge parental decisions through some other agent or decision-maker. The main focus here, according to Freeman, should be on adolescents, and on major, rather than trivial, decisions.

Freeman next outlines a theory of 'liberal paternalism' to justify children's rights, which represents his own position. He states that: 'Paternalism in its classical form does not acknowledge the existence of children's rights. Liberal paternalism, I believe, compels their recognition' (p. 52). Drawing on Rawls's principles of equality and justice, Freeman asks: 'what sort of action or conduct would we wish, as children, to be shielded against on the assumption that we would want to mature to a rationally autonomous adulthood … ?' (p. 57). The answer is that 'We would choose principles that would enable children to mature to independent adulthood. Our definition of irrationality would be such as to preclude action and conduct which would frustrate such a goal; within the constraints of such a definition we would defend a version of paternalism' (p. 57). Constraints must be exercised in such a way as to enable children to develop their capacities. On these grounds Freeman would defend, for example, compulsory education. Robbed of this the young person would be less prepared to become a rationally autonomous person. But a limit on the exercise of paternalism stems from the prospect of the child's eventually seeing the correctness of the intervention. And certain current restrictions require re-examination, Freeman argues. It is clear that Freeman seeks to balance protection and autonomy in a way that would give greater emphasis to protection than the extreme child liberationists would allow; *but* he would support more autonomy than is favoured in the writings of the child protectionist/paternalist school, and is thus placed in the broad 'children's rights' category in this book.

In a later article (1992a) Freeman states a similar line of argument: it is important that children's rights are taken seriously, their rights are important if they are to be treated with equality and as autonomous beings. Freeman subjects to critical scrutiny a number of arguments which would tend to de-emphasise the importance of rights for children. He argues that: 'Children are particularly vulnerable and need rights to protect their integrity and dignity' (p. 55). It is the case that children have needs which are not met by giving them rights on a par with adults, and that children are different from adults, 'but they are not all that different … Age is often a suspect classification … The onus lies on those who wish to discriminate' (p. 66). Freeman, then, stresses the value of equality and autonomy – for children as for adults. Protective structures for children may not be as protective as they seem. Freeman's careful balancing act between protection and liberation is encapsulated in the following: 'In looking for a children's rights programme we must thus recognise the integrity of the child and his or her decision-making capacities but at the same time note the dangers of complete liberation.… To take children's rights more seriously requires us to take more seriously than we have done hitherto protection of children and recognition of their autonomy both actual and potential' (p. 66). As in his 1983 publication, the test of 'future-oriented consent' (p. 68) is introduced – will children when adult accept the restrictions that were imposed upon them?

Eekelaar (1992) may also be seen as belonging in this 'moderate' children's rights category. In a chapter entitled 'The importance of thinking that children have rights' in a book edited by Alston, Parker and Seymour (1992), *Children, Rights and the Law*, Eekelaar offers a theoretical basis on which assertions of children's rights may be grounded. After discussion of a number of authors' approaches to the issue of rights *per se*, and an emphasis on the connection between rights and choice and on the inadequacy of *duties* in fully satisfying rights, Eekelaar summarises his argument by posing a basic distinction between 'welfarism' (where actions are motivated by the purpose of promoting another's welfare), and actions which recognise others' *claims*. Rights and claims are related, and claims go beyond the demand that others act to further one's welfare as *they* define it. Thus: 'to treat someone fully as an individual of moral worth implies recognising that that person makes claims and exercises choices: that is, is a potential right-holder' (p. 228).

Applying this discussion to children's rights, Eekelaar argues that the welfarist model implies that adults should act towards children in accordance with the *adults'* perception of the child's welfare. This: 'fails to give proper respect to the human worth of the child' (p. 228). Having regard to children's claims, on the other hand, involves hearing what children say, and treating this with respect. Attention should be given to what specific children would want if fully informed and mature: It is necessary to observe children for what is important to them and why – 'in direct opposition to the devastating neglect of children's own opinions which has characterised much of the welfarist approach hitherto' (p. 229). But this approach does look forward to the adult that the child will be, and to the choices that the child as an adult might make. Eekelaar acknowledges the similarity of his argument here to Freeman's (1983a). (Franklin's, 1995, criticism of this type of argument is noted above.)

Eekelaar then goes on to analyse the United Nations Convention on the Rights of the Child (see below) in the context of his framework, and concludes; 'It would be a grievous mistake to see the Convention as applying to childhood alone. Childhood is not an end in itself, but part of the process of forming the adults of the next generation' (p. 234). Thus the connection between childhood and later development is stressed. In a later article (1994), Eekelaar expounds how acting towards children with the objective of furthering their best interests can be reconciled with treating them as possessors of rights – thus, again, attempting to reconcile protectionist and liberationist principles. He suggests that the best interests principle should allow scope for the child to determine those interests, and calls this 'dynamic self-determinism' (p. 43). This does not mean simply delegating decision-making to children, but self-determinism: 'is a mode of optimally positioning children to develop their own perceptions of their well-being as they enter adulthood' (p. 58).

Interestingly, the former Norwegian Ombudsperson (see below, on 'the perspective in practice'), Flekkoy (1991), also clearly belongs in this 'moderate' group of commentators. Stressing children's developmental progression, she points out that children are both vulnerable *and* need autonomy: 'They *are* fully equal to adults as persons, and yet it would be maltreatment to burden them with fully equal responsibilities' (p. 224). The office of ombudsperson might itself be seen to embody a children's rights approach in a liberationist sense, so this word of caution is significant.

Brief reference may be made to the historian of child care policy, Hendrick (1994), whose sympathy for a children's rights viewpoint is revealed in comments such as his plea for recognition of ageism, which he takes to mean: 'the repression and oppression of young people, principally through political and economic forces' (p.xi), and his reference to: 'children's powerlessness' which needs to be 'critically examined rather than passively accepted' (p. xiii).

The work of the voluntary organisation the Children's Legal Centre may also be mentioned in the context of the children's rights approach. The Centre was formed in 1979, aiming: 'to promote the recognition of children and young persons as individuals participating fully in all the decisions which affect their lives' through advice and information work, the pursuit of selected cases, research, training and responding to policies. The Centre has since 1983 (apart from a brief break in 1995 – see below) published a monthly bulletin, *Childright*. According to a brief article by Wilson (1988) on the Centre, their view was that in various fields – education, welfare rights, employment, criminal law and many others – children and young people were rarely recognised as a group with the right to have their views considered or their interests represented independently. The content of issues of *Childright* also reflects the Centre's concerns. One major focus of the magazine has been the law enforcement machinery as it affects children – for example, treatment by the police and the treatment of the young in custody. An overlapping area of concern was that of children in care: issues such as locking up children in care, the use of drugs to control them, the general treatment of children in care and care-leavers, and opportunities for them to complain. Another concern has been corporal punishment, whether in care, in schools, or in the parental home. A further prominent issue in *Childright* has been education in its many aspects, but with a children's rights emphasis, for example, in highlighting pupil power in schools and complaints. Articles have also covered a wide variety of other themes: adoption, race, disability, the UN Convention on children's rights, contraception, sex education, age limits, homelessness and young people on the streets, political participation, children's evidence in court, bullying, school exclusions, young carers, and the Child Support Act 1991, to mention a selection. It will be clear that many topics can be examined within a children's rights framework. The magazine has an international orientation, and looks at the position of children in other countries, as well as immigration issues. It has monitored current legislation and policy as they affect children, partly by the useful device of setting out Child Impact Statements for new Acts.

Unfortunately, in 1995 the Centre temporarily closed down due to funding problems, re-opening in a more modest way with reduced staff and *Childright* being published commercially as a supplement to another publication. This down-sizing of the Centre was referred to by one commentator as leaving a 'gaping hole' in the development of children's rights (Neale 1995:19).

Rationale and underlying values

Two themes which seem to be central to the more extreme child liberationist perspective are the perception of children as fundamentally no
different from adults, and the emphasis on freedom from adult control
as children's primary need and right. Both themes give the perspective
much in common with other liberationist writing focusing on, for
example, the freeing of women and oppressed ethnic groups, from the
control of men/patriarchy and dominant ethnic groups. It can be argued
that discrimination against children, and the allocation of a different
legal status on the basis of age, is no more justified than discrimination
on grounds of gender or ethnicity. 'Childhood' is seen as essentially a
social construction, not inherent to the condition of children themselves
– to the extent that the physical, psychological and social characteristics which self-evidently (or from a common sense viewpoint) seem to
differentiate children from adults, tend to be denied. It may be claimed,
for example, as it is by Holt (1975), that children have a far greater
capacity to survive unaided in society than adults give them credit for.
   The general approach of the more extreme children's rights school
seems to be that childhood is not so much a developmental process
through which children gradually become socialised to take their place in
the adult world – learn, in fact, to be adults – as an oppressed state in
which individuals who are essentially no different from anyone else have
become unjustly trapped. If it is indeed the case that children are essentially adults who happen to occupy a smaller body and to have been alive
for a shorter span of years than others, such a critique of childhood would
have great force – denying children the vote, for example, would seem
equally unjust to denying it to adults under five foot, or with black skins,
or with red hair. The question of the *differences* between children and
adults, and between older and younger children, will be explored further
in examining criticisms of this perspective.
   What the children's rights perspective does usefully highlight by
questioning the very concept of childhood is the arbitrary and inconsistent nature of the formal age limits which society sets between
childhood or minority and adulthood in various contexts: for example,
in England, the right to marry with parental consent and work full-time
at 16, to drive at 17, to purchase alcohol and vote at 18, to consent to
heterosexual sex at 16 but to homosexual sex not until 18. It may be
pointed out that such limits can be – and have been – varied by law,
and are clearly a social and legal construction imposed upon young
persons, rather than a biological dividing line relating to any objective
differences suddenly occurring at any of these ages. A similar objection
may be raised to age limits at the other end of the age scale – for
example, a fixed retirement age of 65 is an arbitrary boundary which
makes 'old age' a social construction imposed on people who happen to
have passed a certain age (see, for example, Walker 1980). In so far as
age limits cause resentment because they entail arbitrary discrimination,

and are an entirely socially created barrier bearing little or no relation to people's actual capacities, it seems reasonable to argue for their complete removal. Problems with this approach will also be discussed in considering criticisms of this perspective.

Childhood, then, in this view, is a social construction subjected to arbitrary limits. The artificial construction of childhood allocates to children an essentially passive status in which they cannot exercise the normal rights, or receive the normal respect, of citizenship. In general adult-controlled and adult-defined society does not take seriously what children think, feel, say or do, but attributes different meanings to the actions of children solely because they are children. Linked with this perspective's view of the imposed passivity of childhood is its perception of the primary need and right of children as freedom from adult power. What children need is not, as in the second perspective, good quality care, but autonomy. Their primary problem is the restrictions which adults have imposed on them, and what would benefit children most would be to break free, to make their own decisions, and to lead their own lives. This is the most fundamental difference between the second and fourth value perspectives. Both tend to make children an absolute priority and to disregard, relatively, the interests of adults (which children will eventually become), but while for the second school of thought the obligation placed on adults with regard to children is essentially to care and protect (and indeed, to a degree, to control), for the fourth school the adult obligation is largely to let children go, to listen to what they say, and to respect what they want (rather than – according to an adult view – what they 'need'). Little credit is given to adults for the nurturance role, for adults' ability to care for and make appropriate decisions on behalf of children; in fact the idea that adult attitudes to children are generally benign is explicitly challenged. It is the more sinister and exploitative aspects of adult–child relationships which tend to be highlighted in the children's rights perspective. Even parental 'love' has its suspect side.

While the perspective suggests a particular idea of childhood, then, it also implies a particular notion of adulthood. Adults are perceived rather negatively; their approach to children is seen as chiefly determined by their wish and need to use children for their own ends. Thus children are used to gratify adult needs for power, love, sex, amusement, achievement, and social status. Adults, in fact, are not to be trusted, being the dominant side in a power relationship. This general cynicism about adults in their relations with children can be contrasted with the previous three perspectives discussed where at least some adults (parents in the first and third, various professionals, state agents and substitute parents in the second) are credited with understanding and acting on childen's interests and welfare.

The concept of rights is clearly also crucial to the rationale underlying this fourth perspective. The kinds of child rights with which proponents are characteristically concerned are, as shown, those which are to do with freedom, self-determination, autonomy, and so on, rather than to do with protection and welfare. Such rights of self-determination are claimed as moral rights which should be embodied in the law. Partly, the enforcement of these rights involves legislative action to remove age-related disabilities and parental and other adult power over children. Such action could create for the young rights in the sense of *freedoms*: no legal bar would stand in the way, but no specific obligation or duty would fall on other parties. In the case of certain rights, however, it would seem that particular duties would also have to be created or maintained. It would seem, for example, that at least some adults would have to have an obligation to provide homes for children, if children are to be free to decide where they would live. If children are to be free to work but not to be forced to, some persons or some body must have the obligation to support them financially if they decide not to work. Education must be provided for those children who do choose it. Other examples are Holt's (1975) right to a guaranteed income – which imposes an obligation somewhere to pay it; or Farson's (1978) right to alternative home environments – someone would have to provide them. Where a right involves a particular duty falling on another person or body, different problems of enforcement arise from the case where a right is merely a legal freedom to act in a certain way, such as to travel unimpeded by others. Problems of enforcement constitute one difficulty with the notion of rights in relation to children; another is the over-emphasis on rights and duties in the construction of child–adult relationships, to the detriment of other values. These problems will be considered further in discussing criticisms of this value perspective.

Another point about rights is that those who hold them are usually held to incur a general duty to respect and safeguard other people's rights as well, that is, at least not to impede others in the exercise of their rights. Rights and duties are two complementary aspects of the notion of citizenship, of membership of a community where freedoms can be exercised but freedom itself is curtailed by the rights of others. It is noticeable, however, that Holt (1975) and the other liberationist writers say much about children's rights in the ideal they aim for, but very little about their proposed duties. The position of children aspired to seems to be more favourable in some ways than the current position of adults. This inconsistency will be looked at further later.

Two other underlying aspects of the children's rights perspective concern the view of the family, and of the state. Broadly, there is a low valuation of the family unit as conventionally understood, and a negative perspective of the state which, while it is adult-controlled, is not perceived as generally benign in its treatment of children. On the family first: this institution tends not to be discussed at length, but in its existing form is seen – at least by Holt (1975) – to be oppressive to children. (There is a parallel here with some feminist views of the family as a key site of women's oppression, for example, Barrett and McIntosh 1991, Delphy and Leonard 1992.) For example, Holt is dismissive of arguments that his proposals would weaken the family, seeing the family as often a locus of oppression and of power held by some over others, as claustrophobic and over-burdened with feelings. Parents and children are not necessarily happy in their roles towards each other, and children need other adults besides parents. Holt also draws attention to the historical specificity of the modern nuclear family. But his comment: 'Basically the family was and is a tiny kingdom, an absolute monarchy' (p. 39) captures the flavour of his view; although he also thinks that strong and healthy families could not be threatened by his proposals for children's rights. Holt also suggests loose groups and communities as alternatives for some children; and he favours children having 'extended families' (in a broad sense) of their own.

There are, of course, a number of aspects of the modern family to which children's rights protagonists can point as being unsatisfactory for children – violence, sexual abuse, pathological relationships, isolation, insecurity, disruption and so on. As Macdougall (1985) comments: 'Some will consider the children's rights movement as a necessary response to the failure of the modern family to meet the needs of children' (p. 268). While the proponents of the third value perspective point to the positives in family life for children, the proponents of the children's rights view are very aware of the negatives.

The state, like the family, has a generally poor image in this perspective, and, at the extreme, being actually in the care of the state is likened to imprisonment. Holt (1975) refers to children in 'jails' and children as 'prisoners' of the state, apparently glossing over distinctions between being in care for an offence and being in care for the child's own welfare, or between being held in secure accommodation and living in an ordinary children's home or foster home. Other authors writing from the children's rights perspective are much less simplistic than Holt, but their approach to the state systems which respond, for example, to juvenile offenders and children in need of substitute care, is a critical one. In Franklin's first book a chapter by Lavery (1986) on the rights of children in care sets out 'to highlight some of the ways in which the rights of children in care are violated' (p. 73). Lavery is critical, for example, of some forms of residential care and fostering, and particularly of the denial of children's say in decision-making at that time – for example, their exclusion from reviews of their progress in care. The right to privacy in children's homes, the use of corporal punishment (now banned in homes) and drugs, and locking up children in secure accommodation, are other issues highlighted. In his conclusion Lavery comments that 'the state behaves in some strange, if not positively harmful, ways and, invariably, with paternalism as its hallmark. Its target always seems to be the poor' (p. 90). A subsequent chapter by Adams (1986) on juvenile justice also criticises the overriding of children's rights in specific parts of the system.

The journal *Childright* also reflects a concern about the more oppressive aspects of the state's dealings with children. Using drugs to control children in care would be one striking example, locking them up another; the police and the criminal justice system generally are also a target of interest and concern. The first issue of *Childright* in 1983 reported on young girls in care being forcibly injected with major tranquillisers while in a 'lock-up' (a secure unit), and on solitary confinement as a form of punishment in secure units. There has been some improvement in the prevention of abuse in residential care in the 1990s, following certain scandals, and the establishment of complaints procedures and children's rights officers in local authorities may help (see 'The perspective in practice') but concerns remain. The scandals themselves highlighted the appalling treatment to which some children in residential homes were subject, most notably the practice of 'pindown' or extreme isolation (see Levy and Kahan 1991).

The moderate children's rights author Freeman (1983a) is also critical of the way children are treated by the state, as offenders or as being in need of care, also when their parents divorce. Writing in the early 1980s context, he comments: 'One of the most unsatisfactory features of juvenile justice is that in reality there is very little justice. Neither pre-trial procedures nor the court processes themselves observe the sort of elementary natural justice requirements that are taken for granted in a court dealing with adult offenders' (p. 86). As he points out in his 1992 article, protective structures for children are not necessarily protective.

While not all criticisms of the state put forward by the proponents of the fourth perspective fall strictly into line with a children's rights viewpoint (for example, some of Freeman's, 1983 criticisms of the response to child abuse resemble Holman's (1980, 1988), in general what are emphasised are the areas where the state overrides the rights of children and treats them more unjustly, and more unfavourably, than it treats adults. Those areas where the state treats, or attempts to treat, children *better* than adults are de-emphasised, or interpreted as having the effect of worse treatment despite the intention, most obviously in the field of juvenile justice. The empowerment of children, for example, through the franchise, would, it is argued, induce the state to be more receptive to their needs.

Criticisms of the children's rights and child liberation perspective

See Chapters 4 to 7 of David Archard's book, *Children: Rights and Childhood* (Archard 1993) for an excellent critique of the child liberationist arguments also discussed critically here.

Empirical support

Holt's (1975) manifesto for children's rights was not strongly supported by empirical studies relating to childhood and child care, but drew mainly on individual cases, press stories and anecdotes for backing. Foster and Freed's (1972) position depended mainly on argument and criticism of the existing state of the law (like Holt in an American context), while Worsfold (1974) based his case on argument and theoretical discussion, mainly, as indicated, centred on the work of Rawls on justice. Franklin (1986) brings forward some evidence supporting a rather negative view of the condition of childhood to counter the myth of childhood as a 'golden age', for example, facts concerning child employment, poverty, children in care, and child abuse. Historical evidence on the development of childhood is also cited, to underline its socially constructed nature. There is a reference to research on childhood political socialisation in Franklin's chapter on political rights, research which suggests that the development of political knowledge and attitudes can be traced in three phases in childhood/adolescence.

Chapters by the other authors in Franklin's first book on children's rights bring forward some factual data relating to, for example, school behaviour, children in care, youthful offending, child employment and the enforcement of the child labour laws, child sexual behaviour and schoolgirl pregnancy, girls' educational performance and attitudes, and black children and young people in Britain (including their achievement and under-achievement at school and their employment situation). In the 1995 publication there are chapters on, *inter alia*, street children, children as carers, children's rights in the educational system, the rights of disabled children, and children's rights in their earlier years. Much of the thrust of the argument, however, would seem to depend on a particular interpretation of the evidence, on critical discussion of existing systems for dealing with children, and on the setting out of various arguments surrounding the question of children's rights. Freeman's (1983a) book, similarly, is supported by theoretical argument and by critical discussion of state systems which affect children's lives – when children offend, are victims of abuse and neglect, are actually in care, or are involved in divorce. Data of various kinds are offered on situations affecting children and the state's response.

Two main problems seem to arise with the empirical backing for the fourth perspective (or certainly the more radical version of it). One is the degree to which evidence on developmental growth through childhood tends to be ignored or de-emphasised, and the other is how evidence which is offered is perceived and interpreted. On the first point, the argument that children should have virtually the same rights and freedoms as adults clashes, not only with the world of 'common sense', but with the findings of developmental psychology on how children are different from adults (and older children from younger children) – in other words, on what growth through chronological age means. As Macdougall (1985) comments: 'Psychological research raises significant questions about the decision-making capacity of children – including adolescents' (p. 270). He quotes Teitelbaum (1980) who noted an apparent conflict between the need to socialise an individual, and the demand for individual autonomy: a healthy society will attempt to achieve both. That is, on the one hand children should learn cultural values and conform to social rules; at the same time they need to develop the capacity for choice and autonomous action. Failure to learn social values and rules means that the person cannot join the society; but a person without the capacity for choice cannot usefully participate in it. Freeman in his 1980 article commented:

Although psychological theories of personality and moral development which reflect universal developmental assumptions may be readily challenged as ignoring socio-cultural history and not squaring with anthropological evidence, it cannot be denied that a child matures through a succession of stages and gradually increases his competence, cognitive abilities and moral capacities. That children at an early stage are egocentric is generally acknowledged.

(Freeman 1980:18)

Freeman goes on to say that while a child of seven is arguably capable of exercising self-determination in relation to sleeping, eating or dressing, he or she is hardly able to decide on long-term life goals. Self-determination is a capacity that develops rather than a right to be expressed at any age.

The volume of psychological literature on the various aspects of child development – cognitive, emotional, social, moral and so on – bears witness to the fact that it is not just in that world of 'common sense' that some liberationists deplore, that childhood is seen as a special stage (or, to be more accurate, a series of special stages) where patterns of perception, thought, feeling and behaviour are to some extent different from those of adulthood. Central to human development is the process of learning – and it is in the early stages of life that learning is most rapid and influential. There is a very basic point here emphasised in social science, which is that human beings are not born, but learn to be, members of their society; can learn vastly different things in different cultures; and without human contact (for example, if reared by animals) are not recognisably human in a social sense. It is not suggested that the liberationists would dispute this, but they do perhaps overlook the obvious implications – that as children are not born ready-socialised, there must be some doubt about the validity of extending to them immediately the rights of full members of the society.

However, the children's rights authors correctly point to the absurdity, in a logical sense, of distinct ages or cut-off points below which certain rights cannot be exercised by young people, boundaries which vary for different activities and are constantly shifting (Franklin 1995). How can their powerful arguments here ever be reconciled with the findings of developmental psychology on how children are different? One possible way out of the impasse is to point out that evidence on growth and development through age relates to general or statistical truth rather than telling us anything categorically about any given individual. Of course some individuals below, say, the age of 18, the age of majority in Britain, will be more rational, competent, considerate, independent, and morally, socially and emotionally mature than some individuals above this age. But *in general* a person of 16 will have less of these qualities than a person of 20, a person of seven less than a person of 16, a person of two less than one of seven and so on. Chronological age tells us something about the *probability* that a person will possess a greater or lesser degree of certain qualities which we might subsume under the heading 'maturity'. Similarly, at the other end of the age spectrum, it is statistically the case that being over the age of, say, 75, indicates reduced mental and physical capacity relative to younger ages. The liberationists might respond that no one is proposing to disenfranchise all those who reach their 75th birthday. In reply, it may be said that it is emotionally more distressing and therefore politically more difficult – and indeed, perhaps more unjust – to deprive an individual permanently of something they have had all their adult life, than it is to defer (only) their receiving it initially.

An ironic twist to this issue of the evidence on development and difference is that Holt (1975), in what was perhaps an unintended lapse, does acknowledge the different and asocial nature of children in saying that they are 'animals and sensualists; to them, what *feels* good *is* good. They are self-absorbed and selfish. They have very little ability to put themselves in another person's shoes, to imagine how he feels ... They are barbarians, primitives ...' (p. 86); while Farson (1978) appears to become totally hoist on his own petard in admitting that children may not want rights and that great resistance to children's liberation would actually come from parents, teachers *and children themselves*. Does this not demolish the whole argument, for was not its central plank self-determination, giving children what they want? Furthermore, it is those who know children best who are anticipated to be the strongest opponents of their 'liberation' – why? Because their knowledge of children makes them sceptical of the underlying assumptions, perhaps.

Evidence on what children are like, then, which does not support the liberationist argument about their competence and similarity to adults, is ignored or not adequately incorporated into their viewpoint. There is an overlap between this problem of apparently ignoring contradictory evidence, and the interpretation of the evidence which *is* offered. Franklin (1986), for example, gives considerable space to the evidence for the historical specificity of childhood, drawing mainly on the work of Aries (1962), but also that of Plumb (1972), and refers to these authors again in his 1995 publication. It is argued that childhood emerged as a special phase in life only about 400 years ago in Europe; prior to this there was little differentiation of children from adults, and children were very much a part of the adult world. The relevance of this is to the argument that there is nothing immutable or 'natural' about childhood; it is the product of social definition. Children have been closer to the adult world in the past and therefore could be so again.

While Franklin (1986) does acknowledge that some criticism of Aries' work has been put forward, his own approach to Aries is still, it is suggested, too uncritical. For example, he does not fully take on board the arguments of Pollock (1983) who also studied childhood in earlier centuries, using contemporary sources. Pollock attacks the theory that there was no concept of childhood as a separate state before the sixteenth century, suggesting that there has been considerable homogeneity and continuity in methods of child discipline over time, and that there *was* a concept of childhood in the Middle Ages. She makes the useful point that the fact that past societies may have had a *different* concept of childhood does not mean they had *no* concept of it at all as a separate stage of life. And parents *were* concerned about their children's welfare and education, Pollock claims. She says of the historical thesis of authors like Aries (1962), de Mause (1976) and Stone (1977): 'The sources upon which the received view is founded are obviously suspect and are certainly not a sound enough base to warrant the grand theories which have been derived from them. Aspects of the thesis, especially the assertion that there was no concept of childhood, have been shown by later research to be completely unjustified' (Pollock 1983:52).

A second criticism of Franklin's use of Aries' work is that, while he traces the appearance of 'modern' childhood in Aries' account to the development of capitalism and industrialisation, he offers no clear reasoning as to how we could, in Aries' terms, now revert to a 'mediaeval' incorporation of the child into the world of the adult (if that is indeed what occurred in mediaeval times) while capitalism and industrialisation remain. That is, in so far as Aries is correct in saying that the perception and treatment of children changed from the sixteenth and seventeenth centuries on (though varying with place and social class), and in so far as such change reflected broader social and economic change (the need for a more prolonged period of education, most obviously), it is not apparent that childhood should or could now fundamentally change again, and if so, in what direction. The condition of modern childhood, as the child liberationist authors show so well, leaves much to be desired. But a more searching analysis is perhaps needed of *why* children came to be seen as in need of special treatment, and the relationship of such special treatment to other aspects of social and economic organisation. How realistic or desirable is it to revert to an apparently mediaeval or pre-capitalist concept of childhood without reinstating mediaeval society? This may be an unfair comment, but it seems that Franklin, or certainly Plumb (1972) whom he quotes, is in danger of falling for another type of 'golden age' myth – of childhood long past. (Yet Aries' picture of children in the past is not an altogether favourable one – treating children 'as little adults' is not identified with treating them well.)

An additional and more minor point is that the evidence which Franklin (1986) cites on the political socialisation of children does not clearly support his argument about the similarity of children to adults. This research (Greenstein 1974, Dawson, Prewett and Dawson 1977) shows, according to Franklin's own account, that the development of political knowledge and attitudes can be traced by a tripartite division into early childhood (5 to 9), late childhood (9 to 13) and adolescence (13 to 18). In early childhood, children view political authorities as benign – a more discriminating and critical attitude is developed in later childhood. There is a developmental process at work, in fact. In Franklin's later book (1995) the process of child development seems to be acknowledged; for example, Franklin notes the diversity of childhood across the age range 0 to 18, the growth of skills and so on, and comments: 'Consequently, the period between birth and adulthood is usually divided into four distinct periods; infancy, childhood, adolescence and early adulthood, with different needs, rights and responsibilities being judged appropriate for the different age groups' (p. 8). However, he does not draw from this the implication that children should therefore only gradually acquire rights and responsibilities.

Finally, the evidence offered on the poor treatment of children by society and the state is convincing in its own terms, but does not unequivocally point to a 'children's rights' type solution. It may also point to the need for higher standards of care, and the greater regulation and resourcing of such care, in the paternalistic mode, rather than to more child autonomy. The paternalists might agree, for example, with many of the criticisms put forward of the state in its dealings with children, but differ in what they would see as the solutions. The argument of the children's rights supporters is essentially that the treatment of children would be better if children had more power. While such an argument can certainly be convincingly put on the basis of the evidence, it is not the only conclusion to which the evidence on child mistreatment leads.

Problems with the implications for policy

The implications of this perspective for state policy in the child care field are characteristically not worked through in the same detail as in the three other perspectives discussed, partly because the focus of the fourth perspective is much broader than the other three – it is on the role of children in society in its entirety, and all of the laws, rules, policies and practices which affect children, rather than the more specific role of the state in making decisions and providing substitute care or family support where child welfare is at risk. Nevertheless, it is clear that the children's rights perspective has far-reaching implications for systems of substitute child care and the maintenance of child welfare, as well as for the social rules governing childhood more generally. As indicated earlier, the very existence of a guardianship role for the state, involving decisions about where children should live and who should have rights and responsibilities over them, is called into question by the insistence on children's autonomy and their right to decide for themselves. And some children's rights authors have devoted considerable energy to criticisms of the way the state uses its power in relation to children, as shown. Both the implications for the general treatment of children, and for the specific child care role of the state, will be referred to here.

It is clear that the goals of the child liberationist writers would require sweeping legal changes. For example, Holt's (1975) proposals for the rights which he advocates would require changes in the law to abolish age restrictions on the various activities which he discusses, voting, driving, full-time employment and so on. The implication of Holt's approach would seem to be that all existing statutes on child care and protection, consents, child education and labour, and various other age restrictions, would be swept away; nothing would be forced on children that could not be forced on adults; and children would make their own choices about their guardians. Franklin's (1986) book puts arguments for an extension of children's rights and autonomy in the various spheres discussed. For example, children should have the right to vote; should be freed from compulsory attendance at school; should have more say and better protection of their rights when in the state's care; and should have greater rights to sexual expression and sex education.

One obvious and pragmatic objection to the policy implications of the more radical children's rights position is that the changes intended are so drastic, and so out of line with child welfare as ordinarily understood, that they would inspire little support, and the proposals are therefore unrealistic. Unlike the pragmatic objections to the third value perspective, the argument here is not about cost (some of the proposed changes might well save money in the short-term – through closure of some schools and homes, fewer social workers and court cases, for example). The problem concerns the perceived legitimacy of the changes proposed – they, and the view of children on which they are based, conflict with the world of both common sense and psychological knowledge, and are likely, not just to lack widespread support, but to be actively resisted by those who believe that children do require special treatment, protection and control. It seems unlikely that any government would undertake such a programme of wholesale reform of childhood in the foreseeable future. There are doubts even as to whether children themselves would fully support the changes (as suggested by Farson, 1978, himself a liberationist writer).

Secondly, were such proposals in fact to be implemented wholesale, it may be argued that they would lead to a form of *laissez-faire* more extreme, and far more dangerous to children, than the *laissez-faire* embodied in the first perspective outlined in this book. It is submitted that such an absence of regulation of childhood would very probably lead to more exploitation of children, not less, and that the liberationists are naive in their understanding of the probable actual consequences of what they recommend, as opposed to the enjoyable freedom and excitement for children about which they fantasise. Take, for example, two of Holt's (1975) rights – the right to travel and the right to choose one's own guardian and where one should live. Holt's picture of what this would mean, drawn in the early 1970s, seemed naive by the late 1980s and 1990s, when more was known about violence to, and the sexual abuse of, children. Increasingly, parents and teachers have found it necessary to warn children against the dangers of contact with strangers (see, for example, Franks 1989), although it has to be acknowledged that much known abuse takes place within the family or at least from known adults. Research commissioned by the NSPCC found that 16 per cent of a sample of adults had experienced some sexual molestation during childhood (NSPCC 1995) (with apparently more than half of these abused by a known person). Both Holt's right to travel without adult supervision and to leave home to live elsewhere would place children vastly more at risk from abusers of various kinds, with children being enticed or coerced into various damaging or dangerous situations. Their problems could arise from other children (note instances of murders of younger children by older children, such as the James Bulger killing in 1992 and the Mary Bell case in the early 1970s), as well as from unscrupulous adults. In Holt's scenario it seems that neither parents nor the state would have any special right or power to intervene to protect children who would be reliant on the general law which protects adults from assault. Another obvious example would be the right to work. Holt envisages the right, but not the obligation, of children to work – children would still have the right to be maintained by their parents, and so need not work if they did not wish to. But the creation of an adult-type right to work for children would presumably mean the abolition of all legal restrictions on child employment and the ending of compulsory education. This would leave children formally unprotected from *de facto* coercion by parents and other caretakers who wished – or needed – them to work and bring in an income, rather than be economically dependent. It would, in fact, represent a reversion to the position of children in the early nineteenth century and before.

A third objection links the issue of parental coercion and manipulation, and that of how effectively children's rights could be implemented or enforced, given the physical and psychological vulnerability of children and their forced dependence on adults to at least some degree. Stating rights is one thing, but making them a reality, particularly where rights involve the imposition of duties on others for their realisation, is notoriously difficult, and could be particularly so in the case of children. A useful illustration is the proposed right to vote. How could such an independent right be exercised meaningfully, particularly with younger children? The child's right could simply become an additional right for parents. Admittedly both Holt (1975) and Franklin (1986) see the right to vote as only being exercised when interest is sufficiently developed to motivate the child to vote. Franklin states confidently: 'Of course two-year-olds will not vote, since they are likely to be interested in things other than politics at this age' (p. 41). The problem is that Holt and Franklin are talking about the absence of any lower age limit on a legal entitlement. Presumably if parents wished to place their child's name on the electoral register at birth, there would be no legal obstacle to prevent this. What, then, occurs when the parents arrive at the polling station with their baby or toddler? Are the returning officers to make a lightning judgement as to the genuineness of the child's interest? The right to one's own income provides another example. How could such a right be made effective in the light of the actual physical power of parents and other caretakers over children? Such an income could well be absorbed into general household income. It might be argued that this would be reasonable, given the parental duty to maintain, but such a situation does not correspond to the concept of an independent right to an income for children and young persons as a base for further independence, and highlights the difficulty of establishing the rights that the children's liberation authors seek, without, say, some protective system organised by the state.

This leads to the problems raised by the implications for state child care policy in particular. Holt sees children as choosing their own guardians, and being free to move away from parents and guardians whom they do not like. It seems clear that a developed machinery of state child care and child protection would not be compatible with the scenario of free and self-determining children whose status is like that of adults. This raises all sorts of difficulties. Babies and very small children are physically unable simply to get up and leave to live elsewhere. Older children *may* be physically able to run away but may be forcibly prevented (seven-year-old Maria Colwell, it may be noted, was locked up to prevent her running away), or may lack the psychological strength or the know-how about where to run to – indeed, who would provide the needed resources and alternative homes to enable them to leave? Children can also be emotionally attached to those who ill-treat them and may not wish to resolve their problem simply by leaving. A useful parallel would be the case of women who find difficulty in leaving violent relationships. Legally adult, they may nevertheless remain in or return to an abusive relationship because of an assortment of pressures, ties and obstacles (see, for example, Binney *et al.* 1981). It may, however, be argued that separation from a violent partner is made structurally difficult for women, and that in the general scenario envisaged by the child liberationist authors it would be made structurally easier for children who wanted to leave an abusive, neglectful or unhappy home to do so. Nevertheless, without a protective machinery backed by the force of the law, and an organised system of substitute homes, it seems highly likely that much abuse, neglect and poor child care could not be stopped. Again, children could be returned to the *laissez-faire* situation of the early nineteenth century.

So far, objections to the policy implications of the fourth perspective have been put forward mainly from the point of view of children's interests. Children, it has been argued, would suffer some of the worst aspects of a *laissez-faire* system if paternalism and protection were to withdraw completely, leaving them to the exercise of 'rights' which could in practice spell greater exploitation. However, another practical difficulty facing the implications for policy of the children's rights perspective, is the resistance likely to be encountered from those adults who would see their own interests as threatened by the prospect of children having more power but not necessarily commensurate responsibility. Parents, in particular, might feel that they would face an impossible task, of accountability without adequate control, and even an impossible life, with children who come and go, and do more or less as they please without regard for adult interests. Yet it is adults who are called upon to bring forward the necessary changes which would make children's rights a (legal) reality. Again, this seems unrealistic.

A final objection relates mainly to the abolition of compulsory education, but also to the general reduction of control over children, and concerns the need to prepare individuals for a place in the labour market and society in general. This concerns employment essential to the economy and in various public sector services and the professions; at a broader level, it concerns citizenship, socialised behaviour, and participation in a range of institutions. Without compulsory education at key stages in development, it may be argued, adequate preparation for crucial occupational and social roles would be lacking. There is a limit to the extent to which missing childhood education and learning can be compensated for later. With less control in general over children, socialisation in a broader sense could also be inadequate. To this, however, the liberationists might reply that children would become socialised more rapidly if they were allowed to exercise adult rights earlier. For example, Franklin (1986) says: 'If adults acknowledged young people's capacities to discuss political issues, those capacities would be nurtured, enhanced and, perhaps, show signs of even earlier or accelerated development' (p. 42), and in his 1995 publication he asks: 'If children are not allowed to make decisions because they have no experience of decision-making, how do they ever get started?' (p. 11).

Problems of rationale and underlying values

As indicated earlier, the rationale and underlying values of the fourth, children's rights perspective centre round a perception of children's similarity to adults and their primary need to be free of adult control, the artificiality of the construction of childhood, a pessimistic view of adults and their treatment of children, the concept of rights, and a negative view of both the family and the state. Certain problems surrounding the concept of childhood have already been considered in the section on empirical support, and some of the problems of the withdrawal of the state from children's lives in the section on implications for policy. This section will focus on the problems of advocating rights in isolation from duties and of emphasising rights to the point of neglecting other values, and will also consider further some difficulties in the concepts of childhood and adulthood held by the proponents of this perspective.

First, there are problems in the over-emphasis on rights to the neglect of duties. Writings by political philosophers on rights in general may be drawn on briefly here to show the inter-connected nature of rights and duties. For example, Arnold (1978) argues that the concepts of right and duty can only be elucidated by reference to each other and to the rest of the system. Right and duty are connected to each other as correlatives; they are two different ways of describing a single relation tying individuals together. Flathman (1976) makes a related point, suggesting the inextricable connection between rights and duties, in emphasising that the practice of rights is a social phenomenon which presupposes social arrangements. It seems that individuals only have rights in practice in so far as they exist as part of a set of arrangements and social rules. Ginsberg (1965) argues that rights and duties rest on the same ethical foundation, and like Flathman he stresses that rights and duties define social relations. The point here seems to be that the existence of rights logically entails the notion of a duty to respect those rights, with both the rights and the duties being recognised as part of an ordered social system. Rights are held against others in society (so others' rights are held against us). As has been indicated, the children's rights authors are ambiguous over the question of children's duties. How, in the society they envisage, would children learn, or be made, to respect the rights of others in exercising their own rights? Holt (1975) suggests that children should have the right to choose formally to live as full legally and financially responsible citizens. This would mean that children were fully accountable to their fellow citizens and the law for what they did; they could sue and be sued, be made bankrupt, and so on. However, children could also formally opt back again, to dependent status. Would this allow them to escape some of the consequences of their acts? Holt seems to be saying not, and he does also speak of the burden of citizenship, which can have serious personal consequences, and suggests that young people might be required to meet certain conditions before becoming independent citizens.

In general, though, the emphasis in this perspective is on the institution of rights for children rather than the imposition of duties. This raises the spectre of a section of the community – the least experienced section, by definition – acquiring considerable unaccountable power. Such an end-product seems both difficult to justify and socially dangerous. For example, unsupervised young people with guaranteed incomes and freedom not to attend school, work, or live anywhere in particular, would presumably have more opportunity to commit crimes; but could they then be sued and treated as criminally responsible in the same way as adults? Having made this criticism, it is worth bearing in mind that in the past traditional concepts of children and their role have emphasised child duties rather than rights (see, for example, Pinchbeck and Hewitt 1969, Middleton 1971) – the reverse of the child liberationist emphasis. It is perhaps therefore useful, up to a point, to correct this balance by now emphasising rights.

Another area of difficulty might be a strong focus on rights/duties to the exclusion of other values in human relationships such as love and affection. Freeman (1983a) does stress the importance of rights in enabling us, as Bandman (1973) puts it: '"to demand what is our due without having to grovel, plead or beg or to express gratitude when we are given our due, and to express indignation when what is our due is not forthcoming"' (p. 32 in Freeman), that is, a world without rights would be morally impoverished. However, Freeman goes on to acknowledge (drawing on Kleinig 1976) that 'there are other morally significant values, like love, friendship and compassion ... the absence of these from interpersonal transactions does diminish the moral quality of relationships' (p. 33). Freeman quotes Kleinig's comment that: 'A morality which has as its motivation merely the giving of what is due or what is conducive to the greatest all-round utility, is seriously defective' (p. 33 in Freeman). Freeman suggests that it may be an indictment of contemporary civilisation that rights have assumed such importance; this may reflect the inadequacy or absence of good moral relations (though adding that rights remain important, however benevolent the society).

An emphasis on rights reflects a somewhat legalistic view of human interactions as transactions governed by claims which can be substantiated by reference to legal or moral principle. It suggests a rational and abstract approach in which, in a sense, how relationships should be conducted can be 'worked out', and appears to owe more to a cognitive or cerebral approach to other persons than to the emotions and spontaneity. The relevance of such a legalistic, rational concept of interaction, within the intimate day-to-day relationships of the family in particular, is an issue that should be considered here. It may be argued that a precise calculus of rights and duties in such an intimate setting is not usually possible, and, if attempted, could result in destructive conflicts. It may be thought that relationships between parents and children are more appropriately construed in terms of love and care than rights and duties; the same might be said about relationships between children and adults in certain other roles such as teachers, residential care workers and child minders. However, a word of caution is needed – feminism has shown how, within the private world of the family, an ideology of love and care, often with a denial of the appropriateness of the concept of rights, has resulted in great injustice and exploitation for women (see, for example, Barrett and McIntosh 1991, Finch and Groves 1983, Delphy and Leonard 1992).

Finally, some further problems with the perception of childhood and adulthood can be touched on. It was argued in the section on empirical support that evidence of childhood as a separate developmental stage is ignored or inadequately incorporated into the argument, and that historical evidence on children in earlier times is wrongly interpreted. It is suggested here that another problem with the liberationists' approach to childhood is that, while in a sense they argue for a continuity between childhood and adulthood (for example, no clear cut-off points are definable or acceptable), in another sense they overlook such continuity. One example is the contrast between the positive, optimistic concept of what human beings as children are like and could be like, given more freedom, and the rather negative, cynical view of the state of adulthood which these children will eventually reach. Perhaps, however, it is assumed that freer children would in time become nicer adults than the adults currently existing. Linked with this question of continuity is the tendency of the liberationists, at least implicitly, to perceive childhood's absence of rights and freedoms as permanent. This may be partly why the link with discrimination by race and gender is made. Franklin (1986) in fact states that 'a child, even if foolish enough to desire it, cannot grow old prematurely. In this way exclusion is a "permanent" exclusion, since *all* children are denied rights simply because they are children and can acquire them only when they cease to be children' (p. 25). Later he states the position rather more heavily, saying that the argument that exclusion is temporary: 'rests on a confusion between particular children and children as a social group' (1995:12). Yet from the point of view of the individual person, childhood with its special status is *not* permanent. Individuals only exceptionally find it possible to pass from one racial category or one gender category to another, and therefore racial or gender-based disadvantage must be considered permanent for individuals unless and until some external change occurs. But – barring premature death – all individuals grow from childhood to adulthood and therefore move on from the deprivation of rights and the special status to which the child liberationists object, gradually acquiring the freedoms of adults. In this sense the 'disadvantages' of childhood are different from, and, it may be argued, more justified than, the disadavantages of other groupings. The disadvantages are intentional and directed to a different purpose – socialisation, that is, learning to be adult.

The perspective in practice

As the child liberation/rights perspective is still not as widely accepted within the field of child care law and policy as state paternalism, the defence of the family, or even *laissez-faire*, and is also a much more recent appearance on the child care scene than the other perspectives, it is less easy to point to particular times where this perspective may be said to have been in the ascendant. However, the perspective has been gathering strength in policy and practice in the 1980s and 1990s, and particular aspects of policy which reflect a children's rights view, broadly defined, can be identified in certain countries. This 'in practice' section will look to some other countries and Britain for evidence of a rights approach in practice, in the period from the 1970s to the 1990s.

Norway is one country where the children's rights viewpoint has been taken seriously to the extent that, since 1981, a barneombudet – an ombudsperson or commissioner specifically for children – has been employed, as an independent official but part of the machinery of government. This was the first such government post in the world, and was seen as providing an independent public spokesperson to protect the interests of children and young people (up to the age of majority – 18) (See Children's Legal Centre 1984, Norway Information 1987, Flekkoy 1985, 1988–89, 1991, 1995, Franklin 1989, Philpot 1996). The commissioner's responsibility is to promote children's interests in the private and public sectors and to follow up the development of the conditions under which children grow up. The office deals with individual cases but does not have the power to *decide* cases or change official decisions. The office can be contacted directly, in writing or by telephone, by children or parents, or by groups, with particular times set aside when only children may telephone.

In 1991 the first barneombudet (1981–89), Malfrid Flekkoy, published an account of her experience in office (Flekkoy 1991), and this provides a valuable source on the office in action during the 1980s. The general tone of the assessment is (perhaps predictably) positive. A later article by Philpot (1996) also gives a positive picture of the office's achievements, despite the lack of legal power to overturn decisions; the Barneombudet is: 'backed only by his moral authority, independence, and his command of information and statistics' (p. 23).

Manifestations of the children's rights viewpoint can be found in a number of other countries in recent years (see Flekkoy 1991, Franklin 1995, for accounts of some recent developments). For example, in Sweden (see Children's Legal Centre 1984, Radda Barnen 1987, Franklin 1989) there was a type of children's ombudsperson or barnombudsmannen in existence from 1973, but the system was different from Norway in that the ombudsperson was employed by a voluntary organisation, *Radda Barnen* (Save the Children). From 1993, however, a barnombudsmannen or commissioner for children was established within the Swedish government, this being triggered by the United Nations Convention on the Rights of the Child (also see below). Among other tasks the commissioner was to supervise compliance with the Convention, monitoring the compatibility of government measures with the country's commitments under the Convention. Children were enabled to approach the office (including via a freephone service) if they believed their rights were being violated. The commissioner was to employ a children's perspective, giving chilren a voice, for example, promoting their interests in relation to local and other authorities, and would produce an annual report. However, as in Norway, there were no powers of intervention in individual cases. The role was seen more as one of influencing attitudes. (Swedish Ministry of Health and Social Affairs 1993). In Costa Rica a similar office, the *El Defensor de la Infancia* was established in 1987; this is partly funded by UNICEF

(Flekkoy 1991). In South Australia a Children's Interests Bureau was established in 1983, and in (former) West Germany a Commission for Children's Concerns was set up in 1988. There are a variety of other initiatives at local and national levels (Flekkoy 1991). The idea of an ombudsperson for children seems to be quite widely supported.

In Canada, a Charter of Rights and Freedoms in 1982 gave rise to debate as to whether or not children should be considered 'citizens' under the Charter and therefore be allowed rights such as the franchise. It should be noted that children's voting has been a subject of serious public debate in Canada. Earlier Canadian developments included the office of Official Guardian for children, established in Ontario since 1881. From 1949 the guardian was responsible for investigating arrangements for children in divorce and separation. In British Columbia, family advocates were attached to family courts, and intervened as the child's counsel where the court was of the opinion that the child required representation. The advocates ensured that children had representation in matters affecting their interests or welfare; and one result of their presence was that many cases were settled without the need for a court hearing. The Alberta Child Welfare Act 1984 also provided for separate representation of the child in court. Several statutes in Canada allowed courts discretion in determining the appropriateness of a child's testimony, and a statute in Quebec required that children be given an opportunity to be heard (see below for further discussion of child witnesses) (for Canada up to the mid-1980s, see Levitt and Wharf 1985, Children's Legal Centre 1984).

In New Zealand a Royal Commission in 1986 explored the possibility of lowering the voting age to 16 (Franklin 1989a), and in 1989 a commissioner for children was appointed, close to the Norwegian model (Rickford 1991, Flekkoy 1991).

Another manifestation of the children's rights perspective in practice is the United Nations Convention on the Rights of the Child. Passed in 1989, the Convention's status is an international legal instrument which is more binding than a Declaration, although not enforceable in the courts in the way that the European Convention on Human Rights is (see Byrne 1989–90, Newell 1991). As Newell (1991) says: 'Until the Convention on the Rights of the Child was adopted in 1989, no binding international instrument existed bringing together states' obligations to children.' (p. xv). The Convention was the product of 10 years of negotiation, and contains 54 articles which cover, for example, rights to do with life, freedom of religion and privacy; those requiring protective measures; those concerning civil status such as nationality; those concerning development and welfare, including the right to a reasonable standard of living, health, education and leisure; rights of children in special circumstances including minority children; and procedural considerations, including the setting up of a Committee on the Rights of the Child to monitor implementation and offer advice. UNICEF has divided the rights into four broad categories: survival rights, development rights, protection rights, and participation rights (Flekkoy 1991). (For the Convention, see also Byrne 1989, Hadjipateras 1990, Flekkoy 1991, Children's Rights Development Unit 1994, and Franklin 1995, especially chapter by Freeman.) An emphasis on both welfare and autonomy, on both protection and liberation, can be found in the Convention's provisions. For example, on the protectionist side, there are articles on protection from abuse, on health, education, social security and standard of living. But there is a liberationist bent also. For example, the innovatory Article 12 provides that children be given the right to express their views freely in all matters affecting them (subject to age and maturity), and that in judicial and administrative proceedings affecting them, children shall be provided with the opportunity to be heard. Newell (1991) comments that this article: 'is the cornerstone of the Convention's insistence that children must not be treated as silent objects of concern, but as people with their own views and feelings which must be taken seriously' (p. 44), and Freeman (1995) that the article is the first international document: 'to state explicitly that children have a right to have a say in processes affecting their lives' (p. 73). On the Convention in general, Newell (1991) argues that it is: 'one instrument that can help us all – governments, authorities, organisations and individuals – to improve the status of children, and to ensure that they are treated seriously and accorded rights as people.' (p. xiii) This is clearly a liberationist description.

In late 1991 the Convention was ratified by the United Kingdom (which meant that the government committed itself to implementation), with a progress report made slightly over two years later (February 1994). But the government's commitment to the Convention is, as Franklin (1995) says, 'equivocal' (p. 17). Subsequent monitoring of the UK's performance by the UN Committee on the Rights of the Child gave a less than satisfactory picture. In January 1995 the UK government was required to appear before the Committee to report on progress on implementation of the Convention. As Lansdown (1995a) comments: 'The Committee's highly critical findings represent a powerful indictment of the level of commitment this Government has made to children' (p. 2). On Article 4 – a general article concerned with implementation – concern was expressed that insufficient resources had been allocated and that no mechanisms existed to assess the impact of government policies on children. Another area of criticism concerned the extent of child poverty in the UK. Article 26 sets out the right to social security benefits, and 27 the right to an adequate standard of living, referring to material assistance and support programmes. The Committee queried whether benefit levels were adequate, and addressed the increase in young people living on the streets and the withdrawal of income support rights to 16- and 17-year-olds (Lansdown 1995a). The Committee was also critical of government proposals to build secure training centres for 12- to 14-year-old persistent offenders (see below), of the treatment of children as young as 10 under emergency powers in Northern Ireland, and of the non-prohibition of physical punishment in private schools and in the home (*Guardian*, 28 January 1995, see also below). According to Lansdown (1995a), government was at this point refusing to debate or to disseminate the Committee's findings (see also Lansdown 1995b). For the UK's performance under the Convention, see the Children's Rights Development Unit's critical report (1994) *The UK Agenda for Children*. This reviews the Convention's implications for the UK and the UK's shortcomings. The report comments: 'There has been no attempt to place Government policy as it affects children (and most of it does) within the context of the Convention' (p. xi). The Children's Rights Development Unit, set up in 1992 to promote the Convention in the UK, completed its first programme of work in 1995, and was then funded for a further three years (*Representing Children* 1995).

Concern remains, therefore, that the Convention may not in fact deliver what it appears to promise, although the view is also taken that the Convention is not a 'paper tiger' (van Bueren, quoted by Byrne 1989 and by Byrne 1989–90). Presumably the force of the Convention as a binding international instrument can be used as a powerful means of moral pressure on government by those organisations concerned to further children's rights. As Voegeli and Willenbacher comment on the rights in the Convention (Voegeli and Willenbacher 1993): 'Although these rights have more of the character of political goals and not of immediately justiciable rights and although they are subject to the financial capacity of the state, nevertheless they set the standard against which national family policies and the corresponding body of relevant law are to be measured' (p. 561). And Flekkoy (1991) argues that, even in countries where there is a distrust of legislation: 'the respect for children and the knowledge of children's needs upon which it [the Convention] is built should have some impact, since it can be used as a political platform, help change attitudes, and illuminate the need for child advocacy' (p. 219).

To turn to other fields, in England and Wales the children's rights perspective in child care cases has been expressed in a greater concern for the child's own feelings and views, and increasingly so in the late 1980s and 1990s. As far back as the mid-1970s, however, the 1975 Children Act contained two sections relating to the child's own 'wishes and feelings'. The first was Section 3, which stipulated that in adoption decisions, while first consideration should be given to the need to safeguard and promote the child's welfare, the court or agency should 'as far as practicable ascertain the wishes and feelings of the child regarding the decision and give due consideration to them, having regard to his age and understanding'. The second was Section 59, which embodied a similar provision for decisions relating to children in local authority care. (However, the duty could be waived when there was a need to protect members of the public.) This provision was re-enacted in the 1980 Child Care Act as Section 18 (1). The 1975 Act also made provisions for children in certain cases to be represented in court separately from their parents if there was thought to be a conflict of interests (Sections 64–66). This was achieved by the creation of independent guardians *ad litem*, court-appointed short-term social workers, to represent the child's interests and instruct the child's solicitor.

The 1989 Children Act (see Fox Harding 1991, Lyon and Parton 1995) strengthened the provision regarding welfare, in that the child's welfare now became the *paramount* consideration in court cases relating to a child's upbringing. This was embodied in Section 1, which set out a 'welfare checklist' (Section 1(3)) to guide the court's decisions, in which 'wishes and feelings' were placed at the top. The wishes and feelings of the child were to be ascertained and duly considered in court and local authority decisions about children in proceedings or children being 'looked after' (i.e. in care or accommodation), although the wishes and feelings of parents or anyone else with parental responsibility also had to be ascertained (Section 22). Local authorities also had to inform children of plans for their placement. In reviews of children in care or accommodation the local authority had to discover the child's view and notify him or her of the result of the review (Section 26). Normally the child should attend reviews and case conferences according to Department of Health guidance (1988b). The day-to-day running of children's homes should take account of children's wishes. Such provisions are consonant with a moderate child liberationist position which emphasises that children themselves have a point of view which ought to be formally considered, although it is not necessarily the decisive factor and it may be argued that local authorities still did not enable young people to participate enough (see, for example, Sinclair 1992).

The 1989 Children Act also strengthened the separate representation provisions of the 1975 Act by extending guardians *ad litem* to more categories of children. Guardians were to be appointed routinely in care and emergency protection proceedings, without the need to establish a conflict of interest between parent and child, unless the court were satisfied that it was *not* necessary to appoint a guardian (Section 41); while if guardian and child could not agree, the child's solicitor was to take instructions from the child. The concept of a separate advocate for the child – as distinct from the parents or the local authority – again rests on the notion of the child as an individual, a subject, with separate claims, wishes and feelings which ought to be heard. Guardians were indeed routinely appointed in these proceedings, but the child's position in private law proceedings (cases of separation, divorce and so on) was less fortunate, as children are not independently represented there. This led Wyld (1992) to comment: 'Children are not usually parties to private law proceedings. This contrasts with care and other public law proceedings where the child is a party and is represented by a solicitor in partnership with a guardian *ad litem* … [but] For the majority of children in private law proceedings the appointment of a court welfare officer represents the only opportunity for their voices to be heard. However, there is no requirement for court welfare officers to provide evidence of the child's wishes and feelings.' (p. 18). (The child may also be offered representation by the Official Solicitor.) It may therefore be argued that representation of children's wishes in proceedings affecting them has not been carried far enough (see also Freeman 1992c).

Another provision of the 1989 Children Act which may be mentioned in this context is Section 26, which placed a new duty on local authorities to 'establish a procedure for considering any representations made to them', by a child, the child's parents, a person with parental responsibility or a foster parent, about the authority's functions in accommodation and support of children and families – in other words, a complaints procedure for child care. (The 1984 Short Committee Report, House of Commons 1984, had recommended more rights for children *in* care, and the 1987 White Paper on child care law had recommended a complaints procedure for such children.) The child had to be consulted and notified of the outcome of the investigation and consequent action. The question here, however, is how far the system is being used by children as opposed to other parties. In this context of complaints, it may be noted that by late 1994, the possibility was also opening up of children suing the local authority for negligence (*Guardian*, 11 October 1994).

A new departure in a children's rights direction was that under Schedule 2 of the Act a child in care or accommodation had a right to an advocate or independent visitor (with the child's consent). Where children had infrequent communication with their parents or had not been visited for 12 months, such a person was to be appointed to visit, advise and befriend them if this would be in their best interests. Ogden (1995), describing this as: 'One of the most enlightened reforms to emerge from the Children Act' (p. 21), noted, however, that not all local authorities had set schemes up by 1995. At least one authority piloted a scheme for an independent advocate for children at case conferences (Scutt and Hoyland 1995). A related development in local authority practice, although not one specifically deriving from the Children Act, was the appointment of children's rights officers in a number of local authorities, beginning with Leicestershire in 1987. Partly this step derived from dissatisfaction with existing complaints procedures (Lindsay 1988, 1989). Children's rights officers: 'address the needs of children and young people in the care of a local authority' (Ellis and Franklin 1995:89). By 1993 there were 15 and by the mid-1990s about 30 such officers, and an association was formed in 1992 (National Children's Bureau 1992).

A number of other Children Act provisions are relevant to the notion of children's rights. The fact that the child's racial origins, religion, cultural and linguistic background were important factors which the local authority must take into account in decision-taking (Section 22), may be seen as an element in the support of children's rights, in that these factors uphold the child's own identity. Also, children were no longer subject to care proceedings for non-attendance at school; there was thus a reduction in compulsion, although an education supervision order could be made in such cases (Section 36). Further, a contact order under Section 8 allowed a child to have contact with a named person rather than the other way round; a family assistance order under Section 16 could be made in favour of the child; and adopted children might use the adoption contact register to trace their original family under Section 88 and Schedule 10 (Lyon and Parton 1995).

More significantly, under the 1989 Act children could take certain legal actions themselves – for example, to challenge an emergency protection order (Section 45), seek an order on parental contact when in care (Section 34), seek to discharge a care order (Section 34), challenge the unmarried father's rights – that is, a parental responsibility order or agreement (Section 4), or seek a Section 8 order concerning residence, contact, specific issues or prohibited steps (Section 10). The child had to ask for leave to apply to the court, and a criterion of sufficient understanding applied.

This ability of children to initiate legal action on their own behalf was an area of significant development in the early 1990s after the Children Act came into force in October 1991, and received a good deal of publicity. The provisions were used by children and young people in late 1992 and early 1993 to a perhaps unexpected degree (see Harding 1993). The cases involved adolescents applying for Section 8 orders to redefine their living arrangements – this being sometimes misrepresented by the press as children 'divorcing' their parents (in fact parental responsibility is retained after a Section 8 order). Cases included young people seeking to live with their grandparents, with the non-custodial or non-resident parent, with foster parents, or, in one case, with the girl's boyfriend and his parents (Harding 1993). It should be noted that the children had to jump through a considerable number of hoops in attempting to achieve their desired outcome. They had to get the support of a solicitor and convince a legal aid board that they might have a case; to obtain leave from the court to apply, the granting of this being decided on their age and understanding; and then to convince the court of the merits of their case.

Despite these barriers, there was some controversy over this use of the Act, and over the exact meaning and intentions of the legislation. There was concern at possible abuse of the provisions, at the possibility of children being given more responsibility than was good for them, and about the young age of some of the children involved (down to age 11). There were reservations about the use of the law, rather than softer means such as family conciliation, to resolve troubled family relationships (see Rickford 1992, *Community Care* 19 November 1992, Murray 1992, Phillips 1993). Here the issue connects with wider arguments about the use of the law as a blunt instrument in dealing with close relationships, and the possible oppressiveness of such relationships when unregulated by the law (see, for example, Parkinson 1993). While Dame Margaret Booth, the Chair of the Children Act Advisory Committee, said in 1992: 'once the provisions are there, you expect them to be used. The philosophy of the Act is that the voice of the child is heard' (Dyer 1992), the Committee's first annual report commented that the court should disregard the child's wishes: 'if his future welfare appears to diverge from them; it has to be a decision of the court and not the child' (Children Act Advisory Committee 1992–3:32). This is clearly a protectionist rather than a liberationist understanding of children's rights in this context. For further comment on these cases, see Lyon and Parton (1995). They make the distinction between conferring rights on children and conferring merely strong claims for the child's voice to be heard, and discuss the strong role of the judiciary here.

Even so, it may be argued that children's rights in this sphere of legal action *were* significantly extended by the Act, and that children were merely making use of powers quite clearly spelled out there. However, in February 1993 a practice direction from Judge Stephen Brown (with the concurrence of the Lord Chancellor) laid down that in future all such applications should be transferred to the High Court from the magistrates' courts, as raising issues more appropriate for determination in the former (*Family Law Reports* 1993, Vol. 1). The complexity and formality of a High Court application would tend to be a deterrent to such actions, and indeed there were few further such cases from 1993 (see Lyon and Parton 1995).

Other provisions of the Children Act relating to children as witnesses in court, consents and punishment will be discussed below. Generally it may be argued that the Children Act does widen children's rights in the liberationist, autonomy sense quite considerably; indeed it has been seen as setting out a philosophy of empowerment for children (Hodgson 1990). Frost and Stein (1990) consider that the children's rights lobby was influential in the formation of the Act, this lobby's position having been strengthened by the 'Gillick judgement' on consent to medical treatment of 1986, this case to be discussed below. However, Lyon and Parton (1995) note: 'While various provisions and elements of the Children Act do appear to take children's rights more seriously and provide new opportunities for advancing the wishes, autonomy and independent actions of children and young people, this is very qualified' (p. 53). Certainly, there are also other elements in the Children Act which lead in different directions from children's rights (see Fox Harding 1991 and Chapter 7 here).

Another development has been the giving of greater weight to what children say, first, in facilitating, and listening more carefully to, their disclosures of abuse generally; and secondly, in allocating a larger role to children's evidence when they are witnesses in court in abuse cases, be these criminal cases or civil (care) proceedings. With regard to civil proceedings, where the focus is on the child's interests rather than on the public interest in prosecuting the accused and establishing guilt or innocence, the Children Act 1989 allowed civil courts to accept unsworn evidence from young children in some circumstances, and hearsay evidence of abuse (Section 96). This could include video-taped interviews. With regard to criminal prosecutions, in 1987 the Home Secretary announced his intention to change the law so that a conviction could be obtained on the unsworn and uncorroborated evidence of a child (under 14), something which had not been possible before. Child witnesses were also to be enabled to give their evidence by live video link in some cases rather than actually in the courtroom. These changes were enacted in the Criminal Justice Act 1988, although there was debate about the age of child accepted as old enough to testify. In 1989 a Home Office Advisory Group, the Pigot Committee on Video Evidence (Home Office 1989), recommended that children in general be assumed competent witnesses, but that they should not have to undergo the trauma of giving evidence and being subjected to cross-examination in court. Instead, there should be an informal pre-trial hearing in chambers, and video tapes of this and the initial interview with the child should be accepted as evidence (O'Hara 1990, Fielding and Conroy 1991, Levy 1994a).

The ensuing Criminal Justice Act of 1991, implemented in 1992, allowed children under 14 to give unsworn evidence in criminal proceedings and to be seen as competent witnesses on the same basis as adults. It allowed video recordings to be accepted for the child's evidence in chief, but the child would still have to come into court for cross-examination. This can be a great ordeal for the child (see Levy 1994a, 1994b, Waller 1995). One director of social services commented on the number of cases where: 'the courts have seen prosecutions for child abuse, generally judged as sound, collapse because of the breakdown of children in the witness box faced by the sight of their abusers or under cross-examination by defence counsel' (Waller 1995). And in a similar vein, Levy (1994b) says: 'children who may have experienced physical or sexual abuse are forced to relive it in a daunting public setting, recounting embarassing and painful details, often in the face of defence suggestions that they made up the incident'; and 'One does not need to know of instances of child witnesses breaking down in tears, vomiting, having asthma attacks and, in at least one case, an epileptic fit to realise that there is an urgent need to take children out of the courtroom' (1994a). Levy (1994b) points to the existence of better systems for the child in other countries (for the more child-sensitive system in Canada see Wade 1993, for a number of other countries see Scott 1989).

There is also the question of how far judges are prepared to agree to the use of the video links and tapes which are now allowed by the law. Research by Plotnikoff and Woolfson (reported in *Guardian*, 19 April 1994, 25 May 1994, Plotnikoff and Woolfson 1995, see also Tissier 1995) reported that the reforms were threatened by a backlash from judges and prosecuting counsels. There was some feeling among prosecutors that the child's evidence when given in person would have a greater impact on the jury, and screens rather than video links continued to be used. There was also a concern about the large number of taped interviews being carried out but not leading to proceedings (see, for example, Tissier 1995, Waller 1995, reporting Social Services Inspectorate research).

Here 'treating the child as an adult' – for example, making no allowance for children's age and vulnerability in hostile cross-examining – would seem to work against children's rights in another sense, that is the right to have their experiences and disclosures treated sensitively and given due weight, to have their testimony facilitated. To quote Levy (1994a) again: 'It is ironic that in circumstances where the fact of childhood needs more, not less, recognition, the agenda, often politically motivated, is geared towards equating the child with the fully responsible adult.' The issue highlights how making *no* distinction between children and adults, as the more extreme child liberationist argument would seem to advocate, can be damaging to children.

Enhanced autonomy for children is identifiable in the area of consents – to medical examination and treatment, and to have sex. A celebrated case concerned the campaign of Victoria Gillick in the early 1980s to prevent her own children under 16 receiving advice or treatment relating to contraception and abortion without her consent as a parent. As her health authority was unable to give her the assurances she sought (a position supported by existing government guidance – Department of Health and Social Security 1974), she pursued her campaign through the courts (Gillick v. West Norfolk and Wisbech Area Health Authority (1986) 1 A.C. 112; Gillick v. West Norfolk and Wisbech Area Health Authority & DHSS, HL (1986)). There were several legal stages, but while the Court of Appeal decision went in Gillick's favour, this was reversed in the House of Lords in 1986. That is, medical discretion to advise or treat children without parental consent was *upheld*, subject to the criterion of sufficient understanding in the child, which became known as 'Gillick competence'. Thus the judgement which bears Gillick's name established the exact opposite of what she had wished – children did indeed have the right to consent to contraception and abortion, within certain limits. (For a discussion of the implications of this case, see, for example, Bainham 1993.)

This area of law seems to be a little hazier, however, where the right to *refuse* treatment is concerned, particularly where this is essential or life-saving. Questions arise concerning the true competence of children to make decisions about medical treatment and their own long-term interests (see Dobson 1995). In the case of a 16-year-old girl with anorexia in 1992 (re:W. (1992) 3 W.L.R. 758), the court found that treatment could be ordered for an under-18-year-old against her will, despite her competence to decide – in this case because her life was at risk. This was a controversial decision which might be seen to conflict with the spirit of 'Gillick' (and indeed the Children Act) (see, for example, *Community Care* 9 July 1992, *Social Work Today* 16 July 1992, Freeman 1993, who sees the distinction between consenting *to* treatment and refusing it as 'illogical', p. 19; also *Community Care Supplement* on mental illness, 30 April 1994; and on consents to health care for children in general Montgomery 1993).

It can also be noted in this context that the Children Act upheld the right of the child with 'sufficient understanding' to refuse a medical examination which might otherwise be ordered as part of an emergency protection order, child assessment order, interim care order or supervision order (under Sections 44, 43, 38, and Schedule 3). This is consistent with 'Gillick' – an enhancement of the child's ability to decide what is done to her or his own body.

Finally on consents, the age of homosexual consent was lowered from 21 to 18 years by Parliament in 1994 (having been at 21 since private consenting homosexual acts were legalised in 1967, although there had been pressure to align it with the age of heterosexual consent at 16). There has also been fairly long standing debate about the age for heterosexual consent itself. This was raised from 13 to 16 in 1885, but has been reconsidered on a number of occasions since. It may be questioned why there should be a differential in age for different types of sexuality, but there is also the more fundamental question of why there should be a minimum age for consenting to sexual intercourse at all (see, for example, Davies 1980). Arguments supporting a minimum age for sex may be put in terms of protecting children from abuse: it is not necessary to enter into disputes about consent in abuse cases if all sexual acts with a minor child are illegal. Here the pure liberationist position which opposes an age of consent is apparently at odds with a concern for child protection.

Another area of debate concerns moves towards ending corporal or (the more recent term) physical punishment for children in an increasing number of settings. Such punishment was made illegal in state (but not private) schools in Britain in 1986. Regulations to the Children Act (Department of Health 1991c) provided for the prohibition of physical punishment in residential and foster care settings (this being already the practice in some local authorities prior to this) and in day nurseries and playgroups. The one major exclusion here concerned children with registered childminders, but many authorities also had policies excluding physical punishment in this setting. The issue was, however, tested in the High Court in 1994 when a registered childminder in Sutton wished to uphold her right to smack a child with parental consent, despite the local authority's policy prohibiting this which led them to refuse to register her. The court decision went in her favour (London Borough of Sutton v. Davis, Family Division (Wilson J) 16 March 1994, *Adoption and Fostering* 1994, Haynes *et al.* 1994) and a subsequent circular from the Department of Health upheld this right to smack with parental consent (*Community Care* 8–14 December 1994,

Guardian 3 December 1994), despite its being anomalous in the light of rules covering other forms of regulated day care. However, local authorities apparently found ways of bypassing the government guidelines, for example, by requiring childminders to apply for a special exemption (*Community Care* 16–22 March 1995). There has also been pressure to outlaw physical punishment by parents and parent substitutes (as has been done in some Scandanavian countries and Austria) but this remain legal in Britain at the time of writing (1996).

Arguments on this issue have revolved around the effectiveness or ineffectiveness of physical and other punishments as forms of control, the risk of moderate physical punishment escalating into abuse (and, indeed, the question of whether these two can ever be satisfactorily distinguished), the role models set for children, and the more fundamental question of why it should be legal to 'assault' children when it is not legal to do the same to adults (see, for example, Brown 1994). Freeman (1995) comments: 'nothing is a clearer statement of the position that children occupy in society, a clearer badge of childhood, than the fact that children alone, of all people in society, can be hit with impunity. There is probably no more significant step that could be taken to advance both the status and the protection of children than to outlaw the practice of physical punishment' (p. 76). The main group campaigning against all physical punishment is EPOCH who have publicised the issue extensively (see, for example, Newell 1989a, 1989b). It is argued that the criminalising of all physical punishment would not necessarily lead to prosecution in every case, but would be a clear statement of the unacceptability of such treatment of children (see, for example, Rickford 1993, reporting Newell 1993). The UN Committee on the Convention on children's rights took the stance that all physical punishment of children should be banned (Newell 1994). Counter-arguments to the position have also been publicly aired – in addition to the childminding case cited above, Prince Charles spoke in favour of smacking children in 1994 (Pilkington 1994). It seems then, that while the issue of total prohibition of physical punishment of children is currently unresolved in the British context, the general trend is definitely in that direction. (For this issue see also Barton and Moss 1994.)

It may be appropriate in the context of child punishment to mention the issue of the treatment of young offenders in relation to children's rights. In March 1994 the High Court ruled that in future it should be possible to convict 10- to 14-year-olds of an offence without proof that the young offenders knew their crimes to be seriously wrong (Pilkington 1994, Levy 1994b). Previously the long standing rule was that it had to be positively shown that offenders of this age understood a distinction between 'right and wrong' before a conviction could be obtained, and this had been the case at the time of the notorious child murder case of the early 1990s in which two 10 year olds (11 at the time of the trial) were tried in 1993 for the murder of two-year-old James Bulger. They were convicted, but their knowledge that their offence was wrong had to be demonstrated (Pilkington 1994). Under the subsequent ruling such knowledge would be presumed. This is a move towards treating young offenders more like adults, but not, it may be argued, a move in those children's interests.

The Bulger case also sparked some debate about the age of criminal responsibility in Britain, which has been 10 since the Children and Young Persons Act 1963 raised it from 8 (a clause to raise it further to 14 in the 1969 similarly named Act was never implemented). Pilkington (1994) points out that the two boys in the Bulger case were the first 10/11-year-olds to be convicted of murder for almost 250 years, and that in most European countries children of this age could not have been prosecuted. Levy (1994b) provides a long list of countries where the age of criminal responsibility is higher than in Britain (up to 18 in Romania). In commenting on the Bulger trial, Pilkington (1994) poses a fundamental, if over-polarised question: 'do children exist in a special state, qualitatively different from adulthood, in which they merit unique status and treatment? Or are they small adults, as capable of evil as any grown-up and who deserve to be treated with equal severity?' (see also, Levy 1994b).

Another change of interest in this context is the government's provision in the Criminal Justice and Public Order Act 1994 for particularly tough secure training units for 12- to 14-year-old offenders (Pilkington 1994, Levy 1994b). Again this is a move to meting out more 'adult' treatment but in a way that is disadvantaging to young people. The UN Committee on the children's rights Convention had deplored the idea (*Guardian* 28 January 1995). Finally on this issue, the Criminal Justice and Public Order Act allowed the press to publish details and photographs of dangerous young absconders under certain conditions (Clarkson and Thomas 1995). Thus the traditional right of young offenders to have their privacy safeguarded (also reinforced by the UN Convention) was eroded – again illustrating that 'adultisation' of the treatment of children can be disadvantageous to them; indeed Clarkson and Thomas (1995) describe this measure as 'another *retreat* from respecting children's rights' (my italics).

In another field, the formation of organisations like the National Association of Young People in Care (NAYPIC), and a Voice for the Child in Care, reflected an emphasis on the child's rights in the more positive sense of participation and right to a say. NAYPIC was set up in 1979 as an independent organisation to support local care groups and take up issues at a national level. It originated in a National Children's Bureau initiative of the late 1970s, the 'Who Cares?' project, which helped young people in care to meet nationally as well as starting local 'Who Cares' or self-advocacy groups (NAYPIC 1983, see also Page and Clark 1977, Stein 1983). NAYPIC saw itself as a consumer group, the voice of young people in care. Another organisation, called A Voice for the Child in Care, described itself as a network of people concerned about children in care; it supported, for example, the idea of an independent spokesperson or advocate for the child (A Voice for the Child in Care 1982) and was later involved in such schemes. The establishment of the Children's Legal Centre in 1979, in the International Year of the Child, and the publication of its journal *Childright*, have already been mentioned as an expression of the children's rights perspective. According to Franklin (1995) the Centre was influential in: 'restructuring the discourse about children's rights by advocating children's rights to participate in the decision-making processes and institutions which influence and affect their lives' (p. 4). Another relevant pressure group was Justice for Children, founded in 1978 to bring about reforms in the juvenile justice system. This group has been mentioned in connection with the *laissez-faire* perspective, but in certain respects may be identified with a children's rights viewpoint. That is, it included among its aims the protection of the rights of children, as well as parents, in court, and access by children in care to an independent complaints procedure. The group also supported the principle of separate representation. Another development of a rather different kind was a government advisory committee, the Children's Committee. Originating in a report on child health published in 1976 (Court Committee 1976), this had the function of advising the Secretary of State on health and social services in relation to children. It was, however, short-lived, lasting only from 1978 to 1981, but might represent some kind of model for the future.

The importance of listening to what children say was also recognised in the setting up (within the voluntary sector) of telephone counselling services for children, of which Childline, established in 1986, was the most well-known. Childline attracted an enormous response from children, and was in fact unable to deal with all the demand directed at it. Attempted calls reached the level of 8,000 to 10,000 a day (less than 10 per cent of which were answered) (Doran and Young 1987, *New Society* 1987). Staff more than trebled in the first year. Moving on into the mid-1990s, Childline's newsletter for mid-1995 referred to 10,000 attempted calls daily of which 3,000 (30 per cent) were answered, with problems of under-funding still preventing the service from fully responding to demand. The significance of services such as Childline is that contact is child-initiated, and it is what children say that is listened to and respected.

Other ideas to enhance children's rights in Britain include children's ombudspersons or commissioners, ministers and charters. The Labour Party Policy Review of 1989 proposed the establishment of a children's commissioner who would consider the impact of legislation on children, disseminate information, and ensure that children's needs and rights were protected (Labour Party 1989); Labour also promised a minister for children (Rickford 1991, Lestor 1995), and the European Commission recommended the appointment of such a Minister in each member country (Lestor 1995). A campaign for a commissioner was set up by the Children's Rights Development Unit in 1995, and the idea has been mooted in a number of contexts (see, for example, Rosenbaum and Newell 1991). The Labour Party was said in 1995 to be taking the idea forward (Levy 1995). The Labour Party also launched a charter for children in 1990, encompassing a wide range of areas including access to files and participation in decision-making (Hatchett 1990, Lestor 1990). Another idea came in 1995 – Michael Young advocated a proxy vote for children to be cast by parents (Young 1995).

Finally the English adoption law review of 1992–3 proposed that children of 12 and above should have the right to veto an adoption, while those under 12 would have to have their wishes taken into account (Department of Health 1992, Department of Health/Welsh Office 1993).

This section has considered a number of areas where the expression of a 'children's rights' perspective in action may be identified. These include:

developments in other countries;

the United Nations Convention on the Rights of the Child;

developments under the 1975 and 1989 Children Acts in England and Wales – including recognition of the child's wishes and feelings, separate representation, complaints procedures, advocates, and child-initiated legal action;

the handling of child witnesses in abuse cases;

the question of consents;

the physical punishment of children;

the treatment of young offenders;

organisations and counselling lines for children;

ideas for a children's commissioner, minister and charter.

While not altogether free of paternalism, most developments in these areas do reflect a concern with the child as an individual with an individual set of interests, and with a right to have these interests represented and heard separately. To a degree, then, they reflect a children's rights perspective.

It may be considered whether this is the direction for the future. Considerable space has been devoted to the expression of this perspective in actual policy developments in Britain and elsewhere because it has seemed by the mid-1990s to be the area of most rapid movement. That is, in both Britain and elsewhere, the notion of children as appropriately having a degree of autonomy and right to control their own lives, and in a sense as being entitled to more 'adult' treatment, has found a variety of expressions – in representation and advocacy, in being listened to, in consents and punishment and so on; and it might be inferred that this trend will continue.

This may be broadly welcomed, but a more sinister side to the pursuit of 'children's rights' and adult-type treatment of children must also be pointed to. The damage done *to children* by treating them as adults is most obviously seen when children come into contact with the criminal justice system, either as witnesses to their own abuse or as offenders. But a wider problem concerns whether a diminution in state responsibility for children is identifiable and linked to the propagation of 'children's rights', notwithstanding the emphasis in the UN Convention on children's welfare and standards of living and so on, which do require state intervention. This point may be related to the stress put in Conservative legislation of the late 1980s and 1990s on a particularly tenacious notion of 'parental responsibility' for children (see Fox Harding 1994, also Bainham 1993). It may be asked whether there is a threat of the further withdrawal of the paternalistic, parental state; whether there is an underlying agenda in which, if children behave and are treated more 'like adults', less responsibility has to be taken for them – not only by the state, but perhaps by anyone (notwithstanding government's stress on parental responsibility). The belief or hope may be that children can increasingly take care of themselves. It is instructive to look here at the exclusion of most unemployed 16–17-year-olds from income support since 1988 – these young people seem to fall straight down a hole where neither parents *nor* the state are legally responsible for them, with an increase in numbers surviving as best they can on the streets. One might reflect how in ordinary conversation the phrase 'he (or she) is an adult' may be used to legitimate denying help to someone who obviously needs it. The point being made is that there is a potentially very harsh side to 'children's rights'. The reader is referred back to the criticisms made of this perspective earlier in the chapter, in particular the point that implementation of child liberationist proposals wholesale would lead to an extreme form of *laissez-faire* and that children would suffer if all paternalistic structures were swept away.

CHAPTER 6

Convergences and divergences

The past four chapters (2–5) have each outlined one value perspective on child care law and policy, these being: *laissez-faire*, paternalism and protection, the defence of the birth family, and children's rights. For each perspective particular aspects have been considered: the main elements of the perspective, some of the most prominent authors associated with the perspective, its rationale and underlying values, and some criticisms that can be put. The criticisms have focused on the empirical support for the position, problems with its implications for policy, and problems with its rationale and underlying values. Each perspective has been considered in practice at a particular time. Developments in the 1980s and 1990s in England and Wales have so far been relatively neglected, although there has been some discussion of manifestations of the children's rights perspective at this time; it is submitted that these decades do not reflect any one value perspective in a clear way, but an attempt to analyse them will be made in Chapter 7.

As will be apparent from the discussion so far, the four perspectives contain both themes and ideas in common, and some important differences. This chapter will attempt to summarise both what the perspectives share and where they part company. At this stage the differences between the positions are perhaps more obvious than the areas they hold in common. This higher profile for differences than similarities is a drawback arising from the attempt to define four different perspectives, show how they differ, and categorise child care authors according to one point of view or the other. The author acknowledges that the latter attempt has not been entirely successful. For example, it has been necessary to create a 'moderate' version of some perspectives in order to accommodate certain authors and assimilate them to the framework – Dingwall *et al.* (1983a) are seen as 'moderate paternalists' and Freeman (1983a) as a 'moderate children's rights author' – while there are doubts about classifying Morris *et al.* (1980) and Taylor *et al.* (1979) under *laissez-faire* with Goldstein *et al.* (1979, 1980). Morris and Taylor perhaps occupy a position part way between *laissez-faire* and a liberationist perspective, although the author's conclusion is that they are in fact closer to *laissez-faire* than anything else in the framework developed in this book. Such intermediate positions, however, highlight the problems of attempting to classify authors and their views in any definitive way. It may be noted at this point that the original article by the author under the name of Fox (1982) on which the framework here is based, may be criticised for polarising and exaggerating the distinctions between the two 'value positions' which the article outlined. For example, Holman (1988) commented: 'It should be noted that Fox's categories sharpen the differences between the two camps' (p. 69). However, it should be recalled that Fox's article did devote some space to 'Areas of convergence between the two positions' before going on to enumerate the major differences. It should be helpful at this point, therefore, to consider the important common ground shared by the four perspectives discussed in this book, before outlining how they diverge.

Points of convergence between the four perspectives

The focus on children

First, all four value perspectives must be credited with some genuine concern for the well-being and interests of children. This fundamental orientation is indeed in large part the authors' motivation for writing in the field they do. Goldstein *et al.* (1979, 1980), for example, start from a central interest in healthy child development. The paternalist authors are deeply concerned about child abuse and neglect and good standards of parental care, while the child liberationists are clearly shocked at the general societal treatment of children and desire passionately to improve it. Slightly less unambiguous is the focus of the third, pro-family perspective, but here too a central caring for children does manifest itself. For example, Holman's (1980, 1988) starting point in this field *is* an interest in child care – his sympathy for parents and families has developed from this. The following already-cited quotations from authors in the four camps illustrate their concern for the best for children:

constantly ongoing interactions between parents and children become for each child the starting point for an all-important line of development that leads towards adult functioning.   (Goldstein *et al.* 1980:8)

Whatever beneficial qualities a psychological parent may be lacking, he offers the child a chance to become a wanted and needed member within a family structure.   (Goldstein *et al.* 1979:21)

children are not the property of their parents. Parents are trustees for their children's interests: as with any trust, if they fail in the duties involved, they should be discharged.   (Dingwall *et al.* 1983:19)

(to parents) 1. Give continuous, consistent, loving care ...
2. Give generously of your time and understanding ...
3. Provide new experiences and bathe your child in language ...
                    (Pringle 1975a:159)

the conviction gained ground that a child's own family was, in most cases, the best place for him to be.   (Holman 1988:39) (on families) the normal and rightful lot of most children.   (Holman 1988:203)

children have a right to make just claims, and adults must be responsive to those claims.   (Worsfold 1974:157)

(children) form a large, long-suffering and oppressed grouping in society.
(Franklin 1986:1)

The child-centredness of the thinking is apparent in the desire for children to be normal, healthy, happy, loved, wanted, respected persons whose suffering should be prevented. A value is placed on children and their experiences.

It might be thought that this point is so obvious as not to need stating. Why, after all, discuss and explore child care matters if one does not have a central concern for the welfare and happiness of children? However, in principle it would be possible to write on child care from the point of view of perceiving children as a management or social control problem, whose potential disruption of adult life should be minimised. A purely punitive or oppressive approach is also quite possible in focusing on the issue of children in society. Just as all policies relating to children and young persons are not necessarily benign, so all writing on this issue need not necessarily be motivated by benevolence.

Nevertheless, the authors discussed in this book may be credited with a high degree of concern for children's well-being, even if mixed with other motives at times. The problem, of course, in making sense of these authors' work, revolves around the question of how the child's welfare should be interpreted. Fox's article (1982) referred to some useful comments by Walton (1976) on the interpretation of the 'best interests' of the child. Walton argued that the use of the phrase 'best interests of the child' had often confused rather than helped child care debates, creating the illusion that these interests constituted an objective fact. He, however, saw 'best interests' as contingent, rather than objective, depending on the particular position and assumptions of the person expressing them, and often used as a deceptively simple slogan. In Walton's view there was a need to consider factors to be taken into account if the phrase were to be infused with greater meaning; otherwise there was a danger that it would be used symbolically, to create an illusion of change, to deflect criticism, or to discredit opposition (because no one would want to be seen to oppose 'the child's best interests'). Walton stressed that there was no simple concept or criterion which could be applied in a crude rule of thumb way, and no group or individual which had sole authority to assume that generally it had the best conception of the child's interests. These points would seem to remain valid nearly 20 years later. A much more recent comment on the meaning of the child's interests comes from Parker (1995) in discussing child care policy developments: 'There is the abiding question of what *are* a child's best interests and how are they best secured? Are the short-term interests different from the long-term? When are children best protected by separation and when not? Is one child's best interest necessarily the same as another's – even in the case of brothers and sisters?' (p. 181).

It is clearly on this question of *interpreting* the child's interests or welfare that the four value perspectives diverge. Their central interest in the well-being of children, albeit differently defined, does, however, merit bearing in mind.

The state and the blood tie

A second area of convergence is that the four perspectives would all accept *some* role for the state in intervening between parent and child in order to defend or help the child; while none of them would argue for completely unfettered parental rights, or that the blood tie is always good for the child and ought to be unequivocally supported. The fourth, children's rights perspective is different from the others in that the role of the state it envisages is largely to do with taking steps to free children from any controls at all not imposed on adults. But none of the four perspectives would construe the child's welfare as lying in a return to the legal position of the early nineteenth century in the sense that parents (or fathers) should have virtually absolute control over their children, very much as though they were possessions or chattels, or that the principle of non-interference by the state or anyone else in the dynamics of the patriarchal family should be carried to extreme lengths. Indeed, it is probably the fourth perspective most of all which would find such a system repugnant and deeply antagonistic to children's true interests. Nevertheless the policy implications of the fourth perspective, as has been shown, do in fact seem to lead back to a form of *laissez-faire*, in that compulsory education would be ended, there would be no restrictions on child labour, no specific juvenile justice system, and no system of state substitute care. But the difference from the early Victorian age is that parents, while retaining a degree of responsibility, would not have rights and powers of the same kind. And it is state action through changing the law which would bring this situation about.

The first and third perspectives, while showing a preference for parental control and family autonomy on the whole, do recognise some situations where the force of the law should be used to separate children from their parents and remove parents' rights. Goldstein *et al.* (1980), as shown in Chapter 2, specify the precise circumstances in which this should be done, and the form of intervention envisaged by them when it *is* deemed justified, is draconian (permanent severance from the family of origin). The proponents of the third perspective are vaguer about compulsory intervention and play down the need for it, but would not go so far as to suggest that it should never come into play. For example, one defender of birth families interviewed by Fox and reported in her article (1982) commented on the Maria Colwell case:

I read the majority of that report the other day ... given the obvious protests that she (Maria) made, I just cannot conceive of it (the decision to return her to

her natural parent) ... I don't think any of the reasons were valid ... She did not want to be there ... I just do not understand that social worker's decision.
(Fox 1982:280)

The difference from the paternalist school is one of emphasis, of how and under what circumstances children should be removed and when parental contact should be maintained and restoration to the birth parent attempted. Differences arise, then, about the range and form of state intervention, but the principle of *some* action by the state to safeguard children's interests and rights held against adults, is accepted by all four perspectives.

Areas of convergence in the first three perspectives

Finally, on convergences, certain common ground shared by the first *three* perspectives – laissez-faire, paternalism, defence of the birth family – may be mentioned. One point is that all would give some role to support for natural families stopping short of compulsory intervention, although this is very muted in Goldstein *et al.*'s work. But Morris *et al.* (1980) and Taylor *et al.* (1979) argue for voluntary services to assist parents and children before the point of compulsory intervention. Tizard (1977) mentions the need for support to the natural parents to enable them to care adequately; Pringle (1975b) advocated payment for mothers who stay at home to care; and both Pringle and the British Agencies for Adoption and Fostering in their later writings moved closer to a preventionist position in arguing for support for families to help them care for their own children (*Adoption and Fostering*, Adcock 1983). Again, the difference is one of emphasis: the pro-birth family position is more concerned to press for policy changes such as better day care and financial benefits as urgently necessary; the paternalists perhaps see such changes as more long-term and not immediately related to the needs of the children who are currently the subject of placement decisions, but they are nevertheless not entirely unsympathetic to birth parents. (This is also the case with some moderate children's rights authors, notably Freeman 1983a.)

As has already been made apparent, the first three perspectives converge on not stressing children's autonomy (with the exception of Morris *et al.* 1980 and Taylor *et al.* 1979, who do put some emphasis on this) but on seeing children as different from adults, more vulnerable, of necessity dependent, and appropriately subject to adult decisions. The child's own viewpoint and separate set of interests are thus somewhat overlooked. This, as shown, is the radical difference between the first three positions and children's rights. *Laissez-faire*, paternalism and the pro-family position also converge on accepting some role for adoption and fostering. This is most apparent in the first two perspectives, where good adoptive and secure foster homes have a crucial role in caring for children who are not with their own parents; but the supporters of the third perspective would not deny a role for adoptive and foster parents. However, there are some crucial differences on the type of role envisaged for foster care and adoption, as will be highlighted in discussing 'divergences'. It can be mentioned here that the children's rights authors also see some role for 'substitute homes' – of a kind: those that children choose to go and live in. This is rather different from a home selected and supervised by a child care agency, however. Finally, all the first three perspectives generally favour the nuclear family structure (whether based on biological bonds or not) as in general a beneficial environment for child rearing, and have reservations about alternatives such as residential care, although some role for the latter may be acknowledged.

Points of divergence between the four perspectives

Having indicated these basic points of convergence between the four perspectives, the discussion will now focus on how the perspectives diverge.

The understanding of child welfare

First, as will be apparent, the understanding of the child's welfare, of in what that welfare consists, is different. The first, *laissez-faire* perspective sees psychological parenthood, undisturbed by intrusions from outside except in extreme cases, as of most benefit to the child. This creates a sense of security and commitment and the opportunity for appropriate relationships to develop. The third, pro-birth parent perspective takes a similar approach but places more value on biological parent–child bonds, and envisages the parent–child unit as supported and helped from outside, not just when extremely vulnerable or on the verge of crisis, but at a much lower threshold of need; indeed, in this view, child welfare would be served if society through government extended more help to families with young children in general. While the first perspective stresses certainty, permanence, and a stable bond with a single set of parent figures, the third finds the child's interacting with a number of parent figures more acceptable, indeed often desirable – so the long-term foster child, for example, would usually benefit from contact with birth parents even if they are unlikely to resume full-time care. The second, child protectionist perspective, by contrast, sees child welfare as consisting in receiving the best possible care – as this is construed – which is not necessarily supplied by the original biological or psychological parents. Good care provided by devoted adoptive or foster parents is often preferable to children remaining with their early caretakers; the supporters of the protection position would be more prepared to cut early bonds in the interests of better quality care, and in so doing would give a higher profile to the decisions of professionals and experts as to whose care is preferable. Compulsory intervention to this end is seen as justified. But the first and second perspectives broadly concur on the need for any switch to a new caretaker to be final; 'permanence' must be established in the new home; and the child usually fares best if the original parent figures are excluded. Here they differ from the third perspective. The fourth, child liberation perspective takes the view that the child's welfare consists in maximising children's freedom, including the freedom to choose their own guardians. Whether 'permanence' is more important than retaining contact with more than one home/switching between homes, whether the blood tie is more important than psychological bonds, whether a change of home should only take place in cases of extreme bad care – these issues tend not to be tackled directly by liberationist writing, but would presumably be for children themselves to decide.

The view of the child's welfare is dependent on various underlying ideas and assumptions mainly to do with child psychology. Differences open up as to the child's perceived degree of attachment to neglectful original parents, the child's capacity to relate to more than one set of parent figures, the strength of early bonds and memories, the importance of birth and genetic links, the effects of uncertainty and ambiguity, the effect on the child of intervention in the family by outside experts, the effect on children of changing their home, and the extent to which children can be generalised about at all. Underlying these questions are perhaps three key issues. One concerns the nature of attachment, the second the importance of self-image, and the third the need to look at individual cases individually.

The first problem concerns to what extent attachment is formed in conditions of poor care, the dangers of disrupting attachment, and to what extent attachment needs to be exclusive to one parent or co-resident pair of parents. Also, does intervention from outside and a change of home, or the threat of these things, seriously weaken attachment in a way which is damaging to the child? Secondly, the issue of self-image is important in considering knowledge of and contact with the birth family, and perception of why a breach with the birth family has taken place; are children damaged by loss of genetic links, or a negative view of their origins, even when they receive good care and become attached in other homes? The third point serves as a reminder that children are individuals and psychological theory cannot fully predict the effects of particular steps in every individual case; it is necessary, to some extent, to look at each child as unique and to absorb what he or she appears to be telling us.

The view of the family

A second area of divergence concerns how the family is perceived. The third perspective is the one most obviously concerned about the preservation of the family in a biological or kinship sense. This may include other relatives as well as the parent–child nuclear unit; for example, a respondent reported in Fox's article (1982) talked of children having a right to their own family 'and that doesn't just mean parents, it means grandparents, people who can talk to them about their past, the past of the family' (p. 272). Kinship is seen as of great psychological benefit to individuals; and in this approach the parents' needs and rights are weighted and valued as well as those of the children. Although, as indicated earlier, the rationale for emphasising birth and biological bonds *per se* does not seem fully worked out, it appears to be partly to do with a healthy sense of identity and with what is socially regarded as 'normal'. Children who have lost their original family suffer, in this view; and the parents' suffering in losing their children is also given some weight.

The first and second perspectives set greater store by relationships based on actual psychological interaction of a positive kind, rather than the blood tie. This position is most fully worked out in Goldstein *et al.*'s (1979, 1980) writings, the arguments being largely derived from psychoanalytic theory. In their view, as attachment grows out of relationship, interaction, and day-to-day care, it is the psychological parent figure who is important. When biological parents are not also the psychological parents, they diminish in importance, indeed may be of no consequence for the child. However, the proponents of the third perspective might also draw on psychoanalytic theory to support their view that the primary bond with the birth parents, when they were also the psychological parents, can only be severed at great cost to the child. The dispute arises over how worthy of preservation birth families as such are in the face of poor quality care, weak or non-existent actual relationships, or the disruption of relationships. The second perspective falls broadly into line with the first in advocating the superiority of good 'psychological families' to poor birth ones, but is readier than the first to attempt to create new families based on psychological bonds. These would be adoptive or secure foster homes, probably without contact with the original family. All of these three perspectives, however, as mentioned earlier, see some form of nuclear family structure as appropriate for the care of children and are generally wary about alternatives such as residential care. The children's rights perspective, by contrast, has doubts about the nuclear family structure itself; but it must be said that their view of alternatives is not very fully worked through. However, Holt (1975) thinks that children need 'extended families' (networks of adults) and does propose some possibilities such as groups, communities and organisations where 'young people could live under the loose supervision of some older people who would be responsible for them' (p. 162). These group settings would need to be small and informal. Children are also seen as having the right to go and live in other households if they wish and if the adults there accept them – presumably in nuclear families other than their own. The children's rights perspective does not value any family structure for its own sake, however, but values what children choose for themselves.

In summary, then, differences exist between the perspectives as to whether families should be construed primarily in biological or psychological terms, as to how easy it is to create or recreate families, and, to some extent, on the primary importance of the nuclear parent–child unit.

The origins of child care problems

Related to the differences in the perception of the family are differences of view over the origins of family malfunctioning, problems in families, and poor parenting and inadequate child care. For most writers supporting the first and second value perspectives, problems in families and unsatisfactory care of the children are seen as rooted largely in the parents' own psychological history. In particular, those who have not experienced the right kind of psychological parenting and good care themselves have a weak chance of becoming effective parents in their turn; there is thus a cyclical character to poor parenting. Treatment, therapy, social work and so on, might help, but, particularly for the second perspective, damaged parents are usually better replaced by psychologically healthier ones. The loss they might experience in having their children permanently removed must be offset against the prevention of further poor parenting by *those* children in the future. Young and immature parents may also be seen as a factor predisposing to poor child rearing. In other words, it is factors relating to parents as individuals which are significant in child care matters.

For the third, pro-kinship school of thought, family and parenting problems are to a much greater extent due to external material circumstances such as poverty, environmental stress, and the inadequate provision of services. Parenting behaviour is altered by resources and the opportunities and life chances available, and arises from external factors like social class and geographical area, rather than from parents' own psychology. The lack of child care resources in the home and lack of stimulation arising from low income, poor housing conditions and deprived neighbourhoods, constitute one type of pressure here, which might lead to child care being so poor that the family is separated. Psychological/behavioural and material factors are seen to interact. So Holman (1980) draws on research to show the psychological effects of poverty – lowered self-respect and self-image; and cites data showing two contrasting reactions to this: withdrawal and aggression (Holman 1980, citing Haggerstrom 1964). Both of these may have an adverse effect on child care. And it is the poor whose children disproportionately come to the attention of child care agencies. Holman stresses that poor parents may well share the child care values and objectives of the wider society, but are prevented from achieving them by depriving environments. Construing bad parenting in terms of personal inadequacy, as the first and second perspectives would do, may be seen from this viewpoint as 'blaming the victim'.

In the fourth perspective, the origins of unsatisfactory child-rearing are relatively unexplored, although it should be noted that Freeman (1983a, especially in Chapter 5) shares many perceptions with Holman and the birth parent school. The more radical children's rights proponents are aware of the way that the adult world in general treats children badly, but the reasons for this are not, it seems, enquired into in any depth.

As the causes of poor child care are construed differently, the remedies are seen differently too. In the first perspective, child removal is justified only when standards are extremely bad; certainly in the Goldstein view, little else is offered. For the child protectionists, both help to the individual family experiencing problems and removal of the child to another home might be appropriate at different times and in different cases, but the emphasis would be more on the latter. For the birth parent defenders, the remedies involve help to vulnerable families, reducing social deprivation, and helping families with children more generally. Appropriate means would include child day care, financial support, and community action by groups of parents. Removal is not excluded but is given a lower profile. Loosely speaking, for the proponents of the third perspective, 'prevention is better than cure' (and is presumed possible). The children's rights authors seem to look again to removal of the child to a better home environment – but to self-removal rather than compulsory powers exercised by the state.

These different perspectives on the response to poor child care are linked with different perspectives on the role of the state, as will be shown in the next section.

The role of the state

A number of differences between the four perspectives are found here. In their general view of the state the first three perspectives differ markedly from each other. In the *laissez-faire* school of thought a minimal state is favoured; the state's role in child care is marginal in the sense that it is confined to severe cases, although the state should have very extensive powers in those cases. However, exercise of the power to remove children to, and establish them in, an alternative home, although a strong power for the state, would mostly be followed by withdrawal – the new home having similar autonomy from external intrusion to the first. For the paternalists the state should have a much wider and more controlling role, intervening by compulsion in families on a much greater scale and at a much lower threshold of mistreatment; so in this perspective the state is anything but minimal and may indeed be seen as an over-authoritarian institution in relation to families. Nevertheless its interventions are still individualised, focused on particular families and children rather than concerned with widespread family support. In the third perspective the state's role is seen as wider, yet less authoritarian. The state should be concerned with providing for the welfare of children across a broad front through various supportive services offered on a voluntary basis; but it should use its coercive powers of child removal less. This is broadly consonant with notions of the 'Welfare State'.

The position of the fourth, children's rights, perspective is of interest particularly because, starting from totally different arguments, it comes to resemble the first perspective. In this view the state should take drastic steps to alter the conditions of childhood so as to make it more like the status of adulthood; such legal changes must then be enforced and upheld; but otherwise the state's role reverts largely to *laissez-faire*, with children enjoying adult rights such as the franchise but apparently with no compulsory education, no legal restrictions on child labour, no juvenile justice system, and no child protection system backed by the law. The law would not discriminate between adults and children; it was shown in discussing this perspective how this seems to return us, in some respects, to an early nineteenth century type of *laissez-faire*.

It is the second and third value perspectives which have the most optimistic view of what the state can achieve in the field of child welfare: the paternalists have considerable faith in the decision-making power of courts and social workers, and in the capacities of substitute parents, while the birth parent defenders have faith in the possibilities of broader child policy, preventative and rehabilitative work. The first and fourth perspectives are more sceptical about the state: for the minimalists the law is a clumsy instrument incapable of supervising complex parent–child relationships; while for the children's rights supporters, the state, like individual adults, may get in the way of the child's liberty. For both perspectives, in attempting to improve things for children the state may often in fact make things worse.

The perspectives also differ in how they see the details of state intervention in child care. Some of these differences, relating to removal versus help and prevention, were suggested in the last section when looking at the remedies for poor child care. Two further aspects will be mentioned briefly. The first relates to adoption. The first two perspectives look on adoption as a solution to the problems of inadequate child care much more favourably than the third; in particular, the legal security of adoption is seen as a positive point. To some extent the advocates of adoption can draw on research to support their position. The pro-birth family school, however, tend to have two kinds of reservation about adoption, one relating to the effects of social class and the other to the long-term effects on the child. It may be that if social class is accounted for, and the long-term effects are looked at, adoption *per se* is not the superior form of child care that it appears to be. The second aspect relates to foster care, and has already been touched on in discussing differences over child welfare and child psychology. The divergence of view is basically over whether foster care should resemble (traditional) adoption and birth family care, on the 'exclusive' model, or whether it should be seen more as a partial and temporary quasi-parent–child relationship which is open to contact with the birth parents and eventual return to them. Broadly, *laissez-faire* and paternalism support the first, exclusive approach, and the kinship school the second, more open one. More open fostering has been the favoured form in the late 1980s and 1990s, in line with a general move towards partnership with parents when children are being looked after by the local authority (see, for example, Packman 1993). It may be born in mind also that adoption in Britain in the 1990s was moving towards the open model (Mullender 1991, Department of Health 1992, Department of Health/Welsh Office 1993, Adcock *et al.* 1994, Ryburn 1994a). While the children's rights perspective tends not to tackle this sort of issue directly, it would seem not to support exclusive parent–child bonds of any kind (or the forced exclusion of the child from anybody).

The differences between the perspectives on the child care role of the state connect with their wider views on society and social problems. These will be discussed separately, but firstly a short detour will be taken into the question of how the four perspectives view the concept of rights.

The concept of rights

The four perspectives have different implicit or explicit approaches to the issue of rights in the child care field. It is in the third and fourth perspectives that the term is most likely to be explicitly used. Some supporters of the birth parent school may raise parents' rights as a specific issue; for example, the National Council for One Parent Families (1982) did so in opposing the assumption of these rights by a mere resolution. Booth and Booth (1994) speak of people with learning difficulties having the right to be parents. The fourth perspective, clearly, makes extensive use of the concept of children's rights, defining these as rights of self-determination and essentially the same as adult rights. However, it may be noted that the second, child protection position may also argue in terms of children's rights, although the rights referred to are to nurturance and care, not to autonomy. The moderate children's rights author Freeman (1983a) occupies a midway position. Both the second and fourth perspectives give a very weak weighting to *parents'* rights. Finally, Goldstein *et al.* (1979, 1980) are advocating a model of intervention which in effect shows a strong respect for parents' rights, but their argument is advanced chiefly in terms of what is best for the child. This is also the case with much of the pro-parent writing – parental control is seen as better for the child; at the same time the distinction between what is in the interests of the child and what is in the interests of the parent can be somewhat blurred.

The notion of rights thus occupies an ambiguous role in this debate. Conflicting rights are recognised to a degree; arguments may be advanced in terms of rights but are often put in other terms which overlook rights; the concept of rights is given different meanings; and there is perhaps a well-founded reluctance to understand the child care debate primarily in these terms. At the same time the notion of rights – both parents' and children's – cannot be altogether ignored. Other rights may also complicate the issue – for example, those of substitute parents and of the state.

The view of society and social problems

A final important area of divergence concerns the broader social and political philosophy underlying the four perspectives. A crucial aspect of this is the awareness of social divisions, class and power as significant dimensions to the child care role of the state. It is the third perspective which is most aware of these. Parents who come into contact with child care agencies are seen to be of low social class and in a weak power position, and their child care problems are seen as originating in factors connected with social class. Social workers, judges, magistrates, and often substitute parents too, occupy a higher and more powerful class position, and apply middle-class or upper-class values and norms to child care problems. The result is a class-loaded system in which the poor are at much greater risk than others of losing their children – to higher class homes. Inadequate middle-class parents are less likely to become the object of the child care actions of the state. Ethnicity is also a factor which operates in the system in a similar way. Preferred solutions to this bias in child care are basically an extension of the Welfare State and a reduction in inequality. This is perceived as possible within the framework of a capitalist society (despite the problems seen as generated by such a society). The position may thus usefully be classed as a moderately left-wing view of society and social problems.

By contrast, to the child protectionist standpoint, birth parents appear to have too much rather than too little power, and often stand in the way of the best solution for the child. While not totally unaware of the impact of class and racial factors, the supporters of this position see the first priority as the child, in the sense that the best care must be achieved for her or him now, regardless of the structural antecedents of the problem. As has been suggested, the second perspective, in attempting to be non-political, perhaps only succeeds in being politically naive. Child care problems and solutions are construed largely in personal terms. The social structure is only weakly related to individuals' problems, and is not challenged. The preferred solution is not only individualised but essentially one of social control, and may be seen as treating symptoms while overlooking causes. The state is seen as politically neutral and benign, and its agents as 'a politically neutral expert elite and as legitimate decision-makers in the lives of citizens' (Fox 1982:288).

Interestingly, the first, *laissez-faire* perspective is aware of the class and ethnic element in child placement decisions, and uses this as one argument for minimising state intrusion in families. In many ways, however, a *laissez-faire* stance on child care connects with a right-wing view of a minimal state in general. The approach of Goldstein *et al.* (1979, 1980) would surely be congenial to a right-wing government which wished to roll back the state, curtail public expenditure, and uphold the traditional and self-contained family as a value. The Goldstein perspective legitimates all of these things. Yet Morris *et al.* (1980) and Taylor *et al.* (1979) challenge state intervention from a left-wing position. This confusion is compounded by considering the child liberation perspective. While Freeman (1983a) concurs with the left-wing family defenders at many points, Holt (1975), Farson (1978) and Franklin (1986, 1995), it is suggested, are essentially advocating an anarchist solution which might also be attractive to a right-wing position favouring less state expenditure on welfare and a cheap and biddable labour force. The liberationists, it will be remembered, see oppression and powerlessness in terms of age rather than class. The solution is largely to emancipate children from dependency by giving them adult rights; and in their scenario much state machinery could be dismantled. The provision of a guaranteed income, it is true, would be expensive for government and would be quite incompatible with a right-wing market-oriented approach. But the children's rights proponents' emphasis on independence, and on the adverse effects of paternalism, protection and help, uncomfortably echoes some extreme right-wing propaganda.

In conclusion, of the four perspectives outlined in this book, only one, the pro-parent position, can be clearly located within a political framework, and even this has its own inbuilt contradictions. Both the first and fourth perspectives might be convenient for right-wing governments but cannot be unequivocally aligned with the right. The paternalists, presumably, belong somewhere in the political centre, but are somewhat detached from a broader political debate.

A final comment on convergences and divergences

This chapter has attempted to outline both the convergences and divergences between the four child care perspectives. Two additional general points may also be made. First, there are differences in the degree of empirical support for the four perspectives. The paternalist and pro-family positions appear to be better supported by reference to studies of child welfare and the child care role of the state than the other two. However, this is not necessarily to denigrate the *laissez-faire* and children's rights perspectives; and this leads to the second point, which concerns the quality of the argument. Goldstein *et al.* (1979, 1980) achieve some stature by their link with the respected body of theory associated with psychoanalysis, and have much to say on child psychology which is of great value (in particular, on the child's sense of time). But it is the arguments of the children's rights school, including Freeman (1983a), which the author personally finds most formidable (while not altogether agreeing with them). Holt (1975), perhaps, is a lightweight, but the originality of his ideas still deserves close scrutiny. Franklin (1986, 1995) and Freeman (1983a) present the greatest intellectual challenge. And if the rights perspective does nothing else, it compels us to re-examine our attitude to children in a fundamental way.

CHAPTER 7

Law, policy and practice: an uneasy synthesis

This book has outlined four different value perspectives on child care law and policy which, while sharing certain ideas in common, take different views of child welfare, the family, the origins of child care problems, the role of the state, the concept of rights, and society and social problems. While each perspective has a degree of internal coherence, and while each may be identified as more influential than others in actual policy and practice at different times, the 'real world' of such policy and practice, it is argued, always represents an uneasy and incoherent synthesis of views. That is, the perspectives are not found in practice in anything like their pure forms, notwithstanding the broad prominence of particular perspectives at times. Many factors influence the movements in actual policies. Among these, nevertheless, are swings in professional and pressure group thinking which may correspond to the perspectives which have been outlined.

Such broad swings in thinking may be more apparent with hindsight than when considering contemporary and very recent change. For example, it is now fairly easy to identify the 1960s in England and Wales as the 'prevention' decade when policy and social work practice favoured supporting the natural family and minimising time in care, and the 1970s as the time of 'child protection' spurred on by concern about child abuse. There may be a tendency to over-simplify the past, however. It is perhaps because the 1980s and 1990s are more recent that it seems harder to generalise about these decades. At the same time, it is submitted that the 1980s in England and Wales were genuinely a time of polarisation, of contrasts, and of greater tensions and conflicts in child care policy, while the 1990s saw an attempt to resolve these conflicts under the Children Act 1989, against a background of accelerating family change.

This concluding chapter will attempt to accomplish two tasks. First, the chief factors which seem to be influential in determining the shifting nature of child care policy will be outlined. Secondly, a brief attempt will be made to analyse English child care policy in the 1980s and 1990s in the light of the four value perspectives. The brevity and superficiality of this account is acknowledged; these complex decades merit a far fuller treatment as an exercise in its own right. The reader is referred to other sources for a more comprehensive account, in particular

Parton (1985a, 1991), Stevenson (1989), and Hendrick (1994). The brief account given here may, however, illustrate the extent to which the world of actual policy always represents an 'uneasy synthesis' of views.

Factors influencing law, policy and practice

The following four broad areas are suggested as significant: (a) scandals and enquiries and the response (see Parton 1985a, 1991, and Hallett 1989 as useful sources); (b) interest groups and their thinking (see Parton 1985a, 1991); (c) reviews of legislation and policy; and (d) wider policies and changes.

Scandals and enquiries and the response

It is impossible to overlook the impact of individual cases which achieve 'scandal' status, on the development of child care policy, and difficult to over-estimate their importance in English policy in the 1970s and 1980s in particular. Even as far back as 1870, the case of Margaret Waters, a private foster mother or 'baby farmer' executed for the death of one of the neglected infants in her care, caused a wave of public consternation and prompted the infant life protection movement to press for legislative change to regulate private boarding out (Heywood 1978). It was a scandal case, that of the foster child Dennis O'Neill, followed by a government enquiry (Monckton 1945), which was one factor in the post-war realisation that the child care service was in urgent need of reform. Most famous of all scandal cases, perhaps, was Maria Colwell of 1973 (Secretary of State for Social Services, 1974), which was followed by a public enquiry and much media coverage hostile to social workers. In the 15 years 1972–87 there were no fewer than 34 enquiries (London Borough of Greenwich 1987), some public, some held in private, into deaths of children known to Social Services Departments. Most of these produced recommendations relating to the law, policy and practice. Among these cases the most well-known are probably a cluster in the mid-1980s – Jasmine Beckford, Tyra Henry, and Kimberley Carlile (London Borough of Brent 1985, London Borough of Lambeth 1987, London Borough of Greenwich 1987). These were influential in the preparation for the Children Act.

Three points may be made about the significance of scandal cases, the enquiries into them, the reports, and the media and public response. The first is the degree to which blame for a child's death has been popularly apportioned to the child care agencies of the state rather than the actual killer of the child. The second concerns the determinants of public response to such child deaths and to the responsibility for them. The third point concerns the perception of such child deaths as preventable through the manipulation of the state's response.

First, cases in the 1970s and 1980s were marked by criticisms of the social workers deemed responsible for the care of the children at the time of their deaths, and also seen as largely responsible for not preventing the deaths. These workers were publicly pilloried in the popular press with headlines such as: 'They Killed the Child I Adored' (*The Sun* – see Franklin 1989a), 'Kimberley: Social Workers Failed her and the System Doomed Her to Die' (*Daily Mail* – see Fogarty 1987), and 'Man Who Let Kimberley Die' (*The Star* – see Franklin 1989a). The Social Services Director in the Beckford case of 1984 – herself exonerated by the inquiry report (London Borough of Brent 1985) – had to remind herself that she did not kill Jasmine, Morris Beckford did. Criticisms were based on the view – blindingly obvious with hindsight, but often only with hindsight – that the child victim should not have been left with, or returned to, the birth parent. That is, social workers were castigated for not being firm and authoritative enough in relation to birth parents and children at risk. It may be noted that a reversal of this type of criticism was found in the suspected sex abuse cases in the county of Cleveland in 1987 – not involving child deaths, but also the subject of an inquiry and report (Secretary of State for Social Services 1988). Here social workers were portrayed by the press as over-zealous, as brutally removing children from their parents when there were no good grounds for doing so (see Franklin 1989a). These cases were an important influence on the emergency protection provisions in the Children Act 1989. A similar line of criticism was taken in later cases where abuse was suspected and drastic action taken, most notably in Orkney in 1991 (see Clyde 1992). The issue raised here revolves round the location of blame in those state agents responsible for child protection – almost, in child death cases, to the exclusion of the actual killer of the child.

A second and related point of significance is why the public response to children killed by their caretakers should have been as intense as it was, and should have taken the form it did. An often mentioned point is that child cruelty and child murder are hardly historically new phenomena, yet it is in the years since the 1960s, when the phenomenon of 'baby-battering' was identified, that the public and the media have been highly sensitised to the occurrence of child abuse, and much publicity has been given to discoveries of individual severe abuse cases where social workers were involved. It is not clear whether in fact the incidence of serious abuse has increased or merely that there is more awareness of it. In any event, the degree and nature of social concern, sometimes seen as a 'moral panic' (Cohen 1973, Parton 1985a), requires explanation. Parton (1981, 1985a) is one writer who has set this trend in context – that of a more generalised anxiety about the family and the social order (see also A. Cooper 1995). Another aspect of the context is a general attack on the public sector and the professions under Thatcherite policies in the 1980s (see McCarthy 1989, Johnson 1990, Hills 1991). Child abuse enquiries arguably provided a useful weapon with which to attack one of the least popular groups of public servant. Of interest here also is the seemingly lower profile given to children killed by foster and adoptive parents, than those killed by birth and step-parents.

Thirdly, there is the assumption that severe child abuse and deaths from abuse can be prevented: by more vigilant social work, by changing the emphasis in social work, by changing the law and procedures, by improving training, and so on. Recommendations from inquiry reports assume that steps can be taken to reduce the danger of similar cases occurring again. There are problems with this assumption. First, expectations of social workers are contradictory (as comparison of the child death cases and the Cleveland and other sex abuse abuse cases makes clear). Secondly, the crucial issue of resources in child care work is often not adequately tackled (for example, London Borough of Greenwich 1987). Thirdly, it may reasonably be argued that because of the complexity and unpredictability of human behaviour, no child care agency or child care law can ever completely eliminate severe abuse. Nevertheless, policy and practice have been subject to numerous changes because of scandal cases and their effects. However, at the end of the 1980s Hallett (1989) thought that various factors suggested: 'that the modern era of child-abuse inquiries, stretching from Colwell to Cleveland, may be at an end' (p. 143), with, in the future, greater concentration on low-key internal review.

Interest groups and their thinking

A second factor in policy is the influence of relevant interest groups such as professional and pressure groups. These groups are themselves influenced by research, practice, experience and ongoing discussion, and by the particular interests they represent, as well as by the scandal cases mentioned and the policy reviews and wider changes to be discussed below. From time to time new pressure groups appear, such as Justice for Children, the Children's Legal Centre and the Family Rights Group in the late 1970s, and Parents Against Injustice (PAIN) and the Family Courts Campaign in the 1980s. The thinking of certain groups may be broadly aligned with particular perspectives outlined in this book – for example, the British Agencies for Adoption and Fostering has been broadly identified with the protectionist, 'permanency' position, and the National Council for One Parent Families with the pro-parent view. The social work profession as expressed in the British Association of Social Workers has been, certainly at one time, associated with a position sympathetic to natural parents and preventive work (see Fox 1982); although the effect of child abuse enquiries on the social work profession should not be under-estimated. These have resulted in great anxiety surrounding child abuse work, and some defensive practice. Finally, professional and pressure group thinking is subject to changing trends or, to put it more derogatorily, 'fashions'. As has been suggested, in the 1960s the 'fashion', broadly speaking, was in favour of natural families and preventive work, and in the 1970s, protection and permanence. The continued emphasis on permanence in child care practice in the early 1980s, but with an emphasis on parents' rights also developing, was followed by renewed concern about abuse, but then by a counter-reaction after Cleveland in 1987, and a greater emphasis on partnership with parents in the build-up to the Children Act 1989. It may be that each swing of thinking sets in train its own backlash, giving rise to a 'pendulum' effect.

Interest groups and their thinking may have both a direct and indirect influence on practice – a direct influence on individual decisions and practice at the micro level; and an indirect influence in so far as they feed into the policy-making process at higher levels. They may have a direct influence on the form of legislation, as was the case in the passage of the Children Act 1989 through Parliament (Parton 1991).

Reviews of legislation and policy

Apart from reports of individual case inquiries set up by government, other government documents which review child care policy in general are clearly influential. One category of review is the report of a government committee set up for a specific purpose. In the recent history of English child care policy three reports stand out – the Curtis Committee report, on children in public care (Secretary of State for the Home Department/Minister of Health/Minister of Education 1946), the Ingleby Committee report, focusing on delinquency and child neglect and their prevention (Secretary of State for the Home Department 1960), and the Houghton Committee report, initially on adoption, but coming to include fostering, and children in care (Home Office/Scottish Education Department 1972). The three reports laid the foundations of the 1948, 1963 and 1975 Acts respectively. Their significance lay, broadly, in the construction of a new and better quality service for children in the care of the state (Curtis), the introduction of preventive powers to act on family breakdown, child neglect and delinquency (Ingleby), and the granting of greater powers of child protection (Houghton). In the 1990s there was a major review of adoption law (Department of Health 1992) and another of the Scottish child care law followed by an Act in 1995.

Another type of report is that of a standing body such as the All-Party Parliamentary Select Committee on Social Services (known for a time as the Short Committee), whose report on children in care in 1984 (House of Commons 1984) was influential in the setting up of the review of legislation which eventually led to the Children Act 1989. Consultation papers were issued in 1985 by an inter-departmental working party of civil servants set up immediately after the Short Report to look at options for the codification and amendment of the law. These papers formed the basis for further consultation, for costing, and for a White Paper on child care law and family services published in 1987 (Department of Health and Social Security 1987).

At a later stage of policy-making, White Papers prepare the way for legislation but are also part of the process of consultation. In the 1960s two White Papers on juvenile delinquency (Home Office 1965, 1968) – the first of which met with considerable opposition – fed into the process which eventually produced the Children and Young Persons Act 1969. The 1987 White Paper just mentioned formed, after more consultation, the basis for the Children Act 1989. The adoption review of 1992 was followed by a White Paper (Department of Health/Welsh Office 1993) and by draft legislation in 1996.

Another category of government document which may be mentioned here consists of regulations, circulars, notes of guidance, and codes of practice. These may lack the legal standing of Acts of Parliament, but have considerable force in policy and practice nevertheless. Examples would be a code of practice issued in 1983 on access to children in care, and a circular in 1984 on the passing of parental rights resolutions (Department of Health and Social Security 1983a, 1983b, 1984b). Regulations accompanying legislation are also of crucial importance for practice. There are, for example, volumes of regulations relating to the Children Act 1989, covering family support, day care, residential care, children with disabilities, court issues, private fostering and adoption issues. Also worthy of mention are reports by non-governmental respected bodies such as the Law Commission. The latter has reported on aspects of private child care law such as illegitimacy (Law Commission 1979, 1982, 1986, 1988) and custody/access (now residence and contact) after divorce (Law Commission 1988). Law Commission recommendations on private family law were incorporated into the Children Act 1989.

Wider policies and changes

Two aspects of wider change which impinge on child care policy can be referred to. First, there are other aspects of government policy. One important aspect comprises government approaches to public expenditure in general and social expenditure in particular. Pressure on resources and the search for cheaper solutions have a long-standing history in the field of child care policy, and both foster care and prevention have at times been identified as a means of reducing costs (Heywood 1978, Packman 1981). Where governments seek to reduce state welfare spending in general, social work as a relatively expensive form of labour might be expected to be under scrutiny (see, for example, National Institute for Social Work 1982); but the pressure of public interest in child protection makes it difficult for even an avowedly expenditure-cutting government directly and obviously to reduce work in the child care field. Indirect curbs, however, may stem from reductions in local authority spending in general, adversely affecting child care services unless local authorities choose to divert resources from other areas of work. A preference on the part of government for the 'independent' (that is, private and voluntary) sector in social services may also find an expression in child care work, thus reducing the local authority's direct role and expanding that of voluntary and even for-profit bodies (see, for example, proposals in 1995 to bring profit-making bodies into the field of fostering – Clark 1995). Other relevant aspects of government policy include policies in the fields of health care, social security, education and housing. Many policies here may be said to have implications, short and long term, direct and indirect, for child welfare and child care problems. A useful example of the intersection of policies in different areas is provided by homelessness. Affected by policies in both the income maintenance and housing fields, the phenomenon of homelessness can have severe effects on the health and welfare of children – if families, for example, sleep rough, take refuge in grossly inadequate or over-crowded conditions, or are housed in squalid and dangerous 'bed and breakfast' hotels; and children have come into the care of the state solely because of homelessness (for example, NCH 1989).

More generally, government policy on welfare sets the context and general climate of thinking surrounding child care policy. This is use-fully illustrated by contrasting the situation in the late 1940s and in the 1980s in England and Wales. In the late 1940s newly popular collec-tivist ideas on welfare spread their influence to child care, where a much wider concept of state responsibility for children developed than had been accepted in the past. By the 1980s, although major Welfare State institutions were still in place (see, for example, Hills 1991), there was apparently an end to the post-war 'consensus' on a major state role, and prevalent 'new right' or 'Thatcherite' ideologies favoured free market economics, the reduction of the state's role in welfare, and the encouragement of independence from the state, of private and volun-tary sector alternatives to state provision, and of family responsibility. This did not change significantly in the 1990s following the fall of Thatcher, although some amelioration of the position can be noted in the raising of child benefit under the Major governments. It was still a totally different climate from the 1940s, and logically would not have supported a major state role in child care. However, the effect, as will be shown, was ambiguous, and actual policy did not take the *laissez-faire* form which might have been expected from the ideology.

The other aspect of wider change which is significant for child care concerns wider economic and social change, including levels of pros-perity, poverty, unemployment, and demographic change. To take two examples from the period from the 1970s to the 1990s: increased unemployment and changing family patterns both have profound impli-cations for child care within families and thus for demands on the state child care system. Unemployment has been shown to impose strains, both psychological and financial, on families, and there appears to be an association – though probably not a straightforward causal relation –

between unemployment and referrals to child care agencies (Rapoport 1981, Piachaud 1986, Jackson and Walsh 1987). The poverty associated with unemployment itself causes child care problems, if the proponents of the third value perspective are correct.

Secondly, changes in families connected with the increased incidence of marital breakdown, cohabitation and births out of marriage, are significant – in particular, more lone parent (usually mother-headed) families, and more 'reconstituted' or step-families often comprising a birth mother and 'stepfather'. These changes are themselves probably partially linked with unemployment and the loss of the male breadwinner role. Lone parent families in general experience housing, financial and work-related problems, and their children are disproportionately likely to enter care (Bebbington and Miles 1989); reconstituted families often have severe problems of internal relationships (see, for example, Burgoyne and Clark 1984, Cockett and Tripp 1994); while the prominence of 'stepfather' figures in notorious child death cases has been notable (most obviously Maria Colwell, but also a number of others such as Jasmine Beckford, Kimberley Carlile and Doreen Mason). There has been an increasing proportion of children born to single mothers, and in cohabiting partnerships which may have less stability even than marriage (for the various family change factors see, for example, Fox Harding 1996). Other factors in late post-war society which may be mentioned include the decline in fertility and family size, changes in sexual mores, changing gender roles and the influence of feminism. There are potentially increasing demands on the 'middle' generations by the elderly, and from vulnerable and dependent groups discharged from hospitals into the community at large. To this can be added ethnic and cultural diversity, inner city decline, rising crime, greater poverty for families and children, the social exclusion and indeed destitution of certain groups, and the very pace of social and economic change itself. Many change factors could be listed, and no doubt readers have their own list of those to be considered the most significant. The relationship of all these variables to child care problems and the need for state intervention is complex and is not explored further here; but the general point is that child care problems and the response to them do not arise in a social vacuum.

English child care policy in the 1980s and 1990s

To illustrate the extent to which actual policy is a pragmatic response reflecting a number of different, often conflicting positions, a brief account will be given of the 1980s and 1990s in the light of *laissez-faire*, paternalism, the support of the family, and children's rights. The questions of conflict and balance will be briefly highlighted. Again it is stressed that this is nothing like a full account of these complex decades. Reference should be made to the sources cited at the beginning of the chapter, to the author's other writing on the Children Act 1989 (Fox Harding 1990, 1991, Harding 1993), and to other sources specifically on the Children Act, such as Allen (1992), Bainham (1990), Eekelaar (1991), Freeman (1992b, 1992c).

Laissez-faire

As already suggested, less was seen of *laissez-faire* in English child care policy in the 1980s than might be expected from the government's declared ideology (or from the ideology of family 'traditionalists' like the Conservative Family Campaign). Rigid time limits after which children must be returned to their family or adopted were not imposed, or at least not at a national level; the legal grounds for compulsory intervention were not clearly defined more narrowly as *laissez-faire* would require; the state did not withdraw from all but the most extreme cases; children were not all cut off from their family of origin after a change of home. Certainly, 'permanence' continued to be generally favoured (although with greater grounds for doubt emerging towards the end of the 1980s – Thoburn, Murdoch and O'Brien 1987); but permanence can also be associated with the second, protectionist perspective or, if return to the birth family is preferred, with the third, pro-parent view. Interestingly, while effecting swingeing reductions in local authorities' powers in almost every other field, central government in England in the 1980s did not attempt to remove from local authorities the primary responsibility for child care and protection work. However, as noted, in the mid-1990s there were government attempts to introduce for-profit agencies into the field of fostering.

One way, however, in which *laissez-faire* did manifest itself was in a provision of the Children Act 1989 (Section 1(5)), which set out the principle of 'non-intervention' in both public and private law. This is superimposed on other considerations in the Act. The principle stated that a court should not make an order regarding a child unless it considered it better for the child than making no order at all. This would mean, for example, that in disputes between parents including divorce, parents would in most cases be expected to agree between themselves and their arrangements would not automatically be judged at a court hearing, while in care proceedings a care order would not automatically be made just because the statutory criteria were met. The court has to consider the relative outcomes of making an order or not. Freeman (1992b, 1992c) is one author who sees the non-intervention or no-order principle as particularly significant in the Children Act.

Child protection and state paternalism

While the 1970s in England and Wales have been shown to be the decade in which paternalism in its modern form made the greatest strides, in the 1980s the paternalist and protectionist approach was still influential, especially after the cluster of publicised child abuse cases and the enquiries into them in the middle of the decade – Beckford, Henry and Carlile. One change which may be seen as a step towards greater protection was a widening in the grounds for care and emergency protection proceedings in the Children Act 1989: these now included *likely* significant harm to the child as well as such harm already inflicted (Section 31, Section 44). Where a care order was made, it would mean that mostly children would indeed be in care; the local authority would look after them (Section 33). If a supervision order were made, it would give the social worker greater authority (Section 35). Another change was that the child's welfare should be the paramount consideration in court proceedings relating to a child's upbringing (Section 1); under the preceding legislation welfare was only the first consideration – not quite as strongly put (Sections 3 and 59 of the 1975 Act, Section 18 of the Child Care Act 1980). An extension of local authority powers to care for and assist older 'children' – even up to the age of 21 – under Sections 20 and 24, might be seen as a further expression of paternalism. Another change, which may suggest a fundamental shift in ideology and emphasis, was that parents were no longer defined as having 'rights' but 'responsibilities' (Sections 2 and 3). The Act thus underlined parenthood as a duty to care, although it also conferred the authority and power to do so (Section 3). This is in line with the general paternalist perspective. Another aspect of the Act of interest here is the provision that the emergency protection order – the new shorter order which under Section 44 replaced the old 28-day place of safety order protecting children in an emergency – included a provision for ordering a child's medical examination (Section 44). The EPO was backed up by a child assessment order for non-emergency situations, lasting seven days, and allowing social workers to seek an order for medical assessment (Section 43). Local authority powers of investigation were strengthened in various ways. Residence orders (Sections 8–14) also perhaps reflected a protectionist emphasis, in that, for example, foster parents might ensure some security by this means. A number of sections in the Act thus reflect a paternalist direction.

As far as social work practice in the 1980s was concerned, planning for a permanent home for the child continued to be favoured in general, and it was the early 1980s which saw a considerable shift in this direction in many departments' practice. The social reaction to child abuse continued to exercise a considerable influence, as has been indicated. Awareness of child sexual abuse expanded, partly influenced by greater openness among women abused as children, partly by developments among paediatricians (see, for example, Hobbs and Wynne 1986), and there was more action on this form of abuse by social services departments; however, in Cleveland in 1987 the circumstance of a large number of children being removed compulsorily from their parents in a short time on suspicion of sexual abuse led to something of a public 'backlash' against social workers for being too ready to protect, on insufficient evidence, and the later cases in Orkney in 1991 seemed to confirm this view.

Another practice trend was that foster care became increasingly popular as a form of substitute care, with the percentage of children in care fostered being as high in the mid-1980s as it had been in the early 1960s (over 50 per cent by 1985 – Department of Health and Social Security 1985a), and continuing to increase, reaching 65 per cent of 'looked after' children by 1994 (Secretaries of State for Health and Wales 1994–5). Some authorities closed children's homes. This was at least partly linked with a desire to reduce costs. But at the same time, the number of *adoptions* continued to decrease. By 1983 the number was only just over 9,000 in England and Wales – for comparison, in the peak year of 1968 it had been almost 25,000 (OPCS, various years). In the late 1980s the numbers continued low, being just over 7,000 in 1989 for example (Hansard, cited in *Adoption and Fostering* 1995), in 1991 and 1992 being also slightly over 7,000. Those adoptions which did take place tended to involve children beyond infancy; while both fostering and adoption were expected to be more 'open'. The proportion of the child population in care also dropped; the percentage peaked at 0.77 per cent in 1980, but was down to 0.6 per cent in 1985–87 (Department of Health and Social Security, various years), and decreased further to 0.55 per cent in the early 1990s (Department of Health 1990, 1991d), with the rate not given by the Department of Health for 1993 (Department of Health 1993b) but the numbers still falling. Numbers on child protection registers also went down in the early 1990s (Department of Health/Welsh Office 1993) although they then rose (Secretaries of State for Health and Wales 1994–5). Overall 'less paternalism' is possibly suggested by these trends, although the picture is mixed.

Meanwhile, notwithstanding 'traditionalist' defences of conventional family forms (Dennis and Erdos 1992, Dennis 1993, Morgan 1994), and probably greater scepticism about the 'alternatives' to the nuclear family with which some had experimented in the 1970s, family diversity tended to increase: fewer children spent their entire childhood in the conventional model of a stable nuclear family with breadwinner father and mother at home full-time (Kiernan and Wicks 1990, Fox Harding 1996). As indicated earlier, marriages increasingly ended in divorce; more children were born outside marriage; and more were raised in the context of cohabiting and step-relationships. The stigma of illegitimacy was all but eliminated. Hence – in part – the lack of babies available for adoption; as a result some infertile couples sought out surrogate mothers to bear children for them instead (Rassaby 1982, Department of Health and Social Security 1984c, Montgomery 1986, Harding 1987). Thus, too, perhaps, a greater move to the adoption of older children who had come into care. Instability in family life might be used to justify a more strongly paternalist role for the state; but another implication of family diversity and change is the calling into question of how far a child can ever find permanence. Foster and adoptive families are not necessarily immune to these processes of change (see Garvey, 1992). In general, in the 1990s concern grew about the effects of family disruption and change on children, and evidence was gathering which indicated that, although the picture was not straightforward, the effects were generally negative for children (for example, Burghes 1994, Cockett and Tripp 1994). Whether this will eventually result in a more authoritarian role for the state is an interesting question.

The defence of the birth family

In the 1980s and 1990s the pro-birth family position also made its influence felt, although in a slightly different form from the 1960s, with more emphasis on parents' rights, and more action by aggrieved parents and pressure groups to defend these rights. In the early 1980s there was criticism of the administrative procedure used to take over parental rights by committee resolution, with the then National Council for One Parent Families (later One Parent Families) claiming that this was a contravention of 'natural justice' (National Council for One Parent Families 1982). A circular in 1984 (Department of Health and Social Security 1984b) extended parents' rights in this procedure slightly. Meanwhile, a Section of the 1983 Health and Social Services and Social Security Adjudications Act (HASSASSA) extended the rights of parents of children in compulsory care a little by granting a right of appeal against termination of access. A code of practice on access was also produced by central government (Department of Health and Social Security 1983a). However, this only marginally strengthened the power position of parents in relation to the local authority in the 1980s.

The 1980s saw other developments on the parents' rights front, including the formation of self-help groups such as PAIN, and appeals in child care cases to the local government ombudsman and to the European Court of Human Rights (Eaton 1986, Fogarty 1986). The mobilisation of parents in the Cleveland sex abuse cases should also not be overlooked. Many fought the local authority's decisions on both the legal and a broader public front. Some brought wardship cases; some contacted the MP Stuart Bell who, as shown earlier, became very embroiled in the battle on the parents' side – later he was a prominent participant in Children Bill debates (Parton 1991); and parents spoke to the media and involved other advocates such as a local clergyman. Some proceeded to sue for the damage they considered had been inflicted on their family life (see Parton and Martin 1989). Parents also fought back against the legal actions of the state in the Orkney case and in another Scottish case involving families in Strathclyde in the 1990s (Clouston 1995).

The apparently 'pro-family' elements in the 1989 Children Act also need to be considered. First, it seemed that local authority 'preventive' powers, and powers of assistance outside the substitute care system, were being extended. Section 17 conferred a duty to safeguard and promote the welfare of children 'in need', and to promote their upbringing by their families, by providing services of various kinds, including, exceptionally, cash. Schedule 2 of the Act set out the details. This provision was broader than the old Section 1 of the 1980 Child Care Act (previously of the 1963 Act), in that the duty was not restricted to the diminishing of the need for children to enter care or go before a court. It therefore became easier to assist families, as long as these provisions were supported by adequate resources. However, the local authority had to consider the means of both parent and child, with an eye to repayment, which might be seen as a drawback from a pro-birth parent perspective. There were also some reservations about the possibly stigmatising connotations of the term 'in need' (Jervis 1989). Another important development on the 'preventive' side was that health, housing and education authorities were placed under a duty to comply with requests for help from Social Services, if compatible with their own duties and functions (Section 27), and there was more provision for day care under Section 18.

Secondly, both parental rights resolutions and the need for a parent to give 28 days' notice of removal of a child in voluntary care, disappeared with this Act. Care for the child – or 'accommodation' as it was now termed when on a voluntary basis – was construed more in terms of partnership with the parents. Accommodation was sharply delineated from compulsory care. However, the widened grounds for care proceedings, taking in the *risk* of harm (see the previous section), could be used to protect a child already in accommodation if the local authority thought a parental removal was inappropriate. Apart from this, the local authority was not usually to provide accommodation if the parent objected (Section 20), and in providing accommodation, the local authority had to consult parents about decisions (Section 22). Parents also retain some parental responsibility when there is a care order (Section 33).

The shorter emergency protection order might also be seen as a strengthening of parents' rights. Emergency protection (Section 44) was now based on the more explicit criterion of likely significant harm, and the order lasted for a maximum of eight days rather than 28 (though with the possibility of extension for a further seven), with a right of appeal after three days in some cases (Section 45). The order carried a presumption of reasonable parental 'contact' (Section 44), and additional orders could be made regarding contact, although it could also be refused. The time limit on police emergency protection was also reduced, from eight to three days (Section 46). The provisions helped to satisfy concern about the draconian nature of the former place of safety orders (Ball 1989). There were also restrictions on interim care orders (Section 38). Where children were under Care Orders, the local authority was to be responsible for promoting reasonable contact with the parents, and the court could also order contact (Section 34). Contact was presumed when children were 'looked after'. Under rules pursuant to the Act the parents' position in care proceedings was strengthened, and under Section 26 complaints procedures were set up by which parents, among others, could complain about the local authority in child care cases. Local authority use of wardship proceedings was restricted (Section 100), and the rights of unmarried birth fathers were enhanced, in that the father could obtain parental responsibility either through a court application or formal agreement with the mother (Section 4). These provisions, broadly speaking, enhanced the position of the parents, limiting state coercion.

As far as practice was concerned, in the late 1980s research evidence cast some doubt on policies of permanence (Thoburn *et al.* 1987), and 'shared care' with parents was favoured to a greater degree in social work practice; following the Children Act, the emphasis was firmly on partnership. As noted, both adoptions and numbers in care dropped in the 1980s; it was also the case that fewer were in care under care orders than in the 1970s (Department of Health and Social Security, various years). In the 1990s adoptions continued at a low level. It is true that a marked drop in care orders after implementation of the Children Act in 1991 was followed by a rise (Secretaries of State for Health and Wales 1992–3, 1993–4, Marchant 1992). Care orders were, however, still below the levels of pre-Children Act times, and the National Children's Home (1994) commented: 'Despite the increase in court activity since the implementation of the Children Act 1989 in October 1991, current levels of activity are markedly below the levels prevailing before the Act' (p. 64). Numbers in care/accommodation in the 1990s were also still going down. Shared care and partnership notions favoured by the Children Act were reflected in an increase in children looked after under voluntary agreements (Secretaries of State for Health and Wales 1992–3). Thomas and Beckett (1995) commented on the basis of their research: 'It has become more acceptable to plan for children to remain away from home on the basis of agreements with parents and continuing contact' (p. 23).

On children in need, the Children Act Report 1992 stated: 'most authorities are providing a range of services commensurate with the purpose of the Children Act' (Secretaries of State for Health and Wales 1992–3:35), with a strong showing on family centres, nurseries, respite care, accommodation for children with disabilities, and financial payments. Research reported in the 1993 Report (by Aldgate, McBeath and Tunstill, 1994) found two thirds of authorities providing, for example, family centres, cash payments, respite care and help for care leavers. However, family support work was at risk of being subordinated to child protection work, and in general progress to full implementation of Section 17 was slow. The next annual report, 1994, thought that: 'Some local authorities are in danger of limiting resources to children on the Child Protection Register' (Secretaries of State for Health and Wales 1994–5:1) when the definition of 'in need' was wider. The Department of Health wished for a broader approach.

On balance, it appeared that the Children Act, while containing both state paternalist and pro-birth family provisions, leaned more heavily to the latter perspective, strengthening the parents' position. Indeed, Packman (1993) concludes: 'through the Children Act we are brought full circle, to the place of prevention in the spectrum of childcare services' (p. 234), and Dingwall *et al.* (1995 edn of *The Protection of Children*) comment that the Act has privileged parental responsibility and its associated procedural rights, and reinforced the bias against intervention. As mentioned, the adequate resourcing of the ostensibly wider powers to help families is a crucial issue. The extra resources required to implement the powers were thought to be considerable (Stewart 1989, Richards 1989). Without committing more resources, the Department of Health placed a firmer emphasis on prevention and family support rather than child protection in the mid-1990s, following research summarised in *Child Protection Messages from Research* (Dartington Social Research Unit 1995) which found many families drawn into the complex child protection procedures unnecessarily. However, it was feared that without additional resources, at least in the short-term, diversion of effort away from child protection could be problematic (Brindle 1995).

Children's rights and child liberation

The manifestations of a children's rights perspective in English child care policy in the 1980s and 1990s, including the relevant changes in the 1989 Act, have already been referred to in discussing the rights perspective in practice in Chapter 5, and the reader is referred back to this section. It will be recalled that signs of responsiveness to this perspective were found in the 1980s and 1990s in the ratification of the UN Convention on the Rights of the Child, in facilitating children's evidence in court, in enhanced rights of consent to medical treatment, in moves to end physical punishment, in the formation of pressure groups representing children, in the setting up of telephone lines for distressed children; and in ideas such as commissioners and ministers specifically for children. In the Children Act specifically, there were the provisions to pay heed to the child's wishes, to extend separate representation for children in court proceedings, to enable children to take legal action on their own behalf, and to set up local authority complaints procedures. There were some signs of the liberationist perspective in practice, then, and although it still cannot be regarded as the most dominant viewpoint, there were enough indications to suggest that this was the direction for the future in the short and medium term – with some attendant dangers.

Conflict and balance

The 1980s, as the author has attempted to show, were a period in which both the paternalist and birth parent perspectives were in evidence, while *laissez-faire* and child liberation had a more minor influence. The

1980s appeared to be somewhat polarised with no single perspective dominant. Parton (1991) sees a difference between the earlier and later parts of the decade. In the first half of the 1980s: 'The principles of partnership, family support, shared care, respite care, maintaining links and return to family, were all given pre-eminence' (p. 50). (This remark must be set against the emphasis on permanence at that time, however.) In the latter half, following further child abuse tragedies and inquiries: 'It was as if there were two competing agendas or paradigms for practice and it was the one symbolised by the child abuse inquiries which was dominant' (p. 78). And Hendrick (1994) comments: 'The 1980s were the decade in which long-smouldering tensions concerning the relationship between child care, family responsibility and the jurisdiction of the State finally erupted' (p. 273).

Concerns about both the child care agents of the state doing too much, too coercively, and about them doing too little, too ineffectually, resulted in a wish for legislation and policy to attempt to proceed in two directions at once – both towards better protection of the child and better protection of the parent. This bidirectional policy may be be expressed in terms of conflict, or of balance. From one viewpoint, the two broad objectives are in conflict and cannot be realised simultaneously; more power for social workers in relation to children does mean that parents lose some of their rights. Therefore descriptions of the Children Act 1989 which refer to its providing *both* better protection for children and greater rights for parents (see, for example, the reference to the Prime Minister's introduction to the Bill in Oliver 1988) are simply a denial of conflict, an attempt to avoid the awkward dilemmas that the child care field inevitably throws up. As Dingwall *et al.* (1995 edn of *The Protection of Children*) say, the use of power by child protection agencies is: 'in contradiction to the empowerment of their parents to resist the oppression which is thought to be responsible for their abusive behaviour' (p. 253).

From another viewpoint, however, what legislation and policy is all about here is balance. While there are some conflicting objectives, it may be argued, a better balance can be achieved. Alternative terms might be consensus, compromise or accommodation, although Hendrick's (1994) judgement that the Act: 'slithered on to the statute-book as a tired consensus arrived at between a dispirited, fragmented and largely defunct Left and a morally arrogant Right' (p. 287) is perhaps unduly derogatory. It is perhaps reasonable, and not inconsistent, for the Children Act to attempt to proceed in two directions at once, adding to the power of parents here, strengthening the courts and local authorities there. What will be achieved, it may be argued, is not simply a redistribution of muddle but a genuinely more effective solution correcting tendencies both to over- and under-react, while helping parents and children as a unit where it is appropriate to do so.

It might be premature to ask what the Children Act has achieved by the mid-1990s, when implementation did not occur till October 1991. An immediate drop in court actions (care orders, supervision orders, emergency protection orders as compared with place of safety orders) was followed by a rise but not to the levels of the 1970s and 1980s. This looks like a reduction in the coercive role of the state, therefore. But restrictions on local authority resources prevented family support work from really taking off. Meanwhile, children's rights elements in law and policy did seem to be strengthened in a variety of ways, while the notion of 'parental responsibility' was also developed by government, not just in the Children Act but in the notorious Child Support Act 1991 and other measures as well (see Fox Harding 1994). The wider concept of parental responsibility has not been explored in this book but it is emerging as significant and a pointer for the future.

Postscript: a reply to Harris and Timms

In 1993 Harris and Timms mounted a critique of the first edition of this book, in the context of a chapter called 'The state, the family and the child' within their book *Secure Accommodation in Child Care*, and as most of their critique was directed to Chapter 7, a few points of reply will be made here.

A preliminary point must be that the exposition of the four value perspectives is not offered as an *explanation* of the development of child care policy, either in the post-war period or in general. Although reference is made to particular periods when one value perspective or the other seemed to be in the ascendant, proper explanation of how this came about would be a different exercise. Nor is the account of the four value perspectives offered as a literal description of the state of policy in any one time or place. The perspectives are offered as *ways of seeing* child care issues, each with its own rationale, each with a degree of internal coherence, ways of seeing which are *reflected* in particular policies at particular times, but never in a pure form. Clarifying the perspectives can help us to understand more fully the nature of debates and the reasoning behind certain policies and practices. In response to Harris and Timms' criticism that the perspectives framework is 'weak as social theory' (p. 34), it is replied that it was never offered as this. To use their own terms, the perspectives may be seen as 'culturally conventional (and therefore comprehensible) ways of describing and dividing a social totality' (p. 37). It may be submitted that this is a useful function to perform. Harris and Timms, however, go on to argue that the perspectives are potentially misleading. They say that: 'In the practical world of policy making we still have to accommodate these perspectives in particular "cases"' (p. 37), and with this latter point I can only agree. It is hoped, however, that the perspectives framework may assist in understanding what our underlying values and assumptions are when we find ourselves inclining to one solution rather than another, and in helping us to see the potential problems in any given solution – where we are unclear, where our knowledge is weak, what we have not thought through.

Following this preliminary point, three others are advanced briefly in reply to Harris and Timms. First, they argue that my classification of authors into four different positions does not fully work, because certain authors appear in more than one camp, and 'moderate' categories have been created to accommodate some. This problem of definitive classification of particular authors' writing is acknowledged. It is the ideas that I have attempted to classify rather than (absolutely) the individuals.

Secondly, I have been misunderstood if it is thought that: 'her thesis seems to be that the more "coherent" (in her terms) the policy is, the better it will be' (p. 35). This perception has been misread into my analysis. In fact it is not my view that more 'coherent' policies are necessarily 'better'. Coherent policies can be authoritarian, and in any event we must ask with regard to any policy: 'better for what purpose? for whose interests? in what sense?'. It is, however, helpful for Harris and Timms to point out that the use of the term 'balance' may not be the most appropriate one to use with reference to the Children Act 1989. I would acknowledge that it certainly is not appropriate if it is taken to mean precise 'hydraulic relation' (Harris and Timms 1993:36). Harris and Timms are correct to say that in the field of social policy: 'it is possible simultaneously to increase powers *and* to circumscribe the circumstances in which they may be exercised' (p. 36).

Finally, I acknowledge the limitations of my analysis of the Children Act 1989 in this book. The main purpose of the book is to give an account of four different possible perspectives on child care policy. While this has been applied to the Children Act briefly, the reader needs to look elsewhere for more comprehensive accounts of this extremely complex measure and its implementation.

References

Abbott, P. and Wallace, C. (1992) *The Family and the New Right*, London: Pluto Press.

Adams, R. (1986) 'Juvenile justice and children and young people's rights' in B. Franklin (ed.) (1986) *The Rights of Children*, Oxford: Blackwell.

Adamson, G. (1973) *The Care-Takers*, Brentwood: Bookstall Publications.

Adcock M (1983) 'Working with natural parents to prevent long-term care', *Adoption and Fostering*, 7(3): 8–12.

Adcock, M., Kaniuk, J. and White, R. (eds) (1994) *Exploring Openness in Adoption*, Croydon: Significant Publications.

Adcock, M., White, R. and Rowlands, C. (1983) *The Administrative Parent*, London: British Agencies for Adoption and Fostering (BAAF).

Adoption and Fostering (1983) 'Editorial: BAAF and natural parents', *Adoption and Fostering*, 7(3).

Adoption and Fostering (1994), 18 February: 53–4.

Adoption and Fostering (1995), 19 January: 4.

Aldgate, J., McBeath, G. and Tunstill, J. (1994) *Implementing Section 17 of the Children Act – The First 18 months. A Report for the Department of Health*, Leicester: Leicester University.

Allen, L. J. (1978)'Child abuse: a critical review of the research and the theory', in J. P. Martin (ed.) *Violence and the Family*, Chichester: Wiley.

Allen, N. (1992) *Making Sense of the Children Act: A Guide for the Social and Welfare Services*, Harlow: Longman.

Anderson, D. and Dawson, G. (eds) (1986) *Family Portraits*, London: Social Affairs Unit.

Andrews, C. (1980) 'Is blood thicker than local authorities?', *Social Work Today*, 12(1): 19–21.

Archard, D. (1993) *Children: Rights and Childhood*, London: Routledge.

Aries, P. (1962) *Centuries of Childhood*, Harmondsworth: Penguin.

Arnold, C. (1978) 'Analyses of rights', in E. Kamenka and A. Ehr-Soon Tay (eds) *Human Rights*, London: Arnold.

Asquith, S. (ed.) (1993) *Protecting Children. Cleveland to Orkney: More Lessons to Learn?* Edinburgh: HMSO.

Association of Black Social Workers And Professionals (ABSWAP) (1983) *Black Children in Care*, London: ABSWAP.

Association of British Adoption and Fostering Agencies (ABAFA) (1976) *Practice Guide to the Children Act (1975)*, London: ABAFA.

Association of British Adoption and Fostering Agencies (ABAFA) (1977) *Assumption of Parental Rights and Duties – Practice Guide*, London: ABAFA.

Association of British Adoption and Fostering Agencies (ABAFA) (1979) *Terminating Parental Contact*, London: ABAFA.

Bainham, A. (1990) 'The privatisation of the public interest in children', *The Modern Law Review*, 53(2): 206–21.

Bainham, A. (1993) 'Growing up in Britain: adolescence in the post-Gillick era', in J. Eekelaar and P. Sarcevic (eds) *Parenthood in Modern Society*, Netherlands: Kluwer Academic Publishers.

Ball, C. (1989) '"Carlile factor" overlooked in proposed legislation', *Community Care*, 23 March: 13.

Bandman, B. (1973) 'Do children have any natural rights?', *Proceedings of 29th Annual Meeting of Philosophy of Education Society*: 234–6.

Barclay Committee Report – see National Institute for Social Work.

Barrett, M. and Macintosh, M. (1991) *The Antisocial Family*, London: Verso.

Barton, C. and Moss, K. (1994) 'Who can smack children now?', *Journal of Child Law*, **6**(l): 32–4.

Bean, P. and Melville, J. (1989) *Lost Children of the Empire*, London: Unwin Hyman.

Bebbington, A. and Miles, J. (1989) 'The background of childen who enter local authority care', *British Journal of Social Work*, **19**: 349–68.

Behlmer, G. K. (1982) *Child Abuse and Moral Reform in England 1870–1908*, Stanford, California: Stanford University Press.

Bell, S. (1988) *When Salem came to the Boro'*, London: Pan.

Benians, R. (1982) 'Preserving parental contact: a factor in promoting healthy growth and development in children', in *Family Rights Group, Fostering Parental Contact*, London: Family Rights Group.

Beresford, P., Kemmis, J. and Tunstill, J. (1987) *In Care in North Battersea*, London: North Battersea Research Group.

Berger, B. and Berger, P. L. (1983) *The War over the Family. Capturing the Middle Ground*, London: Hutchinson.

Berridge, D. and Cleaver, H. (1987) *Foster Home Breakdown*, Oxford: Blackwell.

Binney, V. *et al.* (1981) *Leaving Violent Men*, Bristol: Women's Aid Federation Ltd.

Booth, T. and Booth, W. (1994) *Parenting under Pressure*, Buckingham: Open University Press.

Bowlby, J. (1951) *Maternal Care and Mental Health*, Geneva: World Health Organisation.

Bowlby, J. (1953) *Child Care and the Growth of Love*, Harmondsworth: Penguin.

Brannen, J. and Wilson, G. (1987) *Give and Take in Families: Studies in Resource Distribution*, London: Allen and Unwin.

Brewer, C. and Lait, J. (1980) *Can Social Work Survive?* London: Temple Smith.

Brindle, D. (1995) 'Support versus an inquisition', *Guardian Society*, 21 June: 2.

British Agencies for Adoption and Fostering (BAAF) (1985) *Good Enough Parenting*, London: BAAF.

Brown, C. (1994) 'No minor punishment', Guardian, 12 October.

Burghes, L. (1994) *Lone Parenthood and Family Disruption. The Outcomes for Children*, London: Family Policy Studies Centre.

Burgoyne, J. and Clark, D. (1984) 'Reconstituted families', in R. Rapoport, M. Fogarty, and R. N. Rapoport (eds) *Families in Britain*, London: Routledge and Kegan Paul.

Byrne, D. (1989) 'The challenge of children's rights', *Guardian Society*, 22 November: 27.

Byrne, D. (1989–90) 'The rights of the child', *Poverty*, **74**: 13–15.

Campbell, B. (1988) *Unofficial Secrets, Child Sexual Abuse: The Cleveland Case*, London: Virago.

Cawson, P. *et al.* (1978) *Young Offenders in Care. Preliminary Report*, London: DHSS Social Research Branch.

Central Statistical Office (1987) *Social Trends 1987*, London: HMSO.
Central Statistical Office (1994) *Social Trends 1994*, London: HMSO.
Cervi, B. (1994) 'No turning back?' *Community Care*, 17–23 November:14–15.
Chartered Institute of Public Finance and Accountancy (1995) *Personal Social Services Statistics 1993–4 Actuals*, London: Chartered Institute of Public Finance and Accountancy.
Childline (1995) *Newsline*, Spring/Summer.
Children Act Advisory Committee (1992–3) *Annual Report*, London: Lord Chancellor's Department.
Children Act Reports – see Secretaries of State for Health and Wales.
Children's Legal Centre (1984) *Congress '84; Children and their Rights; Discussion Group B: Representation of Children and Young People's Interests*, London: Children's Legal Centre.
Children's Rights Development Unit (1994) *The UK Agenda for Children*, London: Children's Rights Development Unit.
Clark, S. (1995) 'Amendment will allow privatised foster care', *Community Care*, 23–9 March: 8.
Clarke, K., Glendinning, C. and Craig, G. (1994) *Losing Support: Children and the Child Support Act*, London: The Children's Society.
Clarkson, M. and Thomas, T. (1995) 'Into the public eye', *Community Care*, 6–11 January: 7.
Clouston, E. (1995) 'Abused by the system', *Guardian*, 1 March.
Clyde, Lord (1992) *The Report of the Inquiry into the Removal of Children from Orkney in February 1991*, Edinburgh: HMSO.
Cockett, M. and Tripp, J. (1994) *The Exeter Family Study: Family Breakdown and its Impact on Children*, Exeter: Exeter University Press.
Cohen, S. (1973) *Folk Devils and Moral Panics: The Creation of Mods and Rockers*, St Albans: Paladin.
Colton, M., Drury, C. and Williams, M. (1995) *Children in Need. Family Support under the Children Act 1989*, Aldershot: Avebury (reviewed by Weir, A. in *Community Care*, 20–26 July 1995: 33).
Commission for Racial Equality (CRE) (1990) *Adopting a Better Policy: Adoption and Fostering of Ethnic Minority Children – The Race Dimension*, London: CRE.
Community Care, 9 July 1992: 4, 13.
Community Care, 19 November 1992: 3.
Community Care, Supplement on mental illness, 30 April 1994.
Community Care, 8–14 December 1994: 3.
Community Care, 16–22 March 1995: 5.
Conservative Family Campaign (1986) Press release: 'Putting children first', 14 March.
Cooper, A. (1995) 'Part four: child abuse', *Community Care*, 3–9 August: ii–viii.
Cooper, C. (1979) 'Paediatric aspects', in ABAFA, *Terminating Parental Contact*, London: ABAFA.
Cooper, C. (1985) '"Good-enough", border-line and "bad-enough" parenting', in BAAF, *Good Enough Parenting*, London: BAAF.
Cooper, D. (1971) *The Death of the Family*, London: Allen Lane.
Corby, B. (1987) *Working with Child Abuse*, Milton Keynes: Open University Press.
Court Committee (1976) *Report of the Committee on Child Health Services. Fit for the Future*, Cmnd. 6684, London: HMSO.

Creighton, S. J. (1989) *Child Abuse Trends in England and Wales 1983–87*, London: National Society for the Prevention of Cruelty to Children (NSPCC).

Curtis Committee – see Secretary of State for the Home Department *et al.*

Dale, D. (1987) *Denying Homes to Black Children: Britain's New Race Adoption Policies*, London: Social Affairs Unit.

Dartington Social Research Unit (1995) *Child Protection Messages from Research*, London: HMSO.

Davies, J. (1993) *The Family: Is it Just Another Lifestyle Choice?*, London: IEA Health and Welfare Unit.

Davies, L. (1980) 'The age of consent – is it time for a change in the law?', *Social Work Today*, 11(19): 14–16.

Dawson, R. E., Prewitt, K. and Dawson, K. S. (1977) *Political Socialisation*, Boston, Massachusetts: Little Brown.

Delphy, C. and Leonard, D. (1992) *Familiar Exploitation: A New Analysis of Marriage in Contemporary Western Societies*, Cambridge: Polity Press.

De Mause, L. (ed.) (1976) *The History of Childhood*, London: Souvenir Press.

Dennis, N. (1993) *Rising Crime and the Dismembered Family*, London: IEA Health and Welfare Unit.

Dennis, N. and Erdos, G. (1992) *Families without Fatherhood*, London: IEA Health and Welfare Unit.

Department of Health (DH) (1988a) *Survey of Children and Young Persons on Child Protection Registers Year Ending 31 March, England*, London: HMSO.

Department of Health (DH) (1988b) *Working Together: A Guide to Inter-Agency Co-operation for the Protection of Children from Abuse*, London: HMSO.

Department of Health (DH) (1990) *Children in Care of Local Authorities, Year Ending 31st March, England*, London: HMSO.

Department of Health (DH) (1991a) *Patterns and Outcomes in Child Placement*, London: HMSO.

Department of Health (DH) (1991b) *Children and Young Persons on Child Protection Registers, Year Ending 31 March 1991, England*, London: HMSO.

Department of Health (DH) (1991c) *The Children Act 1989, Guidance and Regulations*, London: HMSO.

Department of Health (DH) (1991d) *Children in Care of Local Authorities, Year Ending 31st March, England*, London: HMSO.

Department of Health (DH) (1992) *Review of Adoption Law: Report to Ministers of an Inter-departmental Working Group*, London: HMSO.

Department of Health (DH) (1993a) *Children and Young Persons on Child Protection Registers, Year Ending 31 March, England*, London: HMSO.

Department of Health (DH) (1993b) *Children Looked After by Local Authorities 14 October 1991 to 31 March 1993, England*, London: HMSO.

Department of Health (DH), Welsh Office, Home Office, Lord Chancellor's Department (1993) *Adoption: the Future*, Cm. 2288 London: HMSO.

Department of Health and Social Security (DHSS) (1974) *DHSS Memorandum of Guidance May 1974, HSC(IS)732*, London, HMSO.

Department of Health and Social Security (DHSS) (1983a) *Code of Practice: Access to Children in Care*, London: HMSO.

Department of Health and Social Security (DHSS) (1983b) *LAC Circular on Access*, (**83**)19.

Department of Health and Social Security (DHSS) (1984a) *Second Report on the Children Act 1975*, London: HMSO.

Department of Health and Social Security (DHSS) (1984b) *LAC*, **84** (15).

Department of Health and Social Security (DHSS) (1984c) *Warnock Committee Report of the Committee of Inquiry into Human Fertilisation and Embryology*, Cmnd. 9314, London: HMSO.

Department of Health and Social Security (DHSS) (1985) *Review of Child Care Law: Report to Ministers of an Inter-Departmental Working Party*, London: HMSO.

Department of Health and Social Security (DHSS) (1987) *The Law on Child Care and Family Services*, Cm. 62, London: HMSO.

Department of Health and Social Security (DHSS) (various years, including 1985a, 1986, 1987a) *Children in Care of local Authorities Year Ending 31st March, England*, London: HMSO.

Department of Health and Social Security (DHSS) (various years including 1978, 1987) *Health and Personal Social Services Statistics for England*, London: HMSO.

Department of Social Security (1995) *Households Below Average Income*, London: HMSO.

Dingwall, R., Eekelaar, J. and Murray, T. (1983a) *The Protection of Children: State Intervention and Family Life*, Oxford: Blackwell; 2nd edn (1995) Aldershot: Avebury.

Dingwall, R., Eekelaar, J. and Murray T. (1983b) 'Times change and we change with them?' *Community Care*, 16 June: 18–19.

Dobson, P. (1995) 'Life or death', *Community Care*, 16–22 March: 10.

Donzelot, J. (1980) *The Policing of Families: Welfare versus the State*, London: Hutchinson.

Doran, C. and Young, J. (1987) 'Child abuse: the real crisis', *New Society*, 27 November: 12–14.

Durham, M. (1991) *Sex and Politics: The Family and Morality in the Thatcher Years*, Basingstoke: Macmillan.

Dyer, C. (1992) 'Getting in on the Act', *Guardian*, November 17.

Eaton, L. (1986) 'Parents' rights on trial', *Social Work Today*, 17 November: 3.

Edwards, S. and Halpern, A. (1992) 'Parental responsibility: an instrument of social policy', *Family Law*, **22**:113–18.

Eekelaar, J. (1973) 'What are parental rights?', *Law Quarterly Review*, **89**: 210.

Eekelaar, J. (1991) 'Parental responsibility: state of nature or nature of the state?', *Journal of Social Welfare and Family Law*, **1**: 37–50.

Eekelaar, J. (1992) 'The importance of thinking that children have rights' in P. Alston, S. Parker, and J. Seymour (eds) *Children, Rights and the Law*, Oxford: Clarendon Press.

Eekelaar, J. (1994) 'The interests of the child and the child's wishes: the role of dynamic self-determinism', *International Journal of Law and the Family*, **8**: 42-61.

Elliot, F. R. (1996) *Gender, Family and Society*, Basingstoke: Macmillan.

Ellis, S. and Franklin, A. (1995) 'Children's rights officers: righting wrongs and promoting rights', in B. Franklin (ed.) *The Handbook of Children's Rights: Comparative Policy and Practice*, London and New York: Routledge.

Esterson, A. and Laing, R. D. (1970) *Sanity, Madness and the Family*, Harmondsworth: Penguin.

Family Law Reports (1993) Vol. 1, Bristol: Jordan Publishing Ltd.

Family Rights Group (1982) *Fostering Parental Contact*, London: Family Rights Group.

Family Rights Group (1984) *Permanent Substitute Families. Security or Severance*, London: Family Rights Group.

Family Rights Group (1991) *The Children Act 1989: Working in partnership with families*, London: Family Rights Group.

Farson, R. (1978) *Birthrights*, New York: Penguin.

Fielding, N. G. and Conroy, S. (1991) 'Interviewing child victims: police and social work investigations of child sexual abuse', *Sociology* **26**(1): 103–4.

Finch, J. and Groves, D. (1983) *A Labour of Love: Women, Work and Caring*, London: Routledge and Kegan Paul.

Finkelhor, D. (1984) *Child Sexual Abuse: New Theory and Research*, New York: Free Press.

Firestone, S. (1971) *The Dialectic of Sex: The Case for Feminist Revolution*, London: Cape.

Flathman, R. (1976) *The Practice of Rights*, Cambridge: Cambridge University Press.

Flekkoy, M. G. (1985) 'Speaking for children', *Childright*, **14**: 19.

Flekkoy, M. G. (1988–9) 'Child advocacy in Norway', *Children and Society*, 2(4):307–18.

Flekkoy, M. G. (1991) *A Voice for Children: Speaking Out as Their Ombudsman*, London: Jessica Kingsley and UNICEF.

Flekkoy, M. G. (1995) 'The Scandinavian experience of children's rights', in B. Franklin (ed.) *The Handbook of Children's Rights: Comparative Policy and Practice*, London and New York: Routledge.

Fletcher, R. (1988) *The Abolitionists: Family and Marriage Under Attack*, London: Routledge.

Fogarty, M. (1986) 'Whose son is it anyway?', *Guardian*, 26 November.

Fogarty, M. (1987) 'Cleveland and Kimberley inquiries have at last caused the penny to drop', *Social Work Today*, 21 December: 13.

Foster, H. H. and Freed, D. J. (1972) 'A Bill of Rights for children', *Family Law Quarterly*, **VI**(4): 343.

Fox, L. M. (1982) 'Two value positions in recent child care law and practice', *British Journal of Social Work*, **12**(2): 265–90.

Fox, L. M. (1986) 'Parental rights assumptions, the passage of time and "natural justice": the use of section 3(1)(d) of the Child Care Act 1980', *British Journal of Social Work*, **16**: 161-80.

Fox Harding, L. M. (1990) 'Underlying themes and contradictions in the Children Act 1989', *Justice of the Peace*, **154**: 37 5 September: 591–4

Fox Harding, L. M. (1991) 'The Children Act 1989 in context: four perspectives in child care law and policy (I) and (II)', *Journal of Social Welfare and Family Law*, **3**:179–93; **4**: 285–302.

Fox Harding, L. M. (1994) 'Parental responsibility – a dominant theme in British child and family policy for the 1990s', *International Journal of Sociology and Social Policy*, **14**(1/2): 84–108.

Fox Harding, L. M. (1996) *Family, State and Social Policy*, Basingstoke: Macmillan.

Franklin, A. W. (1982) 'Child abuse in the 1980s', *Maternal and Child Health*. 7: 12–16.

Franklin, B. (ed.) (1986) *The Rights of Children*, Oxford: Blackwell.
Franklin, B. (1989) 'Children's rights: developments and prospects', *Children and Society*, **3**(1): 76–92.
Franklin B (ed.) (1995) *The Handbook of Children's Rights: Comparative Policy and Practice*, London and New York: Routledge.
Franks, H. (1989) 'A world of secrets', *Guardian*, 5 July.
Freeman, M. D. A. (1980) 'The rights of children in the International Year of the Child', *Current Legal Problems*, **33**:1–31
Freeman, M. D. A. (1983a) *The Rights and Wrongs of Children*, London: Frances Pinter.
Freeman, M. D. A. (1983b) 'Freedom and the Welfare State: child-rearing, parental autonomy and state intervention', *Journal of Social Welfare Law*, March: 70–91.
Freeeman. M. D. A. (1992a) 'Taking children's rights more seriously', *International Journal of Law and the Family*, **6**: 52–71.
Freeman, M. D. A. (1992b) *Children, Their Families and the Law – Working with the Children Act*, Basingstoke: Macmillan.
Freeman, M. D. A. (1992c) 'In the child's best interests? Reading the Children Act critically', *Current Legal Problems*, **45**(1): 173–211.
Freeman, M. D. A. (1993) 'Removing rights from adolescents', *Adoption and Fostering*, **17**(1): 14–20.
Freeman, M. D. A. (1995) 'Children's rights in a land of rites', in B. Franklin, (ed.) *The Handbook of Children's Rights: Comparative Policy and Practice*, London and New York: Routledge.
Frost, N. and Stein, M. (1989) *The Politics of Child Welfare: Inequality, Power and Change*, Hemel Hempstead: Harvester/Wheatsheaf.
Frost, N. and Stein, M. (1990) 'The politics of the Children Act', *Childright*, July/August:17–19.
Garnham, A. and Knights, E. (1994) *Putting the Treasury First: The Truth about Child Support*, London: Child Poverty Action Group.
Garvey, A. (1992) 'Adding and subtracting', *Guardian*, 9 June.
George, V. (1970) *Foster Care: Theory and Practice*, London: Routledge and Kegan Paul.
Gil, D. G. (1975) 'Unravelling child abuse', *American Journal of Orthopsychiatry*, **45**(3).
Gill, O. and Jackson, B. (1983) *Adoption and Race: Black, Asian and Mixed Race Children in White Families*, London: Batsford/British Agencies for Adoption and Fostering (BAAF).
Ginsberg, A. (1965) *On Justice in Society*, Harmondsworth: Penguin.
Gittins, D. (1993) *The Family in Question. Changing Households and Familiar Ideologies*, Basingstoke: Macmillan.
Glendinning, C. and Millar, J. (eds) (1987) *Women and Poverty in Britain*, Brighton: Wheatsheaf (2nd edn. 1992, New York, London: Harvester/ Wheatsheaf).
Goldstein J., Freud, A. and Solnit, A. (1979) *Beyond the Best Interests of the Child*, New York: Free Press.
Goldstein J., Freud, A. and Solnit, A. (1980) *Before the Best Interests of the Child*, London: Burnett Books/Andre Deutsch.
Gordon, L. (1989) *Heroes of their Own Lives: The Politics and History of Family Violence*, London: Virago.
Greenstein, F. (1974) *Children and Politics*, New Haven, Connecticut: Yale University Press.

Greer, G. (1971) *The Female Eunuch*, St. Albans: Paladin.
Hadjipateras, A. (1990) 'A step in the right direction', *Social Work Today*, 1 February: 25.
Haggerstrom, W. (1964) 'The power of the poor', in F. Reisman (ed.) *Mental Health of the Poor*, New York: Collier-Macmillan.
Hallett, C. (1989) 'Child-abuse inquiries and public policy', in O. Stevenson (ed.) *Child Abuse: Public Policy and Professional Practice*, Hemel Hempstead: Harvester/Wheatsheaf.
Hallett, C. and Stevenson, O. (1980) *Child Abuse. Aspects of Interprofessional Co-operation*, London: Allen and Unwin.
Harding, L. M. (1987) 'The Debate on Surrogate Motherhood: The Current Situation, Some Arguments and Issues; Questions Facing Law and Policy', *Journal of Social Welfare Law*, January: 37–63.
Harding, L. M. (1993) 'The Children Act in practice: underlying themes revisited', *Justice of the Peace*, **157.38** 18 September: 600–2; **157.39** 25 September: 616–18.
Hardyment, C. (1983) *Dream Babies. Child Care from Locke to Spock*, London: Cape.
Harris, R. and Timms, N. (1993) *Secure Accommodation in Child Care: Between Hospital and Prison or Thereabouts?*, London and New York: Routledge.
Hatchett, W. (1990) 'Not just kids' stuff', *Community Care*, 29 November: 9.
Haynes, G. *et al.* (1994) 'Open verdict', *Community Care*, 30 June–6 July: 25–6.
Helfer, R. E. and Kempe, C. H. (eds) (1968) *The Battered Child*, Chicago: University of Chicago Press.
Hendrick, H. (1994) *Child Welfare England 1872–1989*, London: Routledge.
Hetherington, E. M., Cox, M. and Cox, R. (1982) 'Effects of divorce on parents and children', in M. E. Lamb (ed.) *Nontraditional Families: Parenting and Child Development*, Hillsdale, New Jersey: Eribaum.
Heywood, J. S. (1978) *Children in Care. The Development of the Service for the Deprived Child*, London: Routledge and Kegan Paul.
Hill, M. (1993) *The Welfare State in Britain: A Political History since 1945*, Aldershot: Edward Elgar.
Hills. J. (ed.) (1991) *The State of Welfare: The Welfare State in Britain since 1974*, Oxford: Clarendon Press.
Hobbs, C. and Wynne. J. (1986) 'Buggery in childhood – a common syndrome in child abuse', *The Lancet*, 4 October.
Hodges. P. (1981) 'Children and parents: who chooses?', *Politics and Power*, **3**: 49-65.
Hodgson, D. (1990) 'Power to the child', *Social Work Today*, 12 July: 16–17.
Holman, R. (1975a) 'Unmarried mothers, social deprivation and child separation', *Policy and Politics*, **3**: 25–41.
Holman, R. (1975b) 'The place of fostering in social work', *British Journal of Social Work*, **5**(1): 3–29.
Holman, R. (1978) 'A class analysis of adoption reveals a disturbing picture', *Community Care*, 6 April: 30.
Holman, R. (1980a) *Inequality in Child Care*, London: Child Poverty Action Group, Poverty Pamphlet 26.
Holman, R. (1980b) 'A *real* child care policy for the future', *Community Care*, 18/25 December: 16–17.
Holman, R. (1982) 'Exclusive and inclusive fostering', in Family Rights Group *Fostering Parental Contact*, London: Family Rights Group.

Holman, B. (1988) *Putting Families First. Prevention and Child Care*, Basingstoke: Macmillan.

Holman, B. (1993) *New Deal for Social Welfare*, Oxford: Lion.

Holt, J. (1975) *Escape from Childhood. The Needs and Rights of Children*, Harmondsworth: Penguin.

Home Office (1948) *Circular No. 160/1948*, London: Home Office.

Home Office (1950) *Joint circular from The Home Office (No. 157/50), the Ministry of Health (No. 78/50) and the Ministry of Education (No. 225/50) 31 July*, London: Home Office.

Home Office (1965) *The Child, the Family and the Young Offender*, Cmnd. 2742, London: HMSO.

Home Office (1968) *Children in Trouble*, Cmnd. 3601, London: HMSO.

Home Office (1989) *Report of the Advisory Group on Video Evidence (Pigot Report)*, London: Home Office.

Home Office (various years) *Children Act 1948. Summary of Local Authorities' Returns of Children in Care at 31st March*, London: HMSO.

Home Office/Scottish Education Department (1972) *Report of the Departmental Committee on the Adoption of Children (Houghton Committee Report)*, Cmnd. 5107 London: HMSO.

House of Commons (1984) *Second Report from the Social Services Committee (Session 1983–84) Children in Care (The Short Report)*, London: HMSO.

Howe, D. (1995) 'Adoption and attachment', *Adoption and Fostering*, **19**(4): 7–15.

Howe, D., Sawbridge, P. and Hinings, D. (1992) *Half a Million Women: Mothers Who Lose Their Children by Adoption*, Harmondsworth: Penguin.

Howells, J. (1974) *Remember Maria*, London: Butterworths.

Ingleby Committee – see Secretary of State for the Home Department (1960).

Isaac, B. C., Minty, E. B. and Morrison, R. M. (1986) 'Children in care – the association with mental disorder in the parents', *British Journal of Social Work*, **16**(4): 325–39.

Jackson, M. P. and Valencia, B. (1979) *Financial Aid Through Social Work*, London: Routledge and Kegan Paul.

Jackson, P. R. and Walsh, S. (1987) 'Unemployment and the family', in D. Fryer and P. Ullah (eds) *Unemployed People. Social and Psychological Perspectives*, Milton Keynes: Open University Press.

Jennings, N. (1992) 'All sides must have an equal say in the adoption triangle', *Guardian*, 27 May.

Jervis, M. (1989) 'The stigma of "Children in Need"', *Social Work Today*, 16 February: 35.

Johnson, N. (1990) *Reconstructing the Welfare State: A Decade of Change 1980–1990*, Hemel Hempstead: Harvester/Wheatsheaf.

Joseph, K. (1972) 'The cycle of deprivation', reprinted from a speech given to a Pre-School Playgroups Association Conference 29 June 1972, in E. Butterworth and R. Holman (eds) (1975) *Social Welfare in Modern Britain*, Glasgow/Fontana: Collins.

Katkin, D., Bullington, B. and Levine, M. (1974) 'Above and beyond the best interests of the child: An inquiry into the relationship between social science and social action', *Law and Society Review*, **8**(4): 669–87.

Kelly, G. (1981) 'The lost cord', *Social Work Today*, **13**(12): 7–9.

Keppel, M. Van (1991) 'Birth parents and negotiated adoption agreements', *Adoption and Fostering*, **15**(4): 81–90.

Kiernan, K. and Wicks, M. (1990) *Family Change and Future Policy*, London: Rowntree/Family Policy Studies Centre.

King, M. and Piper, C. (1990), *How the Law Thinks About Children*, Aldershot: Ashgate/Gower.

King, M. and Trowell, J. (1992) *Children's Welfare and the Law: The Limits of Legal Intervention*, London: Sage.

Klenig, J. (1976) 'Mill, children and rights', *Educational Philosophy and Theory*, **8**:14.

Labour Party (1989) *Meet the Challenge, Make the Change – Final Report of Labour Policy Review for the 1990s*, London: Labour Party.

La Fontaine, J. (1994) *The Extent and Nature of Organised and Ritual Sexual Abuse: Research Findings*, London: HMSO.

Laing, R. D. (1976) *The Politics of the Family*, Harmondsworth: Penguin.

Lait, J. (1979) 'Is less worse better than better?', *Community Care*, 14 June: 24–5.

Lambert, L. and Rowe, J. (1974) 'Children in care and the assumption of parental rights by local authorities', *Child Adoption*, **78**(4): 13–23.

Lambert, L. and Streather, J. (1980) *Children in Changing Families*, London: National Children's Bureau/Macmillan.

Land, H (1983) 'Poverty and gender: the distribution of resources within families' in M. Brown (ed.) *The Structure of Disadvantage*, London: Heinemann.

Lansdown, G. (1995a) 'Children's rights and wrongs', *Poverty*, **90**: 2.

Lansdown, G. (1995b) 'Minor offences' *Guardian*, 18 January.

Lasch, C. (1977) *Haven in a Heartless World. The Family Beseiged*, New York: Basic Books.

Lavery, G. (1986) 'The rights of children in care', in B. Franklin (ed.) (1986) *The Rights of Children*, Oxford: Blackwell.

Law Commission (1979) *Illegitimacy*. Working Paper No.74, London: Law Commission.

Law Commission (1982) *Illegitimacy*. Report 118, London: Law Commission.

Law Commission (1986) *Illegitimacy* (Second Report). Report 157, Cmnd. 9913, London: HMSO.

Law Commission (1988) Family Law, Review of Child Law, Guardianship and Custody, Law Com. No. 172, London: HMSO.

Lesley, A. (1996) 'Open adoption in a transracial context', in R. Phillips and E. McWilliam (eds), *After Adoption: Working with Adoptive Families*, London: British Agencies for Adoption and Fostering (BAAF).

Lestor, J. (1990), 'A Charter for Children', *Labour Party News*, November–December.

Lestor, J. (1995), 'A Minister for Children', in B. Franklin (ed.) *The Handbook of Children's Rights: Comparative Policy and Practice*, London and New York: Routledge.

Levitt, K. L. and Wharf, B. (eds) (1985) *The Challenge of Child Welfare*, Vancouver: University of British Columbia Press.

Levy, A. (1994a) 'The end of childhood', *Guardian Law*, 29 November: 12.

Levy, A. (1994b) 'Witness to cruelty', *Guardian Law*, 26 April: 17.

Levy, A. (1995) 'Is anyone minding the kids?', *Guardian*, 6 June.

Levy, A. and Kahan, B. (1991) *The Pindown Experience and the Protection of Children: the Report of the Staffordshire Child Care Inquiry 1990*, Stafford: Staffordshire County Council.

Lindsay, M. (1988) 'Child's rights officer by appointment', *Childright* **49**: 16–19

Lindsay, M. (1989) 'The Children's Advocate', *Community Care*, 25 October: 23–4.

Lister, R. (1996) 'Back to the family: family policies and politics under the Major government', in H. Jones and J. Millar (eds) *The Politics of the Family*, Aldershot: Avebury.

London Borough of Brent (1985) *A Child in Trust: The Report of the Panel of Inquiry into the Circumstances surrounding the Death of Jasmine Beckford*, London: Borough of Brent.

London Borough of Greenwich (1987) *A Child in Mind: Protection of Children in a Responsible Society. Report of the Commission of Inquiry into the Circumstances surrounding the Death of Kimberley Carlile*, London: Borough of Greenwich.

London Borough of Lambeth (1987) *Whose Child? The Report of the Public Inquiry into the Death of Tyra Henry*, London: Borough of Lambeth.

Loney, M. (1986) *The Politics of Greed: The New Right and the Welfare State*, London: Pluto Press.

Loney, M. (1987) 'Pain in a wider world', *Social Services Insight*, 13 November: 20–22

Lord, E. and Weisfeld, D. (1974) 'The abused child' in A. R. Roberts (ed.) *Childhood Deprivation*, Illinois: C. C. Thomas.

Lowe, N. V. and White, R. A. H. (1979) *Wards of Court*, London: Butterworths.

Lyon, C. and Parton, N. (1995) 'Children's rights and the Children Act 1989', in B. Franklin (ed.) *The Handbook of Children's Rights: Comparative Policy and Practice*, London and New York: Routledge.

McCarthy M. (ed.) (1989) *The New Politics of Welfare*, Basingstoke: Macmillan.

MacDougall, D. J. (1985) 'Children's rights: an evaluation of the controversy', in K. L. Levitt and B. Wharf (eds) *The Challenge of Child Welfare*, Vancouver: University of British Columbia Press.

MacLeod, V. (1982) *Whose Child? The Family in Child Care Legislation and Social Work Practice*, London: Study Commission on the Family, Occasional Paper 11.

Magee, B. (1973) *Popper*, Glasgow: Fontana/Collins.

Marchant, C. (1992) 'Fledgling Act floundering?', *Community Care*, 26 March: 8.

Melville, J. (1983) 'Looking for a mother', *New Society*, 8 December: 391–3

Metcalfe, A. and Humphries, M. (eds) (1985) *The Sexuality of Men*, London: Pluto.

Middleton, N. (1971) *When Family Failed. The Treatment of Children in the Care of the Community During the First Half of the Twentieth Century*, London: Gollancz.

Millett, K. (1971) *Sexual Politics*, London: Rupert Hart-Davis Ltd.

Millham, S. (1978) *Locking up Children*, Farnborough: Saxon House.

Millham, S., Bullock, R., Hosie, K. and Haak, M. (1986) *Lost in Care: The Problems of Maintaining Links Between Children in Care and Their Families*, Aldershot: Gower.

Millham, S., Bullock, R., Hosie, K. and Little, M. (1985) 'Maintaining family links of children in care', *Adoption and Fostering*, 9(2): 12–16.

Mishra, R. (1984) *The Welfare State in Crisis: Social Thought and Social Change*, Brighton: Wheatsheaf.

Mishra, R. (1990) *The Welfare State in Capitalist Societies*, Hemel Hempstead: Harvester/Wheatsheaf.

Mitchell, J. (1971) *Women's Estate*, Harmondsworth: Penguin.

Monckton, Sir W. (1945) *Report On the Circumstances which Led to the Boarding Out of Dennis and Terence O'Neill at Bank Farm, Minsterley, and the Steps Taken to Supervise Their Welfare*, Cmd. 6636, London: HMSO.

Montgomery. J. (1986) 'Surrogacy and the best interests of the child', *Family Law*, **16**: 37.

Montgomery J. (1993) 'Consents to health care for children', *Journal of Child Law*, **5**(3): 117-24.

Morgan, P. (1994) *Farewell to the Family*, London: IEA Health and Welfare Unit.

Morris, A., Giller, H., Szwed, E. and Geach, H. (1980) *Justice for Children*, Basingstoke: Macmillan.

Mount, F. (1982) *The Subversive Family: An Alternative History of Love and Marriage*, London: Cape.

Mullender, A. (ed.) (1991) *Open Adoption: The Philosophy and the Practice*, London: British Agencies for Adoption and Fostering (BAAF).

Murray, N. (1992) 'Jackie vs Mum and Dad', *Community Care*, 3 December: 14–15.

National Association of Citizens' Advice Bureaux (NACAB) (1989) *The Social Security Act: First Impressions*, London: NACAB.

National Association of Young People in Care (NAYPIC) (1983) *Sharing Care*, London: NAYPIC.

National Children's Bureau (1992) *Highlight 113 An Introduction to Children's Rights*, London: National Children's Bureau.

National Children's Home (NCH) (1989) *Children in Danger Factfile 1989*, London: National Children's Home (also as reported in *Social Work Today*, 30 March 1989: 4).

National Children's Home (NCH) (1994) *Action for Children 1994 Factfile*, London: NCH Action for Children.

National Council for One Parent Families (NCOPF) (1982) *Against Natural Justice*, London: NCOPF.

National Institute for Social Work (NISW) (1982) *Social Workers. Their Role and Tasks* (Barclay Committee Report), London: NISW.

National Society for the Prevention of Cruelty to Children (NSPCC) (1989) *Child Abuse Trends in England and Wales 1983–87*, London: NSPCC.

Neale, P. (1995) 'Lost voices', *Community Care*, 10–16 August: 19.

New Society (1987) editorial, 18 December.

Newell, P. (1989a) *Children are People Too; The Case Against Corporal Punishment*, London: Bedford Square Press.

Newell, P. (1989b) 'An end to physical punishment', *Concern*, **70**: 8–9.

Newell P. (1991) *The UN Convention and Children's Rights in the UK*, London: National Children's Bureau.

Newell, P. (1993) *One Scandal Too Many ... The Case For Comprehensive Protection For Children in All Settings*, London: Calouste Gulbenkian Foundation.

Newell, P. (1994) 'Open verdict', *Community Care*, 30 June–6 July: 26.

Norway Information Centre (1987) *Commissioner for Children in Norway*, Oslo: Royal Norwegian Ministry of Foreign Affairs.

Office of Population Censuses and Surveys (OPCS) (1992) *General Household Survey 1992*, London: HMSO.

Office of Population Censuses and Surveys (OPCS) (various years) *Adoptions in England and Wales*, London: HMSO (OPCS Monitors cited in *BAAF Annual Review 1985–96*, London: BAAF).

Ogden, J. (1995) 'Help at hand', *Community Care*, 11–17 May: 21.

O'Hara, M. (1990), 'A competent witness', *Community Care*, 24 May: 13.

Oliver, J. (1988) 'Introducing the Children Bill', *Social Work Today*, 1 December: 24.

Packman, J. (1968) *Child Care: Needs and Numbers*, London: Allen and Unwin.

Packman. J. (1981) *The Child's Generation. Child Care Policy in Britain*, Oxford: Blackwell and Robertson.

Packman, J. (1993) 'From prevention in partnership: child welfare services across three decades', in G. Pugh (ed.) *Thirty Years of Change for Children*, London: National Children's Bureau.

Packman, J., Randal, J. and Jacques, N. (1985) *Who needs Care? Social Work Decisions about Children*, Oxford: Blackwell.

Page, R. and Clark, G. (1977) *Who Cares?*, London: National Children's Bureau.

Pahl, J. (1989) *Money and Marriage*, Basingstoke: Macmillan Education.

Parker, R. (1977) 'One parent families and children in care', speech to National Council for One Parent Families (NCOPF) AGM, London: NCOPF.

Parker, R. (1995) 'Child care and the personal social services', in D. Gladstone (ed.) *British Social Welfare: Past, Present and Future*, London: UCL Press.

Parkinson, P. (1993) 'Legal intervention in parent–child conflicts: the emergence of no-fault "divorce" in child welfare law', in J. Eekelaar and P. Sarcevic (eds) *Parenthood in Modern Society: Legal and Social Issues for the Twenty-First Century*, Netherlands: Kluwer Academic Publishers

Parton, C. and Parton, N. (1989) 'Child protection: the law and dangerousness', in O. Stevenson (ed.) *Child Abuse: Public Policy and Professional Practice*, Hemel Hempstead: Harvester/Wheatsheaf.

Parton, N. (1979) 'The natural history of child abuse: a study in social problem definition', *British Journal of Social Work*, 9(4): 431–46.

Parton, N. (1981) 'Child abuse, social anxiety and welfare', *British Journal of Social Work*, 11(4): 394–414.

Parton, N. (1985a) *The Politics of Child Abuse*, Basingstoke: Macmillan.

Parton, N. (1985b) 'Politics and practice', *Community Care*, 26 September: 22–4.

Parton, N. (1986) 'The Beckford Report: a critical appraisal', *British Journal of Social Work*, 16(5): 511–31.

Parton, N. (1990) 'Taking Child Abuse Seriously', in Violence Against Children Study Group (ed.) *Taking Child Abuse Seriously: Contemporary Issues in Child Protection Theory and Practice*, London: Unwin Hyman.

Parton, N. (1991) *Governing the Family: Child Care, Child Protection and the State*, Basingstoke: Macmillan.

Parton, N. and Martin, N. (1989) 'Public inquiries, legalism and child care in England and Wales', *International Journal of Law and the Family*, 3: 21–39.

Phillips, M. (1993) 'Ninety minutes to lose a daughter', *Guardian*, 13 February.

Philpot, T. (1996) 'Child's player', *Community Care*, 14 December 1995–4 January 1996: 22–3.

Piachaud, D. (1986) 'A family problem', *New Society*, 13 June: 15–16.

Pilkington, E. (1994) 'Killing the age of innocence', *Guardian*, 30 May.

Pinchbeck, I. and Hewitt, M. (1969) *Children in English Society* Vol. II, London: Routledge and Kegan Paul.

Plotnikoff, J. and Woolfson, R. (1995) *Prosecuting Child Abuse*, London: Blackstone.

Plumb, J. H. (1972) *In the Light of History*, Harmondsworth: Penguin.

Pollock, L. (1983) *Forgotten Children. Parent–child Relations from 1500–1900*, Cambridge: Cambridge University Press.

Popper, K. (1966) *The Open Society and its Enemies*, London: Routledge and Kegan Paul.

Pringle, M. Kellmer (1967) *Adoption. Facts and Fallacies*, London: Longman.

Pringle, M. Kellmer (1972) 'Better adoption', *New Society*, 29 June: 676–8.

Pringle, M. Kellmer (1975a) *The Needs of Children*, London: Hutchinson.

Pringle, M. Kellmer (1975b) 'Young children need full-time mothers', in Vallender and Fogelman (eds) (1987) *Putting Children First*, London: Falmer Press/NCB.

Pringle, M. Kellmer (1978) 'A ten point plan for foster care', *Concern*, **30**, republished in Vallender and Fogelman (eds) (1987).

Pringle, M. Kellmer (1980) *A Fairer Future for Children*, London: National Children's Bureau.

Quest, C. (ed.) (1992) *Equal Opportunities: A Feminist Fallacy*, London: IEA Health and Welfare Unit.

Quest, C. (ed.) (1994) *Liberating Women ... from Modern Feminism*, London: IEA Health and Welfare Unit.

Quinton, D. and Rutter, M. (1984) 'Parents with children in care – 1. Current circumstances and parenting', *Psychology and Psychiatry*, **25**: 211–29.

Quinton, D. and Rutter, M. (1988) *Parenting Breakdown: The Making and Breaking of Intergenerational Links*, Aldershot: Avebury.

Radda Barnen (1987) *Facts about Radda Barnen. The Children's Ombudsman*, Stockholm: Radda Barnen.

Rapoport, R. (1981) *Unemployment and the Family*, London: Family Welfare Association.

Rassaby, A. A. (1982) 'Surrogate Motherhood: the position and problems of substitutes', in M. Walters and P. Singer (eds) *Test Tube Babies*, Melbourne and Oxford: Oxford University Press.

Rawls, J. (1972) *A Theory of Justice*, Oxford: Clarendon Press.

Representing Children (1995) 8 February: 5.

Rhodes, P. J. (1992) *Racial Matching in Fostering: The Challenge to Social Work Practice*, Aldershot: Avebury.

Richards, J. (1989) 'The Bill: Resource implications', *Family Rights Group Bulletin, Spring*, London: Family Rights Group.

Richards, M. (1986) *Children of Social Worlds: Development in a Social Context*, Cambridge: Polity Press.

Rickford, F. (1991) 'A voice for little people', *Social Work Today*, 3 October: 12.

Rickford, F. (1992) 'Child with a view', *Social Work Today*, 12 November: 13.

Rickford. F. (1993) 'Catch as catch can', *Community Care*, 5 August: 20.

Roll, J. (1986a) *Family Impact: 1986 Social Security Bill*, London: Family Policy Studies Centre.

Roll, J. (1986b) *Family Trends and Social Security*, London: Family Policy Studies Centre.

Rosenbaum, M. and Newell, P. (1991) *Taking Children Seriously: A Proposal for a Children's Rights Commissioner*, London: Calouste Gulbankian Foundation.

Rowe, J. (1977) *Fostering in the Seventies*, London: Association of British Adoption and Fostering Agencies (ABAFA).

Rowe, J. and Lambert, L. (1973) *Children Who Wait*, London: Association of British Adoption and Fostering Agencies (ABAFA).

Ryburn, M. (1994a) *Open Adoption: Research, Theory and Practice*, Aldershot: Avebury.

Ryburn, M. (1994b) 'Contact after contested adoptions', *Adoption and Fostering*, **18**(4): 30-6.

Samuels, A. (1976) 'The Children Act 1975. A critical appraisal: the view of the lawyer', *Family Law*, **6**(1): 5.

Scott, J. (1989) 'Please speak up ... children's evidence in legal proceedings', *Adoption and Fostering*, **13**(3): 49–51.

Scutt, N. and Hoyland, C. (1995) 'My Special Person', *Community Care*, 23 February–1 March: 18–19.

Secretaries of State for Health and Wales (1992–3) *Children Act Report 1992*, Cm. 2144, London: HMSO.

Secretaries of State for Health and Wales (1993–4) *Children Act Report 1993*, Cm. 2584, London: HMSO.

Secretaries of State for Health and Wales (1994–5) *Children Act Report 1994*, Cm. 2878, London: HMSO.

Secretary of State for the Home Department (1960) *Report of the Committee on Children and Young Persons (Ingleby Committee Report)*, Cmnd. 1190, London: HMSO.

Secretary of State for the Home Department, Minister of Health, Minister of Education (1946) *Report of the Care of Children Committee (Curtis Committee Report)*, Cmd. 6922, London: HMSO.

Secretary of State for Social Services (1974) *Report of the Committee of Inquiry into the Care and Supervision Provided in Relation to Maria Colwell*, London: HMSO.

Secretary of State for Social Services (1988) *Report of the Inquiry into Child Abuse in Cleveland 1987*, Cm. 412, London: HMSO.

Seebohm Committee (1968) *Report of the Committee on Local Authority and Allied Personal Social Services*, Cmnd. 3703, London: HMSO.

Seglow, J., Pringle, M. L. K. and Wedge, P. J. (1972) *Growing up Adopted*, Windsor: NFER.

Sinclair, R. (1992) 'Happy Birthday Children Act', *Community Care* 1 October: 18–19.

Small, J. (1991) 'Ethnic and racial identity in adoptions within the United Kingdom', *Adoption and Fostering*, **15**(4): 61–8.

Smith, C. R. (1984) *Adoption and Fostering. Why and How?* London: BASW/Macmillan.

Smith, S. (1995) 'Permanence revisited – some practice dilemmas', *Adoption and Fostering*, **19**(3): 11–16.

Social Security Consortium (1986) *Of Little Benefit: A Critical Guide to the Social Security Act 1986*, London: Social Security Consortium.

Stein, M. (1983) 'Protest in care', in B. Jordan and N. Parton (eds) *The Political Dimensions of Social Work*, Oxford: Blackwell.

Stevenson, O. (1989) *Child Abuse: Public Policy and Professional Practice*, Hemel Hempstead: Harvester/Wheatsheaf.

Stewart, G. (1989) 'Who will foot the bill?', *Community Care*, 8 June: 22–4.
Stone, L. (1977) *The Family, Sex and Marriage in England 1500–1800*, London: Weidenfeld and Nicolson.
Strathclyde Social Work Department (1980) *Strathclyde's Children. 111 Children Whose Parents are the Regional Council*, Glasgow: Strathclyde Regional Council.
Strauss, M. A., Gelles, R. J. and Steinmetz, S. K. (1980) *Behind Closed Doors: Violence in the American Family*, Newbury Park, California: Sage.
Stubbs, P. (1987) 'Professionalism and the adoption of black children', *British Journal of Social Work*, **17**: 473–92.
Swedish Ministry of Health and Social Affairs (1993) Press release; and *The Swedish Children's Ombudsman – A New Epoch*, Stockholm: Ministry of Health and Social Affairs.
Taylor, L., Lacey, R. and Bracken, D. (1979) *In Whose Best Interests? The Unjust Treatment of Children in Courts and Institutions*, London: Cobden Trust and MIND.
Teitelbaum, L. E. (1980) 'Foreword: the meaning of rights of children', *New Mexico Law Review*, **10**: 236.
Thomas, N. and Beckett, C. (1995) 'Striking difference', *Community Care*, 16–22 February: 22–3.
Thoburn, J. (1980) *Captive Clients: Social Work with Families of Children Home on Trial*, London: Routledge and Kegan Paul.
Thoburn, J. (1990) *Success and Failure in Permanent Family Placement*, Aldershot: Avebury.
Thoburn, J., Murdoch, A. and O'Brien, A. (1987) *Permanence in Child Care* Oxford: Blackwell.
Thorpe, R. (1974) 'Mum and Mrs So-and-So', *Social Work Today*, **4**(22): 691–5.
Thorpe, D., Paley, J. and Green, G. (1979) 'The making of a delinquent', *Community Care*, 26 April: 18–19.
Tissier (1995) 'A clouded lens', *Community Care*, 2–8 February: 16–17.
Titmuss, R. (1950) 'Problems of Social Policy', in R. Titmuss *History of the Second World War*, London: Longmans Green.
Tizard, B. (1977) *Adoption. A Second Chance*, London: Open Books.
Triseliotis, J. (1970) *In Search of Origins: The Experience of Adopted Children*, London: Routledge and Kegan Paul.
Triseliotis, J. (1995) 'Adoption – evolution or revolution?', *Adoption and Fostering*, **19**(2): 37–44.
Tunstill, J. (1977) 'In defence of parents', *New Society*, **42**(785) 20 October: 121–2.
Tunstill, J. (1980) *Fostering Policy and the 1975 Children Act*, London: Brunel University Papers in Social Policy and Administration 2.
Tunstill, J. (1985) 'Laying the Poor Law to rest?', *Community Care*, 20 June: 16–18.
Utting, D. (1995) *Family and Parenthood: Supporting Families, Preventing Breakdown*, York: Joseph Rowntree Foundation.
Vallender, I. and Fogelman, K. (eds) (1987) *Putting Children First. A Volume in Honour of Mia Kelliner Pringle*, London: Falmer Press/National Children's Bureau.
Violence Against Children Study Group (1990) *Taking Child Abuse Seriously: Contemporary Issues in Child Protection Theory and Practice*, London: Unwin Hyman.

Voegeli, W. and Willenbacher, B. (1993) 'Children's rights and social placement', in J. Eekelaar and P. Sarcevic (eds) *Parenthood in Modern Society*, Netherlands: Kluwer Academic Publishers.

A Voice for the Child in Care (1982) *Children's Spokesmen*, London: Voice for the Child.

Wade, A. (1993) 'The Canadian experience', *Community Care*, 4 February: 24–5.

Walby, S. (1990) *Theorizing Patriarchy*, Oxford: Blackwell.

Wald, M. (1976) 'Negected children: standards for removal of children from their homes, monitoring the status of children in foster care, and termination of parental rights', *Stanford Law Review*, 28: 622–70.

Wald, M. (1979) 'Children's rights; a framework for analysis', *University of Cailfornia Davis Law Review*, 12: 255–82.

Walker, A. (1980) 'The social construction of poverty and dependency in old age', *Journal of Soial Policy*, 9: 49-77.

Waller, B. (1995) 'The hidden trials of child victims', *Guardian*, 25 January.

Wallerstein, J. and Kelly, J. (1980) *Surviving the Break-up: How Children and Parents Cope with Divorce*, London: Grant McIntyre.

Walton, R. (1976) 'The best interests of the child', *British Journal of Social Work*, 6(3): 307–13.

Walton, R. and Heywood, M. (1975) 'Child care, culture and Social Services Departments', *Yearbook of Social Policy 1974*, London: Routledge and Kegan Paul.

Wasserman, S. (1967) 'The abused parent of the abused child', *Children*, 14:175–9.

Wells, S. (1993) 'What do birth mothers want?', *Adoption and Fostering*, 17(4): 22–6.

Wicks, M. (1987) *A Future for All. Do We Need the Welfare State?*, Harmondsworth: Penguin.

Wilson, R. (1988) 'Protecting children's rights', *New Statesman and Society*, 9 December: 27.

Wolkind, S. (1984) 'Taking a stand: child psychiatrists in custody, access and disputed cases', *British Agencies for Adoption and Fostering (BAAF) discussion series 5*, London: BAAF.

Women's Group on Public Welfare (1948) *The Neglected Child and His Family*, Oxford: Oxford University Press.

Worsfold, V. L. (1974) 'A philosophical justification for children's rights', *Harvard Educational Review*, 44(1): 142.

Wyld, N. (1992) 'Stifled voices', *Community Care*, 29 October: 18–19.

Young, M. (1995) 'For the sake of the kids', *Guardian Society*, 31 May.

Zimmerman, S. (1988) *Understanding Family Policy. Theoretical Approaches*, Newbury Park, California: Sage.

Further Reading

Children Act Advisory Committee (1993–4) *Annual Report*, London: Lord Chancellor's Department.

Department of Health (DH) (1994) *The UN Convention on the Rights of the Child, The UK's First Report to the UN Committee on the Rights of the Child*, London: HMSO.

Department of Health and Social Security (DHSS) (1982) *Child abuse: A Study of Inquiry Reports 1973–1981*, London: HMSO.

Family Rights Group (1986) *Promoting Links – Keeping Children and Families in Touch*, London: Family Rights Group.

Franklin, B. (1989a) 'Wimps and bullies; press reporting of child abuse', in P. Carter, T. Jeffs, and M. Smith (eds) *The Social Work and Social Welfare Yearbook 1*, Milton Keynes: Open University.

Freeman, M. D. A. (1987) 'Taking children's rights seriously', *Children and Society*, 1(4): 299–319.

Freeman, M. D. A. (1988) 'Time to stop hitting our children', *Childright*, 51: 5–8.

Harding, L. M. (1989) 'The hundred year resolution', *The Journal of Child Law*, 2(1): 12–17.

Hodgkin, R. (1986) 'Parents and corporal punishment', *Adoption and Fostering*, 10(3): 47–9.

Jack, G. and Stepney, P. (1995) 'The Children Act – protection or persecution? Family support and child protection in the 1990s', *Critical Social Policy*, 43(15)(i): 26–39.

Jervis, M. (1989) 'The "User-Friendly" Children Bill', *Social Work Today*, 12 January: 14–15.

Mnookin, R. H. (1973) 'Foster care: in whose best interest', *Harvard Educational Review*, 43(4): 599.

Mnookin, R. H. (1975) 'Child custody adjudication: judicial functions in the face of indeterminacy', *Law and Contemporary Problems*, 39: 226.

Morgan, S. and Righton, P. (eds) (1989) *Child Care: Concerns and Conflicts* (Course Reader), London: Open University/Hodder and Stoughton.

National Children's Bureau (1988) *Highlight 80 Child Abuse*, London: National Children's Bureau.

National Society for the Prevention of Cruelty to Children (NSPCC) (1995) Press release: 'Survey of childhood experiences – sexual interference in childhood', London: NSPCC, 13 June.

Open University (1990) *Children and Young People in Care* (Course Reader), London: Open University/Hodder and Stoughton.

Packman, J. and Jordan, B. (1991) 'The Children Act: looking forward, looking back', *British Journal of Social Work*, 21(4): 315–27.

Rogers, C. M. and Wrightsman, L. S. (1978) 'Attitudes towards children's rights: nurturance or self-determination', *Journal of Social Issues*, 34(2): 59.

Wald, M. (1975) 'State intervention on behalf of neglected children: A search for realistic standards', *Stanford Law Review*, 27: 985–1040.

Index